GINGER STRAND

THE BROTHERS VONNEGUT

Ginger Strand is the author of three previous books, including *Killer on the Road: Violence and the American Interstate*. She has written for a wide variety of publications, including *The New York Times*, *Harper's Magazine*, *This Land*, *The Believer*, *Tin House*, and *Orion Magazine*, where she is a contributing editor.

Also by Ginger Strand

FICTION
Flight

NONFICTION
Killer on the Road: Violence and the American Interstate
Inventing Niagara: Beauty, Power, and Lies

THE BROTHERS VONNEGUT

THE
BROTHERS
VONNEGUT

Science and Fiction in
the House of Magic

GINGER STRAND

Farrar, Straus and Giroux

New York

Farrar, Straus and Giroux
18 West 18th Street, New York 10011

The Library of Congress has cataloged the hardcover edition as follows:
Strand, Ginger Gail.
    The Brothers Vonnegut : science and fiction in the House of Magic /
Ginger Strand. — First edition.
        p.   cm.
    Includes bibliographical references and index.
    ISBN 978-0-374-11701-6 (hardback) — ISBN 978-0-374-71154-2 (e-book)
    1. Vonnegut, Kurt.   2. Vonnegut, Bernard.   3. Novelists, American—
20th century—Biography.   4. Scientists—United States—Biography.
5. Weather control—United States.   6. Literature and science—United
States—History—20th century.   I. Title.

PS3572.O5 Z858 2015
813'.54—dc23
[B]
                                                                    2015010126

Paperback ISBN: 978-0-374-53653-4

Designed by Jonathan D. Lippincott

Our books may be purchased for promotional, educational, or business use.
Please contact your local bookseller or the Macmillan Corporate and Premium Sales
Department at 1-800-221-7945, extension 5442, or by e-mail at
MacmillanSpecialMarkets@macmillan.com.

www.fsgbooks.com
www.twitter.com/fsgbooks • www.facebook.com/fsgbooks

1   3   5   7   9   10   8   6   4   2

The most beautiful thing we can experience is the mysterious.
It is the source of all true art and science.   —Albert Einstein

Contents

THE BROTHERS VONNEGUT

1

Autumn Fog

Private First Class Vonnegut prepared to die.

At the bottom of a snowy hollow, he fixed his bayonet and waited, huddled in a group of roughly fifty soldiers. Their unit, the 423rd, had been at battle for three days, since December 16. They'd been lost for most of it. They must be somewhere in Luxembourg, someone said. Now they were surrounded, herded into a small depression in the unfamiliar land. Kurt hunched into his coat—he had a tall man's habit of hunching—but he couldn't get warm. That December—1944— was one of the coldest and wettest ever recorded in Europe.

The Germans were shouting at them. Kurt and the other soldiers couldn't see them, but they could hear accented voices telling the Americans to give up. They were surrounded, the Nazis said. It was useless to resist. The men bunched together, pointing their bayonets out the way soldiers do in the movies. Time slowed down. Kurt had always liked being part of a clan, and here, at the end of the line, the soldiers became almost one being, a big porcupine bristling with steel quills. For a few minutes, it was kind of nice.

He had waded ashore to the European theater less than a month earlier and ground to the front in a truck buffeted by sleet. He was still somewhat in shock. His mother had died of a drug overdose—was it a suicide? an accident?—just before he shipped out. The sadness hung thick over his departure, complicating and deepening his fear. He longed for the feeling that someone loved him, followed his every move with boundless devotion. He hadn't realized how much he needed that until his mother was gone.

Still, for the first time in his life he felt beyond reproach. No longer a flunking chemistry student or a college dropout, he was where he was supposed to be, a soldier putting his life on the line. He was now the sort of person honored in the grandiose Soldiers' and Sailors' Monument at the center of his hometown, Indianapolis. Not even his big brother, Bernard, could say that much. Bernie, the A student, the brilliant scientist, the MIT man like their father. The one who launched the chain of events that landed Kurt here, a pacifist about to be swallowed by war.

The Germans fired on the trees above the soldiers' heads. Branches and splintered steel rained down. A couple of guys were hit. They might be dead. Twenty-five years later, Kurt would introduce a character named Edgar Derby to the world and describe his experience of this very battle. He would call what rained down on him "the incredible artificial weather that Earthlings sometimes create for other Earthlings when they don't want those other Earthlings to inhabit Earth any more."

Come out, the Nazis ordered again. The Americans came out. When he saw the Germans, Kurt couldn't help but note their white snowsuits. That made so much more sense, he thought, than his absurd army drab. The Americans were always in olive, as if wars were never fought in white places, in white weather.

•

The battle had started three days earlier at 5:30 a.m., before dawn crept over the frozen landscape of Schnee Eifel, or Snow Mountain. They were manning a lightly defended spot along the old Westwall, a reinforcement ridge the Allies called the Siegfried Line. It was quiet: no one expected much to happen on this front. Then out of the predawn darkness came the attack, and it sounded like the sky falling in. For eighty miles along the Westwall, Allied soldiers woke up to German artillery raining down on them: fourteen-inch shells from railroad guns, the hacking cough and plunk of mortars, the high-pitched whistles of what the Americans called "screaming meemies" but the Germans called *Nebelwerfer*: fog throwers. The forest along the front was leveled as the Germans fired on trees. Even the Nazis were impressed by their own artillery storm. "A hurricane of iron and fire," one German major called it.

For nearly an hour, the onslaught pounded the American troops. Then, suddenly, there was an eerie silence. As the soldiers tried to get their bearings, they heard a clank, and then they were lit like stage actors from the east. Through the dense fog, the Germans were flooding them with searchlights—a new intimidation tactic they called "artificial moonlight." To the battered Allies, it felt as if the Nazis had commandeered control of nature. Finally, out of the white came snow monsters: German infantry.

Something big was happening, but no one knew what. Telephone lines were blasted; whole divisions lost contact with command. Strategists got garbled and patchy reports; some thought the barrage was merely a "spoiling" attack, a futile lashing out by an enemy who knew he was defeated. After all, the war was meant to be winding down. General Eisenhower had a standing bet with the British field marshal Montgomery that Europe would be won by Christmas. It took days before the Allied generals realized that a major offensive was under way and diverted troops to stop it.

In retrospect, it was clearly a mistake to man twenty-five miles of front with one Allied division. But the Germans were outnumbered and out-armed. Why would they launch an offensive? They had only one thing on their side: the Allies called it "Hitler's weather."

In war, soldiers fight more than the enemy. They fight topography. They fight time. Most of all, they fight weather. Kublai Khan might have overrun Japan, but a typhoon destroyed half his ships. The Spanish Armada fell to Britain because of storms on the North Sea. Napoleon was especially unlucky in weather: he lost Waterloo because of a rainstorm, and his march on Russia was beaten back not by war craft but by winter.

In World War II, weather mattered more than ever. It was the first war in which airpower would be decisive, and the U.S. Army Air Forces were especially vulnerable to bad weather: cloud cover disrupted bombing runs; snow scrambled radio signals; icing forced planes to land. But weather could waylay the Navy too: the day Kurt woke up to the German attack on the western front, the Third Fleet faced a typhoon in the Pacific. The storm sank 3 destroyers, wrecked 146 aircraft on carriers, and killed 778 troops, racking up a higher death toll than any Japanese attack. And weather tormented the infantry: rain and snow slowed tanks, troops, and supply lines. Fog could conceal enemy movements.

Weather forecasting had been part of most militaries since the early nineteenth century, but when World War II broke out, the generals realized they needed more meteorologists than ever. Colleges were enlisted to train thousands of weather officers for the new Air Weather Service. MIT, America's leading meteorology school, established a special program, bumping its enrollment from thirty students to around five hundred. The department head, Sverre Petterssen, left MIT to join General Eisenhower's meteorology team. He played a key role in the war's most famous weather suspense story.

During World War I, a new physics-based school of meteorology had arisen in Norway called air mass analysis. Petterssen was Norwegian and a proponent of this scientifically rigorous new approach. When Ike was poised to invade Normandy, Petterssen told him to wait. The skies looked clear, but the upper air situation was unstable. Petterssen told Eisenhower's team that the weather was likely to turn bad and scuttle the invasion. He based this forecast not just on what he could observe but on the idea that large wind patterns were battling each other high in the sky, atmospheric echoes of the clash of armies below. Such wind patterns are common knowledge today, but in the 1940s not everyone believed that weather was shaped by the huge, invisible air masses that meteorologists had given a warlike name: fronts.

The American meteorologist Irving Krick, who was also on the team, scoffed at Petterssen's approach. Krick, using the classic forecasting technique—looking at weather maps from the past to determine how the future might shape up—declared that the offensive should go on as planned.

The largest invasion in history hung in the balance as the weathermen argued about the winds. Finally, the chief meteorological officer made the call. D-Day was postponed for twenty-four hours, and indeed the weather turned stormy. The next day looked no better, but Petterssen pointed to the changing barometric pressure as a sign that the weather would improve. There would be a window of opportunity before the next bad day. Gambling on Petterssen's prediction, General Eisenhower launched the attack.

Now it was the Germans who were using the weather to their advantage. The attack that would come to be called the Battle of the Bulge was planned for December with good reason. Under cover of heavy cold fog, the Germans had amassed 410,000 troops, 1,400 tanks, and 2,600 artillery weapons for the predawn offensive. The weather had slowed the delivery of Allied troops and supplies to the front, and the bitter cold ensured that the Allied infantry, huddled in foxholes and trenches, was distracted by the need to keep warm. Best of all, the heavy cloud cover would keep British and American planes grounded, depriving the Allies of air support. General Alfred Jodl had foreseen it in the detailed operational plan he drew up for the *Reichsführer*. He called it *Herbstnebel*: Autumn Fog.

•

Kurt's regiment, the 423rd, got the worst of Autumn Fog. Its troops were far enough forward to be on German ground, and before they even realized what had happened, they were cut off. The men of the 423rd, like the entire 106th Division, were green; they had never seen action. Many, like Kurt, had been pulled out of the Army Specialized Training Program (ASTP)—a combined college and military program that was meant to lead to a degree and an officer's commission. It was canceled in 1944 because the Army didn't need more officers; it needed riflemen. Hitler was going to be defeated not by strategists or engineers but by numbers. College boys like Kurt were plucked from classes on thermodynamics, calculus, and mechanical engineering, given a few months' hasty training in combat skills, and shipped to Europe. Kurt tried to get assigned to public relations, but his efforts failed. His unit, the 106th, was the last American infantry division to be mobilized in World War II. Two-thirds of its troops were single men under the age of twenty-three.

The Schnee Eifel was where these young men were supposed to get "blooded"—to practice their battlefield skills before facing actual combat. Now they were thrust in the middle of the very bloody real thing, and they didn't know what to do. Kurt's regiment commander, Colonel Charles Cavender, was told to dig in and hold the Germans back as best he could. He was promised an airdrop of ammunition and supplies. As the Germans moved inexorably forward, the men of the 423rd split into small groups and huddled together like sheep. By nightfall, the sheep were surrounded. For the next two days, they fought as best they could, in small groups or larger ones, while the Germans streamed around them and toward St. Vith.

For three long days, the 423rd and its sister regiment, the 424th, tried to hold their ground, like ants clinging to a boulder in a rising flood. By the morning of December 19, hundreds of men from the 106th were dead or wounded. The promised airdrops weren't coming, and there was no sign of reinforcements either. Colonel Cavender sent six of his men out to reconnoiter. One of them was Kurt. They weren't looking for the enemy; they were looking for their own artillery. Wandering the snowy hills, the six men found about fifty more Americans. And then the Germans found them.

The Americans surrendered as they were taught: they dismantled their weapons and threw them into the snow. Coming out of their gully, they said things like "take it easy" and "don't shoot." They wanted to go on living if they possibly could. Kurt knew a little German; his German American parents spoke it, and he'd had two years of it in high school. He tried out a few words. The Germans asked him if he was of German ancestry. He gave them his last name, Vonnegut.

"Why are you making war on your brothers?" they asked him. The question made little sense. He was a Hoosier, not a Kraut. But they weren't completely off base. When he said his own name, he said it, as his father did, in the German way: *Kooort*.

The Germans pointed their guns at the Americans. They told Kurt Vonnegut Jr. to march.

•

Two years earlier, he had been a relatively carefree undergraduate, writing columns called "Innocents Abroad" and "Well All Right" for *The Cornell Daily Sun*, buying Old Grand-Dad bourbon for a dance he hoped his sweetheart, Jane, would attend. The war meant this to him: Cokes were being rationed on campus. The university was banning house parties and out-of-town dates. Fraternities were going to be strapped for cash. Kurt devoted a whole column to the looming frat-house financial crunch. "It's a nasty picture no matter how you look at it," he wrote in May 1941. "From an abstract point of view it will be interesting to watch, just like bombing."

He'd been sixteen when the war began. He and two friends were wrapping up a summer road trip by spending a few days as the guests of Frank Phillips of Phillips Petroleum. Phillips had a resort in Bartlesville, Oklahoma, called Woolaroc Ranch. Woolaroc was a teenage boy's fantasy, where Kurt and his pals spent their days riding horses, fishing, and swimming, their evenings drinking beer and smoking twenty-five-cent cigars. They goofed around with the lodge's player piano and ransacked their host's library for spicy crime novels and anthropological accounts of the sex lives of primitive tribes while the radio tallied the mounting threat in Europe. It all seemed impossibly far away. The day they drove home, Hitler invaded Poland. As they pounded the road for seven hundred miles, Kurt had looked back on the whole adventure and wondered if he'd ever be that happy again.

His family was pacifist; the Vonneguts had always been freethinkers. Kurt clung to his antiwar conviction long after most others had succumbed to patriotic warmongering. In one column for the *Sun*, he defended the unpopular isolationist sentiments of Charles Lindbergh. In another, he criticized the extreme anti-German bias of the American media. Later, he blasted Wendell Willkie, "political yo-yo from the Hoosier state," for advocating the opening of a second front. It wasn't that he was pro-German. He was just antiwar. He came from a long line of Germans, yes; his grandfather had designed the gorgeous Indianapolis social center formerly known as Das Deutsche Haus. After World War I caused a wave of anti-German sentiment, Das Deutsche Haus was renamed the Athenaeum. But in Kurt's family, ethnicity was less important than ethics, intellect, and wit.

He had learned early that the best way for a third child to be heard at the dinner table was to crack a joke. Being funny was the only way he got them to stop interrupting and *listen* to him. Besides, his brother was brilliant, and his sister was artistic and beautiful. He couldn't compete on brains or talent or glamour. So he nurtured his penchant for humor, and this served him well at the *Sun*. His fellow students at Cornell didn't always agree with his isolationist sentiments, but they liked his snappy writing. In March 1942, he was appointed assistant managing editor of the paper.

He bragged about that to Jane Cox. He was always trying to impress her. They'd known each other since they were small children. In a way, she was his best friend. He recognized things in her—imagination, ambition, idealism—that he saw in himself. They were going to get married and live a blissful life together, full of books and music and smart conversation and ultimately kids—seven of them. He knew all of this, felt it somewhere deep inside him, even if Jane, busy acing her classes at Swarthmore and acting in plays and going on dates with a roster of eligible young men, hadn't come around to it yet. Kurt wrote it over and over in his letters to her. She was alternately encouraging and distant. She was hell to get along with, Jane, but he loved her, and he always would. Nineteen forty-five was the year he had picked for their wedding. He wrote it in one of his columns.

Before he left for Europe, they became lovers.

At Cornell, he had spent all his time working on the newspaper, to the detriment of everything else. His grades in his major—chemistry— suffered. He was supposed to be earning an officer's commission in the ROTC, but he got kicked out after writing an irreverent column: "We Impress *Life* Magazine with Our Efficient Role in National Defense." In it, he claimed that he and the other ROTC boys had little idea what they were doing, but when a *Life* photographer visited, they gamely ran around and disassembled a rifle while shouting things like "Flathatcher! Biffleblock!" to seem like crack militiamen. The ROTC was not amused. It wasn't the first time Kurt had mocked the warlike exertions of the college boys. An earlier column was cast as a letter to the military department from the school's zoologists, who claimed to be just as ready for service as the chemical engineers and advance drill squads.

"Up in the front lines our commanding officer will say 'Vontegal . . .

what the hell kind of butterfly is that,' and we'll be the only man in the trench that can tell him. That's the sort of thing that wins wars!"

It was, on some level, a sly crack at his brother, Bernard, who was doing war work. He'd been asked to leave his peacetime job and go back to MIT to work in the Army's Chemical Warfare Service laboratory there. He was exempted from the draft because of it. He couldn't tell his family what he was working on, but the family was proud of him; they were always proud of Bernard. How could Kurt resist mocking the notion that scientists would win the war? Besides, that was pretty much the only way he ever got a jump on Bernie: he made fun of him.

By his sophomore May, Kurt's grades were so bad he was put on academic probation. He made light of his woes in a column titled "The Lost Battalion Undergoes a Severe Shelling." He was the lost battalion.

Why didn't he just switch his major to English or journalism? He was a newspaperman at heart. In Ithaca, his happiest moments were when he was editing the *Sun*, just as in Indianapolis they had been when he was editing the *Shortridge Echo*, the nation's first high school daily. His experience there convinced him that not only did he like newspaper work, he was good at it. Toward the end of high school, he'd even managed to land a job offer from *The Indianapolis Times*. He wanted to take it. But becoming a newspaperman wasn't what his father and Bernie had in mind for him.

Sure, Kurt senior and Bernie agreed, young Kurt could write, and he was funny—the family clown, the class clown—but when he graduated from high school, it was time to get serious. At one point, Kurt thought he might like to become an architect, like his father and his grandfather Bernard, who had designed the Athenaeum. The opulent building was still the heart of the Indianapolis German American community, and Kurt had spent many a night there as a kid, admiring the elaborate woodwork and leaded glass windows as the adults talked or danced or listened to music. It must be nice to make something so beautiful. But that was before the Great Depression had ruined his father. The disheartened Kurt senior wouldn't hear of Kurt following in his footsteps. Be anything, he said bitterly, but an architect.

When he was a young man, Kurt's dreams—shared with Jane—were all about writing. They both fantasized about being news correspondents in Europe. Sometimes, when Jane was playing along, they envisioned the house they might share: a courtyard with an oak tree at its center and a studio out back where they would sit side by side and type out masterpieces. But even Kurt had a hard time imagining writing for a living. He would have to do something else to support those seven kids.

Bernie knew what Kurt should do; he should be a scientist, like him. So Bernard and Kurt senior decided that Kurt should study chemistry. That was a useful, practical field. Kurt didn't necessarily disagree. He believed, as they did, in science. It had more answers to the questions of life, he told Jane, than fields like psychology or philosophy. Science was going to make the world a better place. To be part of the utopian future, he should do as his brother said.

The older men didn't think Kurt junior was MIT material, so they settled on Cornell. When it looked as if Cornell might not take him, Bernard drove Kurt to Harvard, where he was given a provisional acceptance. But then Cornell came through, and Bernard thought he would have a better time there. That, Kurt said later, "was his idea of me, sort of third rate."

So in the fall of 1940, Kurt went off to Cornell to study chemistry. But he wasn't a born scientist like Bernie. When it came to the actual class work, it just didn't grab him. Not the way writing did. So he ignored his classes and did what made him happiest—keeping late hours in the offices of the *Sun*. Even the warning in his sophomore spring didn't set him straight. By Christmas break of his junior year, he was flunking out. He came down with pneumonia at home and decided not to go back. But his draft number was coming up. In March 1943, he enlisted in the U.S. Army.

So now the whole chain of events boiled down to this: Private Kurt Vonnegut Jr. was a prisoner of war.

•

"The war is over for you," the Germans told the Americans. Kurt joined the long line of Yank soldiers marching east, toward Germany. German cameramen stood filming as the prisoners limped along. This might be the Nazi propagandists' last chance to convince the weary folk at home that victory was still within reach. Kurt saw them pointing their lenses at the broken men. Twenty-five years later, in *Slaughterhouse-Five*, he would describe them as having run out of film—a perfect symbol for the empty pointlessness of it all: the propaganda, the offensive, the Nazi war machine, the whole goddamn war. He picked up his tired feet and marched, past dead soldiers unfurling from tanks, past men frozen in snowy fields, arms stretched toward the sky in fruitless supplication. The Germans did have film. In it, the Americans looked dirty, disheartened, and exhausted. Some supported wounded comrades or lugged makeshift pallets. The rest trudged miserably along. They had survived the German offensive, but many would not survive what lay ahead.

When they came to the top of a hill, the captured men could see a long line of prisoners, as far forward as the eye could see. Seven thousand Allied soldiers had been bagged by the Germans. It would have been different if the Allies had been able to get their planes in the air. Air support could have nipped *Herbstnebel* in the bud. But in all that fog, the airplanes failed them. The weather had fought for the other side.

As they marched into Germany, some of the prisoners must have known the Germans were wrong about one thing: the war wasn't over for them. Kurt and the other captured American troops were marching into a strange gray area, a place where they were neither soldiers nor civilians, neither at peace nor at war. The autumn fog swallowed them whole.

•

Bernard Vonnegut's life had always gone according to plan.

As a kid doing science experiments in the basement, he had planned to go to college and become a scientist. The Depression might have prevented that, but his family didn't let it, keeping him in his elite private high school, Park School. (They economized by enrolling Kurt in public school.) After graduating, Bernard studied chemistry at MIT, publishing his undergraduate chemistry thesis on X-ray analysis of crystalline bromine, then stayed at MIT for grad school, with the help of scholarships and a teaching fellowship. He planned to join his father's fraternity, Kappa Sigma, and by grad school Barney—as his MIT friends had rechristened him—was earning room and board by tutoring Kappa Sigma freshmen.

He hadn't planned for the swim team to lose every meet in his senior year, but he swam gamely anyway. "Vonnegut should be commended for his excellent performance in the 200-yard breast stroke event," declared the yearbook, *Technique*. He swam on a 300-yard medley relay team that set an MIT record. He was a good team player. He never needed to be the star.

After grad school, his plan was to get a good job as an industrial research scientist and start publishing papers, and that's exactly what he was doing as a chemist at Hartford-Empire Company, working on the physical and chemical properties of glass, when war came. And then his plans started to unravel.

Now here he was, stuck on one of his frequent trips to Minneapolis, where he lived at the Hotel King Cole (Royal Guest Rooms! Food to the King's Taste!), away from his Cambridge apartment and Bow. He had married Lois Bowler just over a year earlier, on Christmas Day. They had been set up by friends, and she fit his plans too. His nickname suited her: with her long brown hair and delicately sculpted features, she was extraordinarily beautiful—even Kurt had to admit it—and also somehow fragile, as if she might come untied. Bow didn't like to be alone; she usually went to her parents' home in Elizabethtown, New York, when Bernie traveled.

Now, instead of working at the glass factory, he was traveling back and forth between MIT and the Ice Research Base in Minneapolis, where he spent his days folding his lanky form into the tiny heated compartment he and his team had fashioned for the B-24 they named "the Flying Icing Wind Tunnel." An Army Air Forces pilot would guide the bomber plane into any available freezing clouds, and a sergeant would open the bomb bay doors and lower from the fuselage an ingenious rotating cylinder device Bernie had designed to measure water content and drop size. As the device slowly iced over, bitter wind would whip through the plane. The sergeant would sit casually by the hole in the airplane floor, reading a comic book.

But things were about to get back on track. The war was winding down, meaning his job in deicing would soon end. And Bow had recently told him she was pregnant. So in the quiet of his royal guest room, Bernie took a piece of hotel stationery and wrote the date: February 15, 1945.

One day nearer to victory.

That was the cheery banner message at the bottom of the page in *The Indianapolis Times* that listed his brother, Kurt, as missing in action, unaccounted for after the awful, late-stage offensive, the Battle of the Bulge. The family had found out in January. The paper printed a note that read like an obituary: "He attended Cornell University and after entering the service received ASTP training at the Carnegie Institute of Technology and the University of Tennessee. When the program was closed, Pvt. Vonnegut was transferred to the infantry and assigned to the 106th." That was it, Kurt's twenty-two years summed up in two sentences. The family was not without hope, exactly, but it seemed possible that the war had brought a second tragedy—first their mother, now Kurt—to the Vonnegut family.

His brother's last letter, written on December 15, had been to Bernard.

Bernard was an optimist by nature, not given to brooding or melancholy. The best thing, as he saw it, was to look to the future. He addressed his letter to Chauncey Guy Suits—Guy to his friends—the new director of the General Electric Research Laboratory, the nation's oldest and most renowned industrial research lab. He opened by apologizing for not having written sooner, but he'd been on the go nonstop since leaving Schenectady, New York, ten days earlier.

"I am very favorably impressed with the facilities of the laboratory, its policy and attitude towards research, and the opportunities there for the sort of work that interests me," he wrote. "As you know from our talk, I am not yet in a position to reach a final decision, however . . . I am most interested in working for General Electric."

He couldn't say exactly when he'd be free from his war obligations, but they all knew the war was likely to end soon. He stated that he expected a salary of $5,000 to $6,000 a year.

He was going to have a family to support, after all.

He had been in Schenectady ten days earlier to talk to Irving Langmuir about ice. It had been a heady experience. The brilliant chemist—the first industrial scientist to win a Nobel Prize—crackled with ideas. Some people's eyes glazed over after only a few minutes of speaking with Irving, but Bernie loved it. For the last few months, he had been corresponding with Langmuir and his assistant, Vincent Schaefer, about aircraft deicing, and even though Bernie was director of the MIT meteorology department's deicing project, he was the one doing most of the learning. Langmuir was a chemist, like Bernie, but he had also done significant work in physics and crossed over into biology, mathematics, and even psychology when it suited him. The scientific disciplines were just beginning to divide into a series of silos, their boundaries patrolled by ever-more-focused specialists, but Langmuir was an old-school generalist. Like Bernie, he had never expected to become fascinated by the problem of deicing.

Icing has been a problem since the dawn of aviation. Ice clogs carburetors, adds weight, and interferes with the wings' aerodynamics. An airplane wing's shape provides its lift: add enough ice and it can simply fall out of the sky. With helicopters, it's even worse.

In early days, pilots simply didn't fly in freezing conditions. But as aircraft grew more robust, they were expected to fly in any weather. Methods of deicing were invented and tried. There were coatings, heat applications, inflatable rubber boots that would expand and knock the ice off the wing. Sometimes they worked; sometimes they didn't.

Bernard had never thought much about aircraft deicing, but he had thought a lot about ice. For his graduate thesis, "A Freezing Point Apparatus," he designed a device to measure the exact point at which water with other substances dissolved in it will freeze. Bernie was proud of it. He liked devising tools and gadgets: his first patented invention was an easy-to-clean pipe he designed jointly with his father. The aircraft program required lots of apparatus, because the scientists needed to understand how ice formed. So Bernie once again found himself doing something fun: conducting experiments and coming up with gadgets to get at data in new ways.

As a scientist, Bernie was both old-fashioned and newfangled. He was not unlike MIT in that way. When Bernie's father had attended Tech—as its students called it—the college was a trade school that trained students to design electrical systems or engineer wastewater plants. America's top scientific minds had always gone off to Germany for grad school. But as war with Germany approached for the second time, Americans felt a new urgency about training their own scientists. In the 1930s, MIT's president, Karl Compton, and vice president, Vannevar Bush, began shifting the school's focus from practical skills, such as drafting, to pure science.

By the time Bernie had arrived at MIT, even the undergrad curriculum was centered on pure science. His classes were mostly chemistry, math, and physics, with a smattering of biology and humanities thrown in. He'd had one class in drawing and descriptive geometry, the one required of all first-year chemistry majors. Still, he never shied away from drawing his own illustrations or designing his own instruments. Both imaginative and pragmatic, he actually liked doing paper-clip-and-string kinds of experiments, what he called "Victorian science." When he was first called back to MIT to become a research associate in the Chemical Warfare Service, he was handed a German gas mask and told to reverse engineer it. Bernie got Manhattan District clearance so he could use radioactive tracers to measure smoke penetrations in the mask's filters, then designed an optical apparatus to measure the penetrations quickly. He even applied for a patent on it.

Bernie was a tinkerer. For him, tinkering was what science was about. You played around with something until you understood it. He'd been playing around with aircraft deicing since 1942, when a friend invited him to come work on a meteorology project at MIT. He wasn't trained as a meteorologist. He sometimes joked that he'd never really noticed the atmosphere until someone pointed it out. Meteorology had always been a poor stepsister to hard science disciplines like physics and chemistry. But he recognized right away that the field's puzzles were problems of basic chemistry and physics, manifested in everyday life. Rain, snow, clouds, storms: all were deeply familiar yet fundamentally strange. For a scientist driven, as Bernie was, by curiosity, it was an ideal subject. To study the weather was to ask science's most basic question: Why does the world work the way it does?

Once, when he was in his early teens and the Vonneguts were vacationing in Chatham, on Cape Cod, Bernie wandered down to the beach while the rest of the family slept. He had become enthralled by the dark and the sound of the waves. He walked and walked, passing the lighthouse, winking its beacon into the blackness. When he came to a jetty, he walked out to the end and stood there, surrounded by fathomless dark, hearing only the suck and roar of the ocean battering the breakwater. It was terrifying and thrilling, being so small, so alone in boundless ocean and air.

He never really lost the feeling. The earth's systems—water and weather and atmosphere—were huge and complicated, full of mystery and delight. Bernie had no idea yet that weather would occupy the rest of his life. Or that his interest in ice and his new deicing colleagues would shape not only his future work but also his brother's. He just knew he wanted to keep conducting the kinds of scientific explorations that fired up his brain. GE seemed like a good way to do that.

Awash in government contracts, GE had expanded enormously during the war, especially the Research Laboratory, and the company planned to continue growing. President Charlie Wilson, known as Electric Charlie, directed Guy Suits and other managers to go on a hiring spree. He planned for GE to become a postwar powerhouse and frequently shocked even fellow executives by citing "two billion" as the number he expected net sales to reach before long. But that was going to require new ideas and eager new men. So Suits invited Bernie, among other young men, to apply for a job.

With war winding down and Bow pregnant, the timing of Suits's letter was perfect. Bernie had responded right away and had gone for an interview in early February. There he met some of GE's scientific luminaries: tall, grave physicist Albert Hull, a pioneer of the vacuum tube; plump and outgoing Saul Dushman, one of the earliest experts in quantum mechanics; Gorton Fonda, whose team had famously developed an American version of the radar screen in just fourteen days. Suits had sent Bernie back to Minneapolis with an application form, and he filled it out in his hotel room. Under "available for employment," he wrote, "Probably at termination of war." For racial extraction, he wrote, "German." Under education, he approximated his class standing, with typical modesty, at "lower part top half." On the line for draft status, he wrote, "2B": deferred because of work in a war-related industry.

He had been spared his brother's fate because he was doing critical work: helping get Allied airplanes safely in and out of their bombing runs.

Bernard addressed the envelope and went to bed. There were more test flights to be made on the B-24, more huddling over instruments in the Flying Icing Wind Tunnel. But the war would be over soon; so everyone said. The Russians were moving in from the east, and German cities were being pounded by Allied bombers. The *Minneapolis Star-Journal* had just run the headline "2,250 Planes Hit Dresden." The German city, one of Europe's most beautiful, was already burning after a night assault by the RAF; now American bomber planes were adding fuel to the fire.

An Atlantis, Kurt would call Dresden later, sinking beneath waves of flame.

Did Bernie envision firestorms as he drifted off to sleep in his royal bed at the Hotel King Cole? It seems unlikely. There, in the blank white of Minnesota winter, it would have been quite a leap to imagine the storm of flames his work there was meant to enable. A firestorm is the most complex form of artificial weather warring earthlings can conjure. First there's the search for a target city blanketed in clouds. Then the first wave of planes dropping small explosives, to buckle weaker buildings and blow out windows and doors. The people running for safety. The second wave of incendiary bombs falling with a gentle rain-like patter, then bursting to life. The fires, fed by oxygen circulating through the perforated city, building into currents of wind. Hot gales sweeping through the streets; the city melting, escape routes blocked by a greedy whirlwind of death. The aftermath: blackened husks that were once human beings, and basement shelters turned to tombs.

One thing it is certain Bernard did not imagine: that as he wrote his letter to Guy Suits and laid the plans for his future, his brother was huddled underneath Dresden as the city was wiped from the map.

Bernard, his mind fixed on clouds and water and ice, could hardly have imagined Kurt hiding in a slaughterhouse basement, expecting at any moment to die by fire.

It would be many years before the brothers would learn the code name for the destruction of Dresden: Operation Thunderclap.

2

Precipitating Events

Someone was knocking on the door of Dean Langmuir's apartment on East Forty-Eighth Street. It startled his younger brother Irving. Irving had arrived in New York City the day before, and Dean had put up the usual cot. Hotels had been crowded enough before VE Day. Now with troops on their way home or reassigning to the Pacific, getting a room in New York was downright impossible. Especially on short notice—and short notice was how Irving Langmuir did things.

Dean had already gone to his Wall Street job, so Irving opened the door. In the hallway stood two Army officers, and they were looking for him, not Dean. Once inside, they told him they had come to ask him to change his plans. They would prefer that he decline the invitation to Russia.

Less than a month had passed since Germany's surrender. On May 8, 1945, Langmuir wrote "VE Day" in his GE notebook and underlined it. Then he started a list of meteorology papers he wanted to read. For the last three years, he had been doing war-related research, taking up whatever question the government needed answered. He had designed smoke generators, investigated airplane deicing, and studied precipitation static—the tendency of airplanes flying in snowstorms to pick up electrical charge that disrupts radio communications. Somehow all the projects he had been handed had converged in the fascinating field of weather study. That was what he was going to work on next.

The GE Research Lab encouraged its scientists' fixations the way parents encourage a child's passion for dinosaurs or ants. When Langmuir first started there, in 1909, Dr. Willis Whitney—nicknamed Doc—told him to look around and find something fun to work on. That's what all new scientists were told: Doc Whitney was convinced that was the best way to ensure they produced quality work. He was known for making daily rounds in the lab and asking the scientists, "Are you having fun today?"

After a few weeks of playing around with whatever piqued his interest, Langmuir told Doc Whitney that he was enjoying himself, but he didn't see how this was doing much for the company. Whitney told him not to worry about that; usefulness was Doc's problem, not his. And sure enough, before long, Langmuir's playful experiments had led to a complete redesign of the lightbulb—meaning longer life for customers and a whole new set of patents for GE. Soon after, his goofing around with lightbulbs led to the invention of atomic hydrogen welding. Langmuir had been following his own fancy ever since. And his fancy had led him to weather.

Now the Russians—and who knew more about snow?—were offering him a chance to meet their top scientists. The invitation had come just days earlier, addressed to "Prof. Irving Langmuir, Shenektady, N.Y." Irving and another twenty-five prominent American scientists had been invited on a monthlong, all-expenses-paid visit to Russia to celebrate the 220th anniversary of the Soviet Academy of Sciences. Never mind that there had been no Soviet Union 220 years earlier. Irving packed his bag and phoned his brother. The Russians, he told Dean, were picking him up in two days.

When Irving got to New York, Dean raised a few concerns. The whole thing seemed haphazard. The invite said very little about the program or schedule. Many of the scientists' names were even misspelled. And did Irving know anything about Russian festivities? He would be expected to drink toast after toast of vodka. To refuse would insult Mother Russia. But to comply . . . well, one might find oneself in a compromised position. And what were the Soviets up to, less than a month after VE Day, inviting some of America's most prominent scientists—many of whom had been doing war work—on a junket?

Sure, the Russians were allies, but after the inaugural United Nations Conference in San Francisco, where their petulance had nearly scuttled passage of a UN charter, American suspicions about Soviet motivations were on the rise.

Irving had dismissed all of this. That was politics, and politics did not concern him. He thought the trip would be scientifically interesting, so he packed his bags. That's how Irving was. It was fortunate he had even remembered to pack: a few years back, he showed up for a weeklong sailing trip in a blue serge suit and dress shoes, without so much as a windbreaker. Irving's obliviousness to real-world concerns was legendary. He could walk right by a colleague without so much as nodding. When a woman fell down on the stairs in front of him, he famously stepped over her and continued on. Once, he stepped in a can of paint, pulled his foot out without pausing, and kept on walking, leaving a trail of safety-yellow footprints in his wake.

So Dean thought it reasonable to make sure that his brother knew what he was getting into. Irving had assured Dean that it was all cleared with the State Department, so Dean had shrugged and gone to work. And then the Army officers appeared.

Irving listened with his customary air of unruffled intensity, but beneath his patrician reserve he was livid. Born in 1881, Irving Langmuir had grown up in an urbane and academically inclined family, graduating from Columbia's School of Mines and the University of Göttingen. At GE, he had gone from triumph to triumph. His initial lightbulb successes were just the start. He was one of the first scientists to conduct experiments on ionized gases with strange electrical and magnetic qualities, which he named "plasmas," inventing the field of plasma physics. He improved sonar detection and advanced understanding of the atom's structure, writing a famous paper describing his "concentric theory." He intuited the relationship between winds and ocean circulation. In 1932, he became America's first industrial scientist to win a Nobel Prize, for his work on monolayers—surface films only one molecule thick. The work launched the field of surface chemistry, with applications in mining, aviation, medicine, and water resource management, as well as in understanding the fundamental structure of matter.

As GE's celebrity scientist, his salary rivaled those of top executives. He worked on whatever he wanted and traveled as he saw fit, frequently giving papers at academic conferences and before professional societies. His opinion was sought by radio journalists and newspapermen. People asked for his autograph. He was not accustomed to being bossed around, not even by the Department of Defense.

The officers explained that the Army would prefer that someone with Irving's level of security clearance not visit the Soviet Union at this time. Irving asked if they were ordering him not to go. No, nothing like that, they said. They were *requesting* that he not go. They told him they had made the same request of the physicist Edward Condon and he wasn't going. They neglected to mention that the State Department had helpfully revoked Condon's passport. Later it would be clear why: Condon had worked on the Manhattan Project.

Irving didn't make trouble. But as soon as they left, he phoned GE. He really wanted to go on this trip. A chance to see Soviet scientific labs and talk to Soviet scientists was a rare and thrilling opportunity. Besides, he didn't know half as much as the Army seemed to think he knew about military secrets. None of the war work he had done was highly classified. The smoke screens he had developed were now being openly used in the Pacific to protect ships from kamikaze attacks. It seemed to Irving that the Army was letting a misplaced concern about secrecy get in the way of scientific learning.

Executives made a few calls. As one of the government's largest war contractors, GE had sway with the military. The Army rescinded the request, and Langmuir was free to go to Russia.

On June 10, 1945, one of President Truman's own C-54 transport planes left New York's Air Transport Command airfield. On board were sixteen of America's most prominent scientists: chemists, mathematicians, a hydrologist, and an anthropologist. Conspicuously absent were any physicists. Nevertheless, everyone aboard agreed: once things in the Pacific wrapped up, a new era of peaceful international cooperation would surely begin. And scientists, united by the apolitical pursuit of knowledge, were going to lead the way.

•

"Now, no emotions, please!" Kurt cried. His adored sister, Alice, ran and hugged him anyway, crying, and he too wiped away some tears. His father hugged him after Alice, and his uncle Alex—another favorite—happily pumped his hand. It's unlikely that any of the soldiers eating ice cream, playing the jukebox, or dancing with WACs at Officer Club 1 paid much attention. This was a familiar scene at Camp Atterbury, with its rows of hastily constructed clapboard barracks lined up like hay bales in the Indiana fields. Now that the war in Europe was over, families—the lucky ones, anyway—were turning up daily to pick up their boys.

It was the Fourth of July, and Kurt junior—Kay to his family—was home. His family had only found out he was alive when his letter of May 29 reached Indiana the previous month.

"Dear People," it began. He was alive—not only alive, but still very much Kay, simultaneously mordant and offhand as he reeled off the inventory of horrors he had survived in the last six months. The letter—ten succinct paragraphs—was a masterpiece of concision. It was his first attempt to write about his wartime experience, and it would remain his best for a quarter century. Like one of those seeds that lies dormant until the conditions for germination are perfect, it would wait until the Vietnam era to sprout into *Slaughterhouse-Five*.

"I've been a prisoner of war since December 19, 1944," he wrote, since "seven fanatical panzer divisions" cut his division off from the others. After that, "the supermen marched us, without food, water or sleep," for about sixty miles, then packed them into boxcars and shipped them across Germany. The prisoner train was strafed by the British on Christmas Day; a carload of officers was killed. South of Berlin, the men were unloaded and deloused. "Many men died from shock in the showers after ten days of starvation, thirst and exposure," he wrote. "But I didn't."

He was shipped off to a work camp in Dresden, where conditions were dreadful. One boy starved, and two were shot dead for stealing food. "On about February 14th," he wrote, "the Americans came over, followed by the R.A.F. Their combined labors killed 250,000 people in twenty-four hours and destroyed all of Dresden—possibly the world's most beautiful city. But not me."

The rest of the story was crammed into short paragraphs—his forced labor carrying corpses for incineration, the evacuation as the Russians approached, the Nazis' abandonment of the prisoners, a bizarre wagon ride across Germany, his final repatriation to a Red Cross camp in Le Havre. He hoped to be home, he wrote, in a month.

"I've too damned much to say," he concluded. "The rest will have to wait."

Wait it would. The letter, with its repetitive short phrase, "But not me," was a preview of *Slaughterhouse-Five* with its ironic catchphrase, "So it goes." Its theme of grim good luck—the meaninglessness of both death and survival—would anchor Kurt's lyrical antiwar masterpiece. The letter's evocation of war was brilliant. Even Bernard could see that. He and Lois gave a copy to Lois's hometown newspaper. *The Adirondack Record—Elizabethtown Post* printed Kurt's letter on its front page, under the title "Vet Describes His Experiences as POW of Germany." But Bernard didn't tell Kurt about it. In 2008, after Kurt's death, the letter would be included—incorrectly—in a collection of previously un-published works.

Even before Kurt wrote to his family, though, he had written to Jane. He took a chummy tone, pointing out that they'd parted on pretty friendly terms. He was alluding to the fact that they were lovers and that he'd written to her several times to make sure she wasn't pregnant. That was his typical mode—jokey understatement—when it came to writing about matters of sex.

Jane was by then working in Washington at the OSS—the prede-cessor to the CIA. She had graduated from Swarthmore Phi Beta Kappa in history, even though her thesis was somewhat controversial. She had argued that history teaches us nothing except that history is meaning-less. The historians didn't appreciate that much, but Kurt did. He loved the way her mind worked. Throughout boot camp and Army training, he had continued to write her love letters. As his time in the military wore on, he felt as if all his dreams were dying except one: his dream of a life with Jane.

Jane, for her part, was as busy as ever. She had other suitors, in-cluding a younger man still at Swarthmore, but Kurt was much on her mind. Then her letters of November 27, December 16, and December 27 were all returned to her, with the ominous stamp "Missing." Like his family, she hadn't known if he was dead or alive until she got his letter in late May.

He told her he was still alive, though he looked kind of starved. He was in possession of some money and a furlough and was hoping she hadn't gone and gotten married.

She hadn't.

So Kurt had stopped off in Washington to see Jane on his way to Indiana's Camp Atterbury, and soon she would be back in Indianapolis too. He was planning to ask her once more to marry him, and she was expecting him to ask.

His family had to be shocked at his appearance. He was forty-five pounds lighter, and his skin had been ulcerated by vitamin deficiency. But he was still the same old Kay. He insisted on taking the wheel, and as he drove the forty miles from Camp Atterbury to Indianapolis, he talked nonstop. The family was transfixed as he unfurled a tale of suffering, near starvation, abuse, and dumb luck. He lamented the destruction of Dresden and railed against the cruelty of the SS. When he got to the part where he and three others were forced to dig a grave for Michael Palaia, a fellow soldier executed for stealing a can of pickled string beans, he burst into tears.

"The sons of bitches!" he cried, still driving.

They all listened intently. No one interrupted, as they would when he was little. No one could correct him or gainsay him, because he was the one who was there. Uncle Alex couldn't get over how articulate the young man had become. Kurt's account of the fall of Germany was terrifyingly observant. And his thoughts about the future were bleak.

"I know what's going to happen in Europe," he said. "Now the trouble really starts. The French hate the Americans; the Poles and Russians hate the Germans; the Poles hate the Russians." Uncle Alex told Kurt he'd have to be patient with "civilians," who would have so little idea of what he'd been through.

"Oh, hell," Kurt replied. "I want to be a civilian myself. I'm sick and tired of being in the infantry . . . I've had enough of it. And I'm god-damned sick and tired of the whole damnfool bloody mess."

He was not alone. Many of the citizen soldiers who came back from the war were sick of it. They weren't professional soldiers. They were college boys and local kids, yanked out of normal lives and hurled into a maelstrom. Most who survived just wanted to put the whole thing behind them. Like so many of his fellow vets, Kurt had come home determined to throw himself vigorously into peacetime life. That meant finishing school, getting married, starting a family, and getting a job. The war played no part in any of that. It was time to take up where he had left off, as if the previous two years had never happened.

So Jane Marie Cox came to Indianapolis to see her mother, and when she went back to her job in Washington, she was wearing an engagement band made from Kurt's mother's ring. The original ring, an artifact of the family's affluent pre-Depression life, had boasted two large diamonds. Bernard and Kurt each got one to give to their wives.

Kurt couldn't wait to get on with married life. He was full of dreams and plans for their future, which would begin the minute he got his discharge. The only reason he stayed behind in Indianapolis instead of spending his precious leave in Washington, near his future wife, is that he was stuck at home waiting for Bernie.

Bernard had not been there to greet Kurt; he and Lois were in Elizabethtown, New York, awaiting the birth of their first child. They were still living in Cambridge while Bernie wrapped up his deicing work, but Bow wanted to have the baby at the Community House hospital near her parents. Three days after Kurt's homecoming, Peter Vonnegut was born. Bernie sent photographs of the baby, and Kurt and Alice were amazed to see how much like Bernie he looked. It was hard to believe, Kurt told Jane in a letter, that there were now two such creatures on earth.

He wrote to her every day. After such a long separation, it was nearly unbearable to be apart once more. But Bernie kept delaying his trip. And he was hoping that after his trip to Indy, Kurt would come back to Cambridge with him, to visit and meet his son. Kurt agreed, planning to spend a few days with Bernie and Bow before heading to Washington and Jane. He wanted to see his brother, but he was eager to start his new life. He consoled himself with the thought that maybe the know-it-all Bernie would pass on some explicit marital tips. If so, he promised to relay them to Jane pronto.

While awaiting Bernie's arrival in Indianapolis, Kurt went downtown to the offices of *The Indianapolis News* and asked to see issues from the second week of February. He wanted to find out how the bombing of Dresden had played in America. Later he would describe finding a column half an inch long, a tiny paragraph merely noting that Dresden had been bombed and two American planes had been lost. He had experienced a life-altering cataclysm, and Americans hadn't even heard about it.

In fact, the paper's reporting on Dresden was much more thorough than he claimed. Strategic bombing was the front-page story, under a banner headline: "Great US and RAF Air Raids Drive on Reich." The paper reported that 2,250 American bombers had attacked industrial centers in Germany, including delivering "one of the biggest blows of the war" to Dresden, which was "already burning from a night assault by heavy R.A.F. bombers." The next day the paper reported that Dresden lay in ruins.

It's not that Kurt lied or even misremembered. The newspaper's story was simply not enough. Surrounded by movie listings, sports scores, bond prices, and ads for hats, given equal billing with Indy getting a new airport and the manpower shortage in trash collection, how could it suffice? All that heavenly life had been going on back home while he was huddled in hell. And the paper, like all American wartime newspapers, took the standard patriotic tone. The morality of firebombing civilians was not brought up. Kurt had watched Atlantis disappear beneath the waves, and the newspaper had merely reported a fruitful rain. Schoolgirls had boiled to death in water tanks; zoo animals had charred to blackened husks. Kurt saw the giraffe and wished he hadn't. To cause that kind of suffering without feeling shame could only be considered a sin.

•

Bernie arrived in Indianapolis on August 7, 1945. He had repeatedly delayed the trip because Bow was having terrible headaches after Peter's birth and he didn't think he should leave her alone with the baby. Finally, on Monday, August 6, he left, heading to Indianapolis by rail. The trip took the better part of two days. On Tuesday afternoon, the train stopped in Dayton. He called the family to tell them he'd be in Indy at 4:40.

Somewhere in there, he must have seen the newspapers. A single bomb had been dropped on Hiroshima, and banner headlines were declaring that the world had changed. "Atomic Bomb May Spell Annihilation for Japs," proclaimed that morning's *Indianapolis Star*. A drawing just underneath the headline showed a uranium atom being exploded into two new atoms.

The article called atomic energy "the most terrible destructive force ever harnessed by man." And it was now in U.S. hands. The president was insisting on immediate surrender, or the Japanese could expect "a rain of ruin from the air, the like of which never has been seen on this earth."

Bernard knew they weren't posturing. He understood atomic fission; any scientist working at his level did. He had used radioactive tracers in his work with gas masks at MIT. So he knew why the *Star*, like papers across the nation, had very little to report about what actually happened to Hiroshima. No trains were going in or out, and the city was under an impenetrable cloud of dust and smoke. The Japanese were reporting that Hiroshima lay in ruins, but many Americans thought they must be exaggerating. Scientists like Bernie knew better. A city had been wiped from the map, and with that the atomic era had begun, born not in the war rooms of Hitler or Hirohito but in America's halls of science. Born in places like the one where Bernie was about to start work. This wasn't Victorian science: this was something completely new and appalling. The usually unflappable Bernie was sick at heart.

Hiroshima cast a pall over the brothers' reunion. Bernie took in Kurt's emaciated appearance, and Kurt took in Bernard's horror at the day's news. Kurt hadn't realized, until he saw his brother's face, how dramatically the world had changed. Just that morning, he had written a cheerful letter to Jane with a 7 inscribed in pencil behind the typed words. Seven for the date, for the seven kids they planned to have. When he saw Bernie, his mood changed.

Like everyone else in the nation, Bernie followed the newspapers' race to piece together the story in the days that followed. The United States, in secret from its citizens and Congress, had entered "the battle of the laboratories." It was a two-and-a-half-year effort, employing more than 125,000 people, costing $2 billion, and requiring the construction of three top secret cities—Oak Ridge, Hanford, Los Alamos—but in the end America had won the war of the labs. The White House called it "the greatest achievement of organized science in history."

Two days later, on Thursday, organized science annihilated Nagasaki.

The war was over: so the president and the military were saying. Families surged with new hope of seeing their sons. Many Americans, worn down by months of harrowing reports from the front lines of Iwo Jima or the liberation of the Japanese prisoner of war camps, felt a grim satisfaction: The Japs had gotten what they deserved. And it had been American know-how that gave it to them. *The Indianapolis Star* ran a breathless story under the headline "Scientists' Dream Comes True— the Atom Is Split!"

It was a dream, but it was a nightmare too. In the days following the two atomic attacks, the nation experienced a kind of cognitive dissonance. The newspapers and radio could talk of nothing but nuclear fission, but the conversation ricocheted between hope and dread. On the one hand, there were stories about atomic airplanes and atomic cars, about atomic medicine that would cure cancer and atomic energy that would power the nation for pennies. The National Press Club in Washington introduced an "atomic cocktail," and Hollywood publicists christened the voluptuous new starlet Linda Christian the "anatomic bomb." On the other hand, there was fear. What would happen when some other nation got its hands on the terrible new weapon? That was inevitable, Bernie told Kurt. There was no keeping this secret. War had grown more frightening than ever: it had commandeered the power to destroy the earth. When the Japanese agreed to surrender, revered radio personality Edward R. Murrow summed up the national mood. "Seldom, if ever," he intoned, "has a war ended leaving the victors with such a sense of uncertainty and fear, with such a realization that the future is obscure and that survival is not assured."

Bernie's soon-to-be employer was mentioned in many stories about the bomb; GE's contributions had been critical. And lest anyone think that the scientists could now turn to peacetime pursuits, GE was running ads in papers nationwide pointing out that "military and naval power drove this enemy to defeat down a road built by research." Democracy owed its survival to scientific know-how. That work must not cease with the end of war. "Scientific progress and productive efficiency," declared the ads, "are the most wonderful weapons of all time because they do not have to be laid aside when the fighting ends. *They must not be laid aside.*"

Bernie returned to Cambridge earlier than he had planned and without his brother. With the end of the war weeks if not days away, he had to get busy wrapping up his government contract. D. E. Chambers, assistant director of the GE Research Lab, had already written to him asking when he intended to report to his new job. Scientific progress, as the ads declared, must remain on the march.

•

Kurt and Jane took the small, leaky rowboat out onto Lake Maxinkuckee. It was called the *Beralikur*—for Bernard, Alice, and Kurt—and it had been the boat the kids used every summer, when the family spent weeks at their cabin on the lake and the three kids spent their days running around with a gaggle of cousins and friends. Those were some of the happiest days of Kurt's life.

The honeymoon trip had a valedictory feel: this boat ride would be the last in the *Beralikur*. The cottage, a final vestige of the family's pre-Depression prosperity, had been sold; Kurt and Jane would be the last Vonneguts to stay there.

The papers were still full of atomic horror as the newlyweds rowed out into the lake. They were adrift in a world gone mad, but at least they had each other.

"I swam all the way across this lake when I was eleven years old," Kurt told his new wife.

"You told me," she said.

"I don't think you believe I could really do a thing like that," he insisted. "But you ask my brother and sister if it isn't true." Bernard and Alice had been there, egging him on. He was tall and gangly, a kid once given a Charles Atlas bodybuilding set by a sadistic high school coach. But in the water, he felt beautiful. As he swam across the lake, he'd felt buoyed up not just by water but by his siblings. For once he'd earned their admiration. He wanted Jane's admiration too, but she wasn't about to hand it over for something as banal as swimming across a lake a decade earlier. She had higher hopes for him, the kinds of hopes he barely dared hold for himself.

Sometimes he could hardly believe they were married. But it had been real, all of it, the silver vases full of white gladioli on the Cox backyard terrace, the shimmery chords of a harp, modest words spoken by a minister from First Friends Church. The wedding had been moved from September 14 to September 1 after Kurt received orders to report to the Miami Beach Redistribution Center. There was not enough time for Bernard to get there, so Kurt's high school friend Ben Hitz took his place as best man.

In the newspaper announcements of their wedding, Jane's academic accomplishments—Tudor Hall, Swarthmore, Phi Beta Kappa—outshone Kurt's. He had only "attended Cornell." But there was also a write-up on the *Indianapolis News* society page where the columnist Filomena Gould had gushed over the young private's "fresh and cogent humor." He even showed her some of his writing about the war, which she declared "surpasses any firsthand account of an American soldier's existence in enemy hands."

Jane liked his writing too. She wanted him to keep doing it, and he was; in his free time, he worked on short stories and humorous essays and fired them off to *The New Yorker* or *The Saturday Evening Post*, reporting on his submissions—and rejections—to Jane. He assured her, however, that he had no illusions about trying to write full-time, as a career. He'd get a good job to provide for their seven kids.

A loon popped out of the lake and gave its long, mournful cry, and the newlyweds were silent.

It was all an ocean. That was one of Jane's favorite sayings, from a book Kurt hadn't read: *The Brothers Karamazov*. The priest Father

Zossima says it to the youngest Karamazov brother, Alyosha. The elderly monk is explaining why someone would ask forgiveness of the birds. "It's all an ocean," he says, meaning the birds, the sky, the clouds, even himself; it's all part of one big surging life force, and the name of that force is God.

"It's all an ocean!" Jane would cry when she was struck by how everything was interconnected. It made her happy to believe, fervently, in things that lent mysterious magic to the world. She thought Dostoyevsky's treatise on the human need for that magic was the most brilliant book ever written. She suggested Kurt start reading it on their honeymoon.

The lake, the loon, the forgiveness of birds, the rain-like patter of incendiary bombs, the exploding sun over Hiroshima: It *was* all an ocean, but how did it fit together? Kurt knew there were currents connecting the ruin rained down on Japan with the firestorm that haunted his dreams. The link between Hiroshima and Dresden was indiscriminate bombing, what the Allies called total war. But it was deeper than that; it was something about man's inhumanity to man, about technocrats who valued demonstrations of know-how so much they lost sight of the fact that they were killing *people*: schoolgirls and geezers and mothers pushing babies in prams.

Dresden, Hiroshima, Nagasaki: the world was spinning off into a series of atrocities, each one worse than the last. It was enough to make a man lose his faith. Kurt's buddy Bernard V. O'Hare had told him on the ship home that the war had killed his faith in God. Kurt didn't believe in God, but he still thought that was too much to lose. But now he too was losing his own faith, faith in knowledge and technology. As a child, Kurt had drawn pictures of futuristic cars and planes and houses. As a young man, he had acquiesced in his brother's and father's desire that he dedicate his life to science. Now it seemed that the urge to discover, to invent, was not noble at all, but evidence of a sickness in the human soul. "Scientists' Dream Comes True." What kind of dream was destruction and death in industrial quantities? This could only be the dream of a species that hated the earth and hated itself too.

Jane said they could build a life of poetry and art and beauty. They could go back to school, leaving science to others, and throw themselves into the study of the human soul. They could have friends and raise kids and build a home filled with music and books, rich conversation, and a well-stocked bar. They could make paintings and write stories and make those things their life, a life that, in its own small way, would help change the world. She showed him another of her treasures, a slip of paper given to her by a professor who copied a quotation for each student at semester's end and tucked it into a walnut shell. Jane's quotation was "Some good sacred memory, preserved from childhood, is perhaps the best education."

Right there on their honeymoon, Kurt painted his first painting. For his subject, he chose a chair—something solid, and homey, and redolent of possibility. And he started reading *The Brothers Karamazov*.

"My brother asked the birds to forgive him," Father Zossima told Alyosha. "That sounds senseless, but it was right for all is like an ocean, all is flowing and blending; a touch in one place sets up movement at the other end of the earth."

•

Irving Langmuir took his seat in a room full of people who had just changed the world. It was September 19, 1945, and every famous physicist in the nation—along with eminences from other sciences and humanities as well—seemed to be here at the University of Chicago. Langmuir had seen some of them at a dinner the previous month for the American-Soviet Science Society. Now they had all been summoned to Chicago by the university's dynamic young chancellor, Robert Hutchins, for a secret conference on the scientific and social ramifications of the atomic bomb.

Chicago had played a critical role in the Manhattan Project: Enrico Fermi and Leo Szilard had achieved the first self-sustaining nuclear chain reaction there in 1942. Now many of the nation's most prominent physicists were headed for Chicago to join its new Institute for Nuclear Studies. But it was crucial that the bomb be contemplated not just as a technical problem but as a social one. The atomic era had begun, and no one knew what came next.

The general mood was grim. A terrible thought was troubling many scientific minds: not every scientific advance was necessarily good for humanity. Leo Szilard set the conference's tone with a speech full of foreboding. The bombs that had fallen in Japan, he said, had a one-mile radius of destruction. Atomic bombs in ten years would have a destruction radius ten times greater. The Soviets would inevitably get the bomb, probably in two and a half years, and in six years they would have enough of them to destroy every major city in America. The United States by that time would have built enough atomic bombs to destroy every major city on the planet. The only hope was international control of all atomic energy, which required something drastic: world government. This would probably only come about through World War III: he estimated the chance of instituting world government without war at only 10 percent.

Some in the audience objected to such a dire forecast, arguing that world peace could be possible without world government. Others argued that Szilard was probably wrong about the Soviets getting the bomb so soon. Irving Langmuir spoke up then. He had been to Russia just a few months earlier, he said, and he agreed with Szilard. The Soviets would catch up in less than five years, probably more like two or three. Their science would surpass ours in ten. The critical question was how much information the United States should share with them. In his opinion, the United States should share its science freely.

Many scientists agreed. Science abhors secrecy. It was said that the Army was going to seek legislation giving it total control of all atomic bomb research so it could continue to keep the details classified. But to the scientists, the idea of keeping the atomic secret was absurd. Other nations would get atomic capability; the only question was when.

What the scientists hoped for was international control, including an inspection system that would keep nations from building more bombs. Langmuir pointed out that it wasn't such a bad thing that the Russians would have the bomb soon: once other nations had nuclear weapons, it would be less likely that the United States would use them. The military strategist Bernard Brodie was there, and he agreed with Langmuir. The following year, he would publish "War in the Atomic Age" in a collection called *The Absolute Weapon*. The essay would be a founding text of what came to be known as the theory of nuclear deterrence.

But many in the room recoiled from the idea of peace through a balance of power based on fear. To most of those present, seeing atomic war as a kind of *game* was morally repugnant. Worse still would be a world in which nations raced to out-arm one another, building bigger and more fearsome weapons. Already the Manhattan Project physicist Edward Teller was advocating building a "Super bomb," a hydrogen atomic bomb that would make the first A-bombs look puny. But not many in Chicago agreed with him. Most of the scientists gathered there were convinced that an atomic arms race would be nothing less than the end of the world.

In fact, many seemed to feel guilty about their role in having created the first superweapon. This seemed illogical to Irving. The atomic bomb had ended the war and unquestionably saved many lives, Japanese as well as American. Yet many of the Chicago scientists seemed to feel it shouldn't have been dropped or even that they shouldn't have made it. "The physicists have known sin," the head of Los Alamos, J. Robert Oppenheimer, would later declare, "and this is a knowledge they cannot lose."

Many scientists had read H. G. Wells's 1914 novel *The World Set Free*, a story that takes place in a future where scientists have harnessed atomic energy. Rather than ushering in a new era of ease and enlightenment, atomic power causes massive social upheaval and world war. The world is finally "set free" when humans realize that a technological advance as momentous as atomic power calls for an end to nationalism and a new era of world government in which science becomes "the new king of the world."

Szilard was so taken by the book that he ordered a copy of it for the Chicago scientists. Along with most of the conference participants, he agreed with Wells's main thesis: once scientific knowledge reaches a certain level, separate sovereign states are no longer possible. In the atomic era, nations would go the way of coal: they would be replaced by something better.

At the conference, the scientists hammered out a consensus based on three simple points: there was no secret that could be kept, there was no defense against the bomb, and there must be international control of atomic energy. They decided to form a group, the Federation of Atomic Scientists (later changed to the Federation of American Scientists), dedicated to educating the public—and the government—about this new technology. It was, the anthropologist Robert Redfield declared, their moral duty. With that, what was known as the Scientists' Movement was born. It made its public debut with a two-page statement published in *Life* magazine. The statement hewed to the three main points: no secret, no defense, international control.

As one of America's most famous scientists, Irving Langmuir was in a position to take their message to the people. He stuck to the script, at least at first. In October, he testified before a Senate subcommittee, predicting that Russian science would trump America's in ten to twenty years. In November, he addressed a joint meeting of the American Philosophical Society and the National Academy of Sciences, insisting that an atomic war could make the earth uninhabitable and that "world control of all atomic energy seems the only alternative." But in late November, back before the Senate to argue for an international agreement, he urged that "the Governments of the United States, Britain and Canada make immediate contacts with the Russian government to secure, if possible, their tentative agreement instead of relying solely on the more cumbersome machinery of the United Nations."

At heart, Irving was a pragmatist. Sure, he'd had his youthful flirtation with socialism, but like so many men of his age and status he had settled into a low-key laissez-faire conservatism. Theoretically, he had no problem with the concept of world government. But instituting it was likely to be difficult. Science would progress most smoothly if the Western powers simply stuck together and did their best to pacify the Russians.

Also unlike many of his colleagues, Irving knew and accepted that science would never return to its prewar openness. He was not an academic but an industrial researcher at one of the nation's biggest defense contractors. Government security clearance had always been an informal requirement at the GE Research Lab. Soon it would become mandatory for employment. This didn't worry Irving. He didn't see how it could possibly become a problem.

•

Kurt stood in the shower, thinking of Jane. His wife, Woofie. That was her old nickname. "Woofie on the dance floor or Woofie in a seminar or Woofie in a bull session or Jane Marie out for tea," declared the 1944 Swarthmore *Halcyon*, "is the same piquant treat." Jane was putting a stop to that now, though. Sometimes he called her Wifey. He was trying out other nicknames too: Lovey, Sweety, Dear Heart, Darling, Lamby-kins. They were jokey, but his love was real.

Water was drenching him in a shower stall in Kansas, but he was seeing Jane standing in the Florida ocean. Her dress was hiked up around her hips—oh, how he loved those hips—and her ankles were being licked by the waves. She had come down to Miami Beach while he was there awaiting his post-combat reassignment to Fort Riley. They had stayed at the Roney Plaza Hotel: palm trees, cabanas, pool, ocean beach, and their own bed; it was bliss.

What other shores, she had wondered there in the surf, had the water molecules that were touching her touched before? She was always saying things like that, brilliant things that emerged from the part of her he thought of as her fourth dimension, the part full of wisdom and inspiration and poetry. There was Jane, the smart, charming woman the world knew, and there was Jane Marie, his Jane Marie, lyrical and spiritual and capable of depths that other people could only imagine.

At Fort Riley, he had been assigned the job of clerk-typist. In between typing up reports of correspondence received, he was writing to anyone he could think of to speed up his discharge. At least he had finished reading *The Brothers Karamazov*. Here, in the miserable flat Kansas landscape, where he cycled between apathy, depression, and joyful memories of Jane, the book was like a beacon of sanity. Dostoevsky was saying something he had always suspected: that if there wasn't a God, humans would have to invent him. They needed that order, that illusion that things made sense. But the real salvation, the true holiness of the world, came only from the world itself.

Next up, he was going to read *War and Peace*. Also a life of Beethoven and a textbook on calculus. He had to be worthy of Jane—and of the University of Chicago.

The day the acceptance letter arrived was the happiest in his life. He was going to finish his undergraduate degree on the GI Bill, and this time it wouldn't be in science. He would study anthropology—which at Chicago was a program that led to a master's degree, not a bachelor's. And Jane had been given a fellowship for grad school in Slavic languages and literature. They would enroll—if his damn discharge papers would finally come through—in the winter semester. They would finally start living the beautiful, intellectual life they had always wanted.

Chicago had been an easy choice. Kurt had thought about going to its law school even before going to war. His cousin Walter, a close friend, was studying philosophy there now, also on the GI Bill. Walter came from the "artsy" side of the Vonnegut family: his parents were actors. And he and Kurt had another thing in common: Walter had been a navigator on B-17s during the war, and after being shot down, he'd been a German POW for two years.

Kurt couldn't wait to be done with the Army. Fort Riley was dreary, and he had little to do. The only good part was he had enough free time to write short stories. One of the very first he attempted was "Atrocity Story," a thinly disguised account of his fellow POW Michael Palaia's execution. Kurt changed his name to Steve Malotti and set the story in the Red Cross camp at Le Havre, where the narrator and a couple of others try unsuccessfully to get the bureaucrats in the War Crimes Commission tent interested in Malotti's case. The story ended—as the real event had—in a frustrating lack of closure. But Palaia's story haunted Kurt, and it would until he got it right.

Paper was scarce, so he typed his stories on the backs of the meteorological briefs that rolled off the office Teletype: "Scattered thundershowers occurred early this morning in Minnesota, northern Wisconsin and western Upper Michigan, and are occurring again this afternoon in Northern Minnesota." On the flip side of the weather report, he typed another attempt at his war material: "Brighten Up!" This time, he aimed for a lighter tone than in "Atrocity Story," focusing on the black marketeering of a "dissipated little weasel" named Louis Gigliano, who manages to use his time as a POW to rack up massive profits. It was an improvement, story-wise, funnier and not so pedantic. Friends of his at the base who read it said he could write.

When he finished his stories, he sent them to Jane. It was her critical eye he really cared about. She had been an editor on Swarthmore's literary magazine, *The Dodo*, and could write herself. He trusted her. She typed up his stories, editing them in the process. She picked out a selection to send to the "writer's consultant" Scammon Lockwood to get some advice. Kurt waited anxiously, fearful of what she might think of him if Lockwood said he was a hack. Fortunately, Lockwood thought he had promise and for another twenty dollars, would help edit his work. They declined, because they didn't have the cash. But Lockwood's praise convinced Jane more than ever that Kurt could write for a living one day. He protested: How could he support seven kids on a writer's income? He thought he should get a job in a newsroom or a school. He knew from his misery at Fort Riley that an office job wasn't for him. But something steady and salaried, that's what he wanted. Jane was wonderful, but she was impractical. He told her she didn't understand finances. She said that she just knew it would all work out.

Sometimes it scared him, Jane's conviction that he would become a great writer. She told him he was a modern-day Chekhov, that if he'd lived in the Elizabethan age, he'd have been Shakespeare. She believed his works would help create the literature of the postwar era. He thought that was pushing it. It was easy to believe he was a genius when he and Jane were daydreaming, but now, as he toiled away as a clerk-typist in Kansas, it seemed like mere fantasy. They were just normal people, he told her; they should not aim for greatness. Bernie was the great one in the family, the one who was going to make a contribution.

But one day in November, reading the foreign affairs section of *Newsweek*, he had a strange sensation. He *knew* about these things. In fact, he knew more than the writer did. He knew what Europe looked like, how it tasted. He knew what artillery sounded like coming in, what it felt like to be crammed into a boxcar with sixty smelly men, what it sounded like to be bombed, what it felt like to begin to starve. He knew how to make iron ration soup, how a man who had given up hope stared into space with blank despair. He knew all this because he was there. His experience had taught him things that were important. Writing about them wouldn't be just for him. People should hear about what he knew if they were going to make better decisions in the future. He told Jane in a letter that he would take his writing seriously. She had given him the courage at least to do that.

When his discharge finally came, he was ready. He was going to go back to school and to write. From this point on, he was going to live his own life.

3

Head in the Clouds

Schenectady, New York, was divided into three parts. South of downtown lay neat rows of modest homes, where almost all of the workers lived. In the east, just beyond the leafy campus of Union College, was the GE Realty Plot, where the managers and executives had stately homes. And in the center, just south of the Mohawk River, belching and clanking at the end of Erie Boulevard, were the machines.

The sprawling Schenectady Works, as the industrial complex was known, was GE's world headquarters and one of its largest factories. A brick and steel compound ringed by a fence, the hulking, humming city within a city contained forty thousand employees in more than two hundred buildings. The Works had a hospital, a fire station, a power plant, and a foundry. It had clubhouses, restaurants, employee stores, its own sound studios, and a radio station, WGY. Blinking down on all of it through the smokestack haze was the sign atop Building 37: yellow letters ten feet tall spelling out "General Electric," crowned by the giant red GE insignia. "The initials of a friend," the company called its logo. Employees called it "the meatball."

For the last three years, the Works had turned out the tools of war in quantities never before imagined. Now its three daily shifts cranked out the fruits of peace: the steam turbines, generators, motors, electrical equipment, and control systems that would help build the nation's postwar prosperity. Americans and foreigners alike came to gape at the wonder of it. Tour groups clutching maps followed guides from building to building, wide-eyed at this mecca of American industry.

Bernard wanted to be close to work, but he didn't want to live in the noisy, bustling factory town. Bow had grown up in a sylvan village in the Adirondacks. They had a dog that needed room to romp. He ran ads in the *Schenectady Gazette* for a farm or a home in the country. Postwar housing was tight, so when something came on the market that was almost in the country, he grabbed it. The house was in Alplaus, a tiny village right across the Mohawk River from Schenectady. It sat on the village's main street but was set far back on a big lot, and one whole side hung out over a tangle of trees and vines at the edge of Alplaus Creek. It was a peaceful spot, just a short walk to the block-long village center, with its firehouse, grocery store, and post office at the back of a bike shop. Most of Alplaus's residents worked for GE. It was a short drive to the Works, and if Bow needed the car, Bernie could take one of the daily buses that ran from Alplaus to the GE gate.

The buildings at the Works were numbered so people could navigate the sprawling complex, but Bernie was lucky: he only had to get himself to Building 5, right near the gate. The GE Research Lab's cozy connection with management was reflected in its location right next door to Building 37, the main administration building; the two brick office blocks were connected by an arched sky bridge. In the midst of the sprawling Works, the Research Lab stood apart, a cluster of workrooms where brainy Ph.D.'s cooked up experiments with little regard for their practical value. It was a temple of science lodged in a city of trade. Yet the Research Lab was the branch of GE most essential to proving the company motto: "Progress is our most important product."

The General Electric Research Laboratory was the brainchild of GE's first celebrity scientist: Charles Proteus Steinmetz. A four-foot-tall, hunchbacked, cigar-puffing socialist, the eccentric Steinmetz was a mathematical and electrical genius who dominated GE in the early twentieth century. GE's generators wouldn't have been the same without him. One of the most famous stories told about Steinmetz is probably apocryphal, but it conveys the reverence in which he was held. Mid-career, the story goes, Steinmetz was called in to look at a broken generator in one of GE's plants. Steinmetz asked for the generator's mechanical drawings and spent a couple of days poring over them. Then he approached the machine and put his ear to it. After a few moments, he took out a piece of chalk and marked an X on the side. Open the generator there, he told the engineers, and remove so many turns of wire from its turbine. Asked the fee for his services, he said $1,000. Shocked by the amount, the plant engineers insisted on an itemized invoice. Steinmetz sent them a bill. It said,

> Marking chalk "X" on side of generator: $1.
> Knowing where to mark chalk "X": $999.

That was Steinmetz's particular genius: knowing where to mark the X. And yet the company was initially reluctant to embrace his plan for a research lab—until 1900, when GE patents began to expire. Facing the loss of market dominance in lightbulbs, management suddenly saw Steinmetz's point: keeping a group of research scientists on the payroll meant anything they invented or discovered would be the property of GE.

Other industrial labs were narrowly focused on churning out new or improved products. GE's was different. In a radical new approach to industrial research, the scientists worked only part of the time on practical tasks like coming up with new patentable types of lamp filaments. The rest of the time they were allowed to conduct pure research.

It was a fantastic success. Given the opportunity to explore freely, the scientists came up with all kinds of new inventions. By World War II, the GE Research Lab could claim responsibility for the electric range, transoceanic radio, the portable X-ray machine, the turbo-supercharged jet engine, and autopilot. Its contributions to both world war efforts further boosted its importance to a company whose growth was increasingly driven by government contracts. GE dubbed it "the House of Magic." The scientists hated the name—they were doing science, not magic tricks—but the boys in PR loved it.

Bernard fit the place temperamentally. The Research Lab was sometimes described as having a university atmosphere. But in its early days, it was more like a salon, a mecca of what Bernie called Victorian science: the eccentric but brilliant researchers followed their curiosity wherever it took them, moving easily between physical, material, and even biological sciences. Having a Ph.D. in physics didn't mean you couldn't work in neurology if you liked; having a Nobel Prize in chemistry didn't mean you left statistics to the mathematicians. The scientists discussed their work with each other in weekly cross-disciplinary presentations and frequently had far-flung hobbies outside the lab as well: Steinmetz had kept a greenhouse full of strange plants and a menagerie of deadly animals, including alligators, black widow spiders, and rattlesnakes. The lab's director, Doc Whitney, was famous for his obsession with turtles. Albert Hull taught Greek before becoming a physicist and contributed the many classical coinages for the lab's new inventions— thyratron, magnetron, kenotron, dynatron—that one inventor later dubbed "Graeco-Schenectady." Irving Langmuir spent much of his spare time studying the hydrodynamics of the Adirondacks' Lake George, where he had an island house, and his assistant Vincent Schaefer collected arrowheads, archaeological artifacts, and natural history specimens.

"Research is appreciation," Doc Whitney liked to say. He often told the story of how, as a young professor at MIT, he had given students an assignment in which they combined the elements of sulfur and iron in a glass tube and heated them over a Bunsen burner. As the iron and sulfur combined into iron sulfide, the vessel was suffused with a bright glow. Students writing up the experiment almost inevitably reported that the elements had combined. When they did, Whitney would send them back to the lab with the instructions "Repeat and note the glow."

Bernard never had to be told to note the glow. Like Whitney, he considered research an expression of appreciation for the natural world and its principles, and he couldn't wait to get down to doing it. But almost as soon as he arrived in Schenectady, he was denied the opportunity. GE was on strike.

Almost before the VJ Day celebrations wound down, the nation was swept by a wave of strikes. Throughout the war, laborers had accepted wage controls and strike bans, even while upping production, and profits had soared. Workers expected corrective wage increases once the war was won. Instead, after VJ Day, employers, fearing the loss of government contracts, began laying off workers and cutting hours. So in the fall of 1945, union members across the nation—oilmen, coal miners, autoworkers, truckers, meatpackers, newspaper printers, phone and telegraph operators—began walking off their jobs.

Bernie probably hadn't expected to see it happen at GE, any more than President Charlie Wilson had. The company was supposed to be a liberal, employee-friendly place: it was widely known that in 1937, while other corporations were fighting unionization, GE had willingly hammered out a contract with the United Electrical Workers. Employees called it the "Generous Electric Company"; management didn't think its workers would strike over a smaller-than-requested pay raise. Yet in early January, a hundred thousand of them did.

The strike hobbled the entire company. Dozens of factories, including the Schenectady Works, were effectively shut down as picketing electrical workers denied access to everyone, including non-union, white-collar employees. Bernie, along with all the Research Lab scientists, was told to work from home.

Public opinion favored the striking workers. Desperate to avert a public relations disaster, GE settled with the union on a wage increase of eighteen and a half cents an hour. Now at last Bernie could start his new job—by looking around for a good problem to work on. If he didn't find something quickly, someone would assign him something, and he preferred to choose a research project himself. So, after years of wartime interruption, he finally got his life back on track.

•

Chicago was a dream come true. Kurt and Jane's apartment on Ellis Avenue was within walking distance of the university and from Walter and his wife, Helen, who lived on Lake Park Avenue. The cousins were frequently at each other's homes or strolling down to Lake Michigan together. Kurt and Jane loved the lake. They loved having Walt and Helen in town, and they loved the university. Chicago was a heady place to be. The school had always been a magnet for leftists, skeptics, bohemians, and civil rights activists; now the issues raised by the bomb gave its intellectual life a new urgency. But Chicago's thinkers weren't wallowing in atomic dread. They were stepping up to help shape this new atomic age. Hyde Park buzzed with a new prospect: that, just as in H. G. Wells's novel *The World Set Free*, humanity had learned its lesson at last.

Kurt and Jane embraced the idea. The horror of Hiroshima could at least bring this new hope: that human beings might finally change, might finally move beyond the outmoded nation-state and form a world government. If so, there might be hope for the elimination of war. Some scientists were even acting on their conviction that they must lead the way in renouncing violence. In the spring of 1946, as the government prepared to test atomic bombs by dropping them on a fleet of captured enemy ships at Bikini Atoll, some prominent scientists, including J. Robert Oppenheimer, refused to take part.

It was gratifying that Chicago was at the center of this movement. Chicago chancellor Robert Hutchins and physicist Leo Szilard were leading spokesmen for the world government cause. The Chicago-based Federation of American Scientists published the first issue of its journal, the *Bulletin of the Atomic Scientists*, the month after Kurt and Jane arrived. Soon after that, it put out the bestseller *One World or None: A Report to the Public on the Full Meaning of the Atomic Bomb*, a collection of passionate essays advocating international control of atomic energy. Contributors included Albert Einstein, J. Robert Oppenheimer, Leo Szilard, Edward Condon, and Irving Langmuir.

Kurt's own anthropology professor Robert Redfield had helped form the University Office of Inquiry into the Social Aspects of Atomic Energy and had joined Chicago's Committee to Draft a World Constitution. He believed that the social sciences—especially anthropology—were going to be critical in helping humanity adjust its institutions for the new atomic age.

Kurt admired Redfield, whose work he began to follow when he switched his specialization to cultural anthropology. He had started off studying physical anthropology, which had charts and maps and measurements and all kinds of complicated theories, making it comforting to someone who valued scientific thinking. But there were also tedious scientific tasks, like measuring the size of early human brains by pouring grains of rice into their skulls, then measuring the rice. Disappointed,

Kurt had gone to his adviser and confessed that the science bored him; he would rather study poetry. The adviser had recommended cultural anthropology, "poetry which *pretends* to be scientific." Kurt liked the idea, and he threw himself into the new field.

He filled his notebooks with cramped notes: phases of different cultures; notes on cultivation, ceramics, human sacrifices, and metallurgy; ideas about literacy, agriculture, the development of moral orders. He learned about a vast array of cultures: Finns, Kazakhs, South Pacific Islanders, Mayans, Incas, ancient Chinese, Turks, Native Americans. He devoured journal articles, marking them up with red pencil. He studied Turkish linguistics. It was still rigorous and precise. But now all that precision was being directed toward something he actually cared about: not molecules or cells or atoms, but human beings and the cultures they made.

He was especially taken with Professor Redfield's ideas about the changes and dislocations that result when small isolated communities— Redfield called them folk societies—evolve into sprawling, heterogeneous cultures. Culture, Professor Redfield declared, was in a constant state of flux; even the moral order was always forming, dissolving, reforming. Culture wasn't something that simply happened to humans; it was something they could tinker with. You could see it happening as the atomic age washed over Chicago and the university's best minds worked on reshaping the culture to accommodate it.

Kurt could play his part in that by writing. So he attempted, once more, to write about his Dresden experience in an essay called "Wailing Shall Be in All Streets." It was, like his letter home, pointed and concise. It began with an account of basic training and how the infantry were urged to "kill, kill, kill," without being told very clearly why they were fighting. "A lot of people relished the idea of total war," he wrote; "it had a modern ring to it, in keeping with our spectacular technology." But the war, he wrote, had left him "sick at heart." The reason was simple: "In February, 1945, Dresden, Germany, was destroyed, and with it over one hundred thousand human beings. I was there."

I was there. It was something he would say again and again.

He went on to tell of his experience helping to find and burn bodies after the firestorm. But then the essay devolved into several pages of outright moralizing.

"There can be no doubt that the Allies fought on the side of right and the Germans and Japanese on the side of wrong. World War II was fought for near-Holy motives. But I stand convinced that the brand of justice in which we dealt, wholesale bombings of civilian populations, was blasphemous."

He sent "Wailing" to *The American Mercury*, which rejected it, but editor Charles Angoff suggested Kurt send the magazine something else.

He tried a different tack in an essay called "I Shall Not Want," where he tried to convey what it felt like to starve. Here he tried to keep the tone light, thinking maybe he could sell it to *Gourmet*. Some parts worked, such as his account of how the prisoners kept journals full of fantastical descriptions of meals they would eat once free, arguing about whose imagined menus were best. But other parts were over-formal, tendentious even. Jane went through it with a pen, striking out stilted constructions and wordiness. It helped, but not enough. Kurt sent it off to *The New Republic*'s college essay contest. The prize was a summer internship at the magazine. He didn't win.

In July, Kurt and Jane vacationed at Lake Maxinkuckee with Walt, Helen, and their baby son, Kit; Kurt and Jane were his godparents. The two couples played cards and stayed up late talking about politics. That month, Congress passed an act creating the Atomic Energy Commission. It felt hopeful: like the first step on the road away from madness and toward sanity through world government.

•

Not long after his arrival at GE, Bernie dropped in on the lab of his old deicing acquaintances. Irving Langmuir was away for most of the spring, giving the prestigious Hitchcock Lectures at Berkeley, but Vincent Schaefer was in Schenectady, moving forward with their new investigations. Bernie told Vince that he had grown interested in the process of supercooling: lowering the temperature of a liquid or gas without converting it to a solid. Vince said he and Irving were working on the same thing. Specifically, they were trying to figure out if they could manufacture snow.

Snow had brought Vincent Schaefer and Irving Langmuir together. Vince was president of the Schenectady Wintersports Club, and Irving, who also adored skiing, was a member. In the early 1930s, Vince got the idea of sponsoring a snow train for skiers out of Schenectady. Irving, an avid pilot, offered to take him up to look for likely routes in his open-cockpit Waco plane. Before long, the startled Vince found himself flying the plane—banking, turning, diving, even practicing stalling and recovering, all under the tutelage of the brilliant scientist. They flew over the Catskills and scouted out ski hills. By the time they landed, Vince was groggy with incipient hypothermia. Langmuir took the younger man to his own house, and Marion, Irving's wife, fed him hot tea and cookies until he felt better.

To some people, Vince seemed an unlikely assistant for Irving Langmuir: he had never even finished high school. His father was sickly, and Vince had to leave school at sixteen in order to help support the family. On the advice of an uncle, he joined the GE apprentice program and trained as a machinist, landing a job as a drill press operator. Eventually graduating to model maker for the Research Lab, he quickly became known as the person who could put together any kind of apparatus the scientists needed. Intelligent, ambitious, and with a burning desire to be a "real" scientist, he was soon not simply making lab machinery but helping in the design of experiments.

In 1932, when Langmuir's old assistant retired, Vincent became his right-hand man. Vince called Irving "the Boss," but they were really scientific partners. Irving put little stock in degrees or credentials: he cared about whether a person was curious and thoughtful. Bernie was the same way: it never seemed odd to him that Vince had made himself indispensable.

Like Bernie, Irving and Vince had grown intrigued by supercooling during the war. In their work on precipitation static, they had attempted to conduct experiments at the research station on New Hampshire's Mount Washington, home to some of the worst weather in the world. One day, as they were hiking up—they preferred to hike up and ski out when they had work to do at the summit—Langmuir stopped and indicated some clouds that hovered on the mountain's peak. They were heavy and ominous, but only one lone snowflake drifted to the ground.

"Look, Vince," he said. "With all these clouds everywhere, there's only a flake here and a flake there. Why? I think we ought to do some more studies on that."

They knew that the clouds on the mountain peak were often supercooled. Objects at the summit research station could amass ice three feet thick without a drop of rain or snow falling. Irving intuited that this must happen because the clouds passing over the peak contained large numbers of water droplets that were colder than 32 degrees Fahrenheit. Those droplets didn't freeze until something disturbed them, such as sudden contact with a metal surface. It was the same process that caused airplanes to accumulate ice when flying through supercooled clouds. But were there ways to force the supercooled water droplets in a cloud to freeze spontaneously, after which they would fall as snow or rain?

People have dreamed of inducing precipitation for as long as they have been thirsty. But efforts to make rain were usually mystical, not scientific. Military men had long claimed that rain tended to fall after big battles, leading to the idea that firing cannons into the sky might "bust" the clouds. In the nineteenth century, some scientists argued that filling the air with particulate matter was likely to bring down rain; James Pollard Espy, the nation's first government meteorologist, proposed burning large swaths of the nation's forests to make rain for the arid West. But most purported rainmakers were charlatans and con men. No one really knew how to make rain because no one understood how rain happened.

Snow and rain seem like some of the most basic phenomena on the planet, yet they were still largely mysterious. Meteorologists knew that clouds form when moist air cools to its dew point, converting its water vapor to cloud droplets. At some point, some of those droplets would convert to ice crystals. The ice crystals would collect water and grow until they were heavy enough to fall. But what made those first droplets turn to ice?

In the 1930s, the meteorologist Walter Findeisen proposed that they required a nucleus—a small atmospheric particle of dust or salt spray for the water to cling to. Findeisen suggested that if he was right, it should be possible to introduce artificial nuclei into clouds to stimulate rain. Langmuir and Schaefer had not yet read Findeisen's foundational work; they preferred to start their work with experiments, rather than the literature. But they had guessed correctly that the cloud droplets require a nucleus to convert to ice. So, with the war over, they had decided to test different chemical substances for their ability to do just that.

Because Vince was already conducting experiments on supercooled water, Bernie decided that he would focus on supercooled metals. But he kept in touch, dropping in on Vince periodically to see how he was progressing. In the early summer, Vince had an idea that was startlingly simple. He requisitioned a GE chest freezer. When it arrived, he lined it with black velvet and aimed a light at its innards. He chilled it to 10 degrees below freezing and breathed into it, and voilà—his breath made a cloud! Because cold air is heavier than warm, the cloud stayed there in the freezer, even with the lid open. Now, with a laboratory cloud, he could begin trying to make laboratory snow.

For several weeks, Vince assailed his cloud with substances that might function as ice nuclei: sulfur, magnesium oxide, volcanic dust, talc, diatomaceous earth. As the summer heated up, his lab partner Katharine Blodgett—the first woman to receive a Ph.D. in physics from Cambridge University—noted that his experiment was cleverly timed: it required him to spend sweltering days in the lab hanging the upper half of his body into a freezer. But one day in July, it got so hot the freezer couldn't keep up. To get his freezer back down to the right temperature quickly, Vincent got a large block of dry ice, which the Research Lab always had on hand, and threw it in. To his surprise, the entire cloud inside instantly converted into shimmering crystals of snow. After all the substances he'd tried, dry ice—nothing more than solid carbon dioxide—had nucleated the cloud.

Vincent wrote up the experiment in his lab notebook: "I have just finished a set of experiments in the laboratory which I believe points out the mechanism for the production of myriads of ice crystals." When he wandered into the adjoining lab, he was less circumspect. To the astonished scientists he announced, "Now I know how to make it snow."

When Langmuir returned to Schenectady in late July, Vincent

showed him the freezer experiment. The Boss saw the point at once. In his GE lab notebook he wrote, "Control of Weather."

They both knew this was their next big project. Irving had recently heard that his name was on the list of prominent figures President Truman was considering to head up the Atomic Energy Commission. But now nothing could be further from his mind than atomic bombs and nuclear power. He was onto something even more important. In his small notebook, he recorded his plans. They would fly to the tops of clouds and seed them with pellets of dry ice or a stream of liquid carbon dioxide. They would make flights through various types of clouds measuring wind speed, temperatures, vertical currents, and the distribution of water droplets. "Develop theory of growth of rain drops," he wrote. "Can we cause cloud of uniform droplets to give rain?"

He spoke to Guy Suits about getting a plane. But he would also need instruments to record all the data they would collect. Then he had another thought.

"What is Vonnegut doing?"

•

On the last day of August 1946, *The New Yorker* dedicated its entire issue to John Hersey's thirty-one-thousand-word article "Hiroshima." Rather than report on the event in the traditional way, Hersey followed six characters in detail from the moments just before the bomb fell, documenting their activities in the horrific days that followed. Written in a flat, almost clinical tone that avoids overt moralizing or rhetorical flourish, the piece piles detail upon detail until the cumulative result is far more harrowing than any attempt to sermonize. The issue sold out at newsstands in a few hours. Rarely has a magazine piece—which soon became a book—caused such powerful soul-searching. Albert Einstein sent a thousand copies to fellow scientists, urging them to consider its implications.

It was the sort of response Kurt would have liked to provoke with "Wailing Shall Be in All Streets." But his little piece on Dresden was not gaining traction. After *The American Mercury* rejected it, he sent it to *Harper's*, *The Atlantic*, *Time*, and *The Yale Review*. Edward Weeks at

The Atlantic was positive enough that Kurt revised it and sent it again. But in the end, no one wanted it. He threw himself back into his anthropology studies at Chicago.

And then, before the fall semester could even get going, Jane told him she was pregnant. It had happened: an atom of Kurt and an atom of Jane had smashed together and split into two new cells. Two to four to eight to sixteen to thirty-two and on and on—a chain reaction bringing life, not death.

She would drop out of school. That's what women did. Together they went looking for her adviser, a gloomy Russian who had fled Stalin and washed up on the shore of Lake Michigan to bestow the pearls of Russian culture on frat boys, ex-GIs, and coeds. They found him in the library. Jane told him she was going to resign her scholarship and drop out of grad school. And then—she couldn't help it—she broke down and wept.

"Mrs. Vonnegut, pregnancy is the beginning of life, not the end of it," he sniffed.

Yes, it was a beginning, the beginning of a life they had imagined together, their married life with seven kids. But it felt like the end of something too. They shared so many dreams: to write, to learn, to travel, to help cure an ailing world. Having seven kids was among their dreams, but now it was cutting to the head of the line, especially for Jane.

•

When he heard the whine of an airplane over the village of Alplaus, Bernie rushed outside. He had come home for lunch; his house was just a mile from the airport. Vince and Irving were still at the airstrip, experimenting. In fact, that might be Vince overhead. Bernie peered at the airplane intently. Sure enough, a long unnatural trail of something that looked like ice crystals was streaming out behind it. He ran for his camera.

Bernie was now officially part of Langmuir and Schaefer's team. They had invited him to join them soon after Schaefer's freezer experiment. For months now, Vince had been conducting more freezer tests while Bernie scoured the crystallographic tables, trying to find other substances that might nucleate ice crystals. Meanwhile, Langmuir was filling his notebook with theoretical calculations of the number and size of snow crystals likely to be produced in different circumstances.

They had all been longing to try out dry ice nucleation on a real cloud. But the fall had been frustratingly mild: sunny, warm days, with barely a cloud to speak of in the heavens. The bright blue Schenectady skies deepened to a rich royal tone at dusk, and the stars blinked the promise of another clear day. Every morning, Vincent was up at dawn, scanning hopefully for clouds. He told the others he was so eager to test his theory he couldn't sleep.

By November 12, unable to bear the suspense, they had decided to make a practice flight. They rented a single-engine Fairchild plane and got Curtis Talbot of the GE test flight division to fly it. Using a motorized dispenser he had designed, Vince released crushed dry ice into cumulus clouds at three to five thousand feet. But the cloud temperature was nowhere near cold enough to produce snow. There were some more promising stratus clouds at around twelve thousand feet, but Talbot told them the single-engine plane could go no higher than ten thousand feet.

A day later, the weather had finally given them what they wanted. The temperature was around freezing, and the sky to the east and north of Schenectady was filled with parallel bands of thick stratus clouds. An excited Vince had called Talbot as soon as he stepped outside, then driven to the local dairy and bought six pounds of crushed dry ice. Now he was up there, dispensing it.

Bernie retrieved his camera and went back outside. He fumbled with the aperture setting, then searched the sky again for Curtis and Vince in the Fairchild. Langmuir had had a two-way radio installed on the plane after the previous day's flight, so he was probably talking to them now from the tower.

The plane Bernie was watching flew in an odd pattern, the trail of snow behind it tracing its path. The path was growing more elaborate. It almost looked like a *P*. Then it looked like an *E*. Suddenly his heart sank.

P . . . E . . . P . . . S . . . I . . .

It was not Vince and Curtis at all. Bernie couldn't help but laugh at himself. Ruefully, he went inside and put his camera away.

But when he got back to the lab, everything was in an uproar. Vincent had not done any skywriting that morning. He had done something even better: he had made snow.

Irving and Vince recounted the story over and over. The stratus clouds were high up in the sky, so after takeoff Curtis had begun climbing, taking forty minutes to reach ten thousand feet. Vince spotted a promising cloud in the vicinity of Mount Greylock, over the Massachusetts border. Its base was well above them at around thirteen thousand feet.

"Can we get to it?" he asked Talbot. Curtis, getting into the spirit, nodded and urged the little plane upward.

The plane's single propeller churned away. It seemed to take forever. The last four thousand feet took half an hour to climb. Looking into the cloud, Vincent saw shimmering iridescent ice crystals around its edges—a sign that the inside was probably supercooled. He checked the thermometer. It read −17.5 degrees, and its bulb was beginning to ice over. Curtis swung the airplane around, and they flew into the cloud. Vincent dispensed three pounds of dry ice. Then his ice dispenser jammed. He was breathing heavily. His head swam, and his heart pounded—the effects of altitude in the unpressurized plane. He picked up the cardboard box and opened the Fairchild's window. Wind sucked the remaining dry ice into the white.

After that, they made a big loop and flew back through the cloud again. This time, they were surrounded by glinting crystals of snow.

"We did it!" Vince cried over the roar of the engines. He and Curtis shook hands on their triumph.

In the tower, Langmuir had his field glasses glued to his eyes. Shortly after the plane disappeared into it, the cloud almost seemed to explode. Then it began to split horizontally, dividing into two parallel clouds. Falling from the space between them were long streamers of snow.

"It works," Irving wrote in his notebook. When the plane landed, he rushed across the tarmac to greet Vince.

"This is history," he said.

Back at the lab, the normally reserved Langmuir could hardly contain himself, glowing with excitement as he described the snow they had made.

"I could see it forty miles away," he marveled.

Guy Suits pointed out that they would soon need a better plane to continue the experiments. He had worked closely with the military during the war, heading up GE's war research division, and had many close contacts there. He proposed bringing in General Curtis LeMay. Surely the Air Force would be interested in a technique for dissipating fog and clouds.

Before long, the phones were ringing. GE's publicity department, the News Bureau, was staffed with real journalists, and like reporters everywhere they had a nose for breaking news. Before long, two men from the News Bureau had arrived at Building 5 with portable type-writers and were tapping away as fast as Langmuir could talk. The PR men returned to the News Bureau that evening, bursting with reports of man-made snow. An assistant editor at *The GE Monogram*—the company's in-house magazine for managers—was there to hear the tale.

"Well, Schaefer made it snow this afternoon over Pittsfield!" he reported to his colleagues back at the *Monogram*. "Next week he walks on water."

The GE press release went to the papers the very next day: "Scientists of the General Electric Company, flying an airplane over Greylock Mountain in western Massachusetts yesterday, conducted experiments with a cloud three miles long, and were successful in transforming the cloud into snow."

The release quoted Langmuir's estimate that a single pellet of dry ice the size of a pea "might produce enough ice nuclei to develop several tons of snow." He went on to give a primer in cloud physics. When a cloud was seeded and its water droplets froze, he said, latent heat was released. Ironically, the freezing process generated heat in the cloud, which would produce turbulence, the kind that causes cumulus clouds in thunderstorms to billow upward. The turbulence, he said, "enables the process to spread as a type of chain reaction and draws more moisture into the active region."

It was typical of Langmuir's brilliance that, although not trained as a meteorologist, he had intuited something fundamental about clouds. They are not, as most people think, reservoirs of water hanging out in the sky. They are hives of activity, constantly taking on water vapor from the atmosphere, the ground and surface water, and sometimes converting that water to precipitation. Langmuir had figured out that seeding did more than force clouds to release stored water. It could literally make clouds more efficient. He and Schaefer had discovered a method not of "milking the skies," as it was sometimes described. They had found a way to build better clouds.

The newsmen were less interested in cloud physics than in what this all meant for the man on the street. They packed the press release with thrilling claims. Scientists could now fill reservoirs, deliver more water to hydroelectric dams, clear dangerous clouds that iced airplanes, make snow over ski resorts, and divert storms from urban areas. A new era of managed climate was dawning.

It was headline news. "Snowstorm Manufactured," announced *The Boston Globe* in inch-high banner type. "Three-Mile Cloud Made into Snow by Dry Ice Dropped from Plane," said *The New York Times*. "Man Does Something About Weather—Makes It Snow," declared the *New York Post*, and *Newsweek* quipped, "Deliver One Blizzard." *Time* described the event as if the dry ice had been an atomic bomb and the cloud had succumbed to radiation sickness: "Almost at once the cloud, which had been drifting along peacefully, began to writhe in torment. White pustules rose from its surface. In five minutes the whole cloud melted away, leaving a thin wraith of snow."

File clerks struggled to keep pace as more than ten thousand clippings descended upon GE. Delighted newsmen took publicity photographs of the News Bureau snowed under with news.

For Bernie, Vince, and Irving, the next few weeks were a whirlwind. Letters and telegrams poured into the Research Lab. It seemed almost everyone had ideas about how to use this fabulous new tool. Airline meteorologists wanted to dispel icing clouds and dissipate fogs. Water managers and irrigation districts wanted to produce more rain. A Chilean government agency requested a team of GE scientists to draw up a plan for fixing Chile's arid areas. A U.S. Marine Air Corps navigator offered to fly the GE scientists to Seattle to dispel fog that was slowing rescue efforts for a plane that had crashed near Mount Rainier. Ski clubs and ski resorts offered their slopes to further the work. A classroom of California schoolkids sent postcards requesting a snowstorm. A film crew wanted snow for a shoot in Buffalo. Buffalo itself wanted snow sent back over Lake Erie.

There were naysayers, but not many. The *Boston Herald* editorialized that "bringing more snow to snowy New England is very much like carrying coals to Newcastle . . . Can the General Electric create a snow-repellant as well as a snow-producer?" A columnist in the New York *Sun* had more philosophical objections to monkeying with nature, asking, "Who wants to see a child look out the window at the crystals from fairyland on a winter morning and exclaim, 'Oh, mumsy! Look what General Electric is doing'?" Vincent, riding high on his new fame, sent the columnist a sardonic apology, claiming that he was "repenting inside the igloo doghouse" to which he'd been consigned and assuring the columnist that "the day will never come when each and every snowflake carries a G-E monogram."

But most of the world seemed giddy at the prospect of GE snow. And why not? Only a year earlier, scientists had harnessed the most fundamental power in the universe and used it to end a seemingly endless war. Why shouldn't they move on from mastery of atoms to atmosphere? This was just the next step in man's taking control of nature.

One letter sounded a different theme, one of particular interest to Guy Suits. Simon Goldstein, an insurance broker from New York City, wrote to warn GE about the many injurious effects that a manufactured snowfall might cause: car accidents, falls, floods, property damage, even the expense of snow removal. "This is likely to produce lawsuits against your Company," he wrote. "It would therefore seem dangerous to leave yourselves unprotected in these circumstances. May I hear from you?"

•

"Time to go home, Barney," Katharine Blodgett called out as she gathered her things. It was 5:30, and everyone else had already left. But Barney—Bernard's undergraduate nickname had followed him to GE—was huddled over Vincent's freezer. Approaching him, Katharine realized he wasn't likely to be heading home anytime soon. He was on the trail of something interesting and was determined to see it through.

That was the quality in Bernie that made him such a good scientist—and also at times such a frustrating husband, father, or brother. Once he got some new idea in his teeth, no force on earth could tear him away from it. Now his obsessive nature was zeroing in on a new method of cloud seeding: silver iodide.

He had paged through the entire crystallographic handbook, looking for things with crystal structures similar to water. He had found three promising substances and tried them in Vince's freezer. Only one seemed to have any effect. So he had been trying it in different forms, including smoke. When he vaporized silver iodide, it worked like a charm. Not only that, but the ice nuclei created with silver iodide lasted for half an hour or more. They lasted even after more moist air was added to the freezer. The effect was as striking as what happened with dry ice, and it was likely to be even more durable.

He was trying, he told Katharine, to figure out if silver alone would do the trick, or iodine alone, or if it had to be silver iodide. He had hours of experimenting to do, and he wasn't about to stop now. Bernie would stay in the lab for as long as it took, because he was onto something big. Dry ice seeding was causing a national sensation. But Bernie might have found something even better.

The next time Vincent went up in the Fairchild, Bernie went with him. They conducted two days' worth of inconclusive tests with dry ice. On the second day, Vincent thought perhaps they had over-seeded the cloud, producing so many ice nuclei that they were too small and light to fall. But Bernie couldn't help but notice that even when their seedings produced immediate and dramatic results, they did not propagate further snow. Dry ice worked, but only for a short time.

Back in the lab, he built a small smoke generator based on the ones Langmuir and Schaefer had made during the war. He put silver iodide in it and ran it for fifteen seconds, and the lab filled with nuclei. When he blew a puff of air into the freezer, it filled with ice crystals. The effect persisted for an hour. Bernie put the device on a windowsill and let it blow silver iodide smoke out into the atmosphere. But it was late in the day and dark, so there was no telling if the chemical had any effect on the clouds.

In early December, Bernie, Irving, and Vince met with the Army. After a formal lunch downtown at the Hotel Van Curler, they gave Dr. Michael Ference of the Signal Corps a tour of the lab. Vincent created an ice crystal fog in the freezer. Bernard brought a balloon filled with silver iodide smoke he had produced in the boiler of Building 37, and they created another round of ice crystals with that. Ference was impressed. He thought they could work out a contract for at least a year, including the long-term loan of a bomber plane and its crew.

On December 20, Vincent and Curtis went up in the Fairchild again. Bernie and Irving were in the tower, but the airplane radio failed, so they had to wait for the plane's return to hear how the seeding went. After landing, Vince reported that they had made four runs dispensing dry ice and liquid carbon dioxide. On their way back to the airport, they saw a new cloud full of fine crystalline snow hanging just below the cloud deck. They figured it had been made by seeding.

The first snowflakes fell shortly afterward. Snow fell all afternoon and into the evening. By the time it stopped, around 11:00 p.m., Schenectady was buried under nearly ten inches of snow.

"A very interesting storm," Langmuir wrote in his notebook.

For the next couple of days, they researched it. Bernie collected data on snowfall times and measurements for all Weather Bureau stations within two hundred miles of Schenectady. They made maps showing the storm's development. Irving woke up before dawn with equations filling his head, waiting until 9:00 a.m. before calling Vincent or Bernie to talk it through. Once they felt certain, Irving called Guy Suits and told him what they had concluded: their seeding had caused the unusually heavy snowfall in the Schenectady region and beyond.

Suits told him not to tell anyone.

But on the day after Christmas, Irving wrote to C. N. Touart in the Air Weather Service of the Army Air Forces. "Schaefer made some seeding runs Friday morning, Dec. 20," he wrote, "which look as though they may have produced wide-spread effects upon the development of the snow storm that swept over parts of New York state and New England." If Suits didn't want to go public, the best way to ensure continued research was to keep the military interested.

•

The meteorologist Harry Wexler, chief of scientific services for the U.S. Weather Bureau, respectably liveried in flannel suit and wire-framed glasses, sat up in his conference chair and gaped. He had come to Boston to learn what could be learned for the good of his governmental agency, but he hadn't expected anything as dramatic as this. At the front of the room, Vincent Schaefer was showing slides of man-made snow while Irving Langmuir predicted GE's imminent victory over the climate.

Wexler was at the joint meeting of the American Association for the Advancement of Science and the American Meteorological Society (AMS). The whole conference was abuzz with the GE scientists' bombshell. The night before, GE had hosted a cocktail reception in the Georgian Room of the posh Statler Hotel. Vincent had brought the laboratory freezer he had used to make his early experiments, and as the assembled reporters and scientists drew near, he had breathed into the box to create a cloud. Ice cubes rattled in glasses as the gods of this miniature world waved their hands and filled its sky with shimmering snow.

Now Langmuir was talking in sweeping terms about their experiments outdoors and what would come next: deserts would bloom, storms would be quelled, snow would fall where people wanted it and not where they didn't. After the official paper was over, he spoke even more broadly. He told people about the flight of December 20 and the unusual snowfall that had followed. Cloud seeding, he was telling people, had created a spectacular snowstorm.

Harry Wexler had studied meteorology at MIT, under the supervision of pioneering Swedish meteorologist Carl-Gustaf Rossby, and gone on to become an editor at the *Journal of Meteorology* and a member of the council of the AMS. He had joined the Weather Bureau in 1934, and he was now on a mission to bring the new, mathematically rigorous meteorology of the Scandinavians to the United States. He had an ally in the Weather Bureau chief, Francis Reichelderfer. Long a bastion of old-school weather mapping and forecasting, the government's weather service was undergoing a makeover under Chief Reichelderfer. He was going to drag it—kicking and screaming, if necessary—into the new scientific age.

As Harry and Chief Reichelderfer saw it, the facts were simple. The laws of physics underlay all weather, from the tropical hurricane to the sudden gust of wind. The planet spun, the sun shone, the tides rose and fell, the winds blew, all of it following basic equations of hydro-dynamics that had been around for two hundred years. With enough study, it must be possible to come up with a mathematical model of the atmosphere that would enable accurate forecasts of its future behavior. This, after all, was the scientific revolution's great insight: that the universe could be described—all of it—in purely numerical terms. In other words, it was knowable, and if it was knowable, it was predictable.

Scientists had a name for this insight: the clockwork universe. In 1814, the French mathematician Pierre-Simon Laplace had imagined a creature intelligent enough to "comprehend all the forces by which nature is animated . . . an intelligence sufficiently vast to submit these data to analysis." For that creature, "nothing would be uncertain and the future, as the past, would be present to its eyes." Scientists had made up a name for this mystical being with perfect knowledge. They called it "Laplace's demon."

Harry Wexler had dreamed of being able to modify the weather. What meteorologist hadn't? But one of his favorite quotations was from Ben Franklin: "He who would master nature must obey her laws. He must learn her laws and then obey them." If weather control ever became real, Wexler knew it would be the result of what he had dedicated his life to: learning the physical dynamics of the atmosphere. It would happen when humans had learned enough to become like Laplace's demon. That's what the atomic scientists had done: they mastered nature's laws to master nature. But here, at the AMS meeting, scientists who knew nothing about the mathematics of atmospheric circulation were announcing they could make snow—when they didn't even know how nature made snow! It was as if the nuclear physicists of 1942 had been approached by a couple of chemists who claimed to have gone outside and smashed some atoms.

The GE scientists' revelations were the "outstanding contribution" of the meeting, Harry Wexler reported to Chief Reichelderfer. But they were meteorologically naive, and their approach was downright primitive. The real way to take charge of the climate was through something more rigorous—like the ten nonlinear equations on punch cards Harry had right there in his briefcase. He had brought them to Boston to see if he could get some time on Harvard's high-speed calculating machine.

Once the equations were solved, he would take them back to Princeton, New Jersey, where the Weather Bureau was taking part in an all-out mathematical attack on the weather. Because as Harry Wexler saw it, the future was not in experiments but in equations—equations so complex they had to be worked out by an artificial brain. Laplace's demon might finally be coming to life, not at GE, or in any human mind, but in the tiny, electrically ignited glow of a vacuum tube.

•

"I promise to scrub the bathroom and kitchen floors once a week," Kurt typed, "on a day and hour of my own choosing. Not only that, but I will do a good and thorough job, and by that she means that I will get *under* the bathtub, *behind* the toilet, *under* the sink, *under* the icebox, *into* the corners; and I will pick up and put in some other location whatever moveable objects happen to be on said floors."

The baby wasn't even born yet, but things would never be the same. Jane missed going to class, and she had terrible morning sickness. She pestered Kurt so much about the household chores that in January he finally typed up a contract in which he promised, in addition to scrubbing the kitchen and bathroom floors weekly, to take out the garbage promptly, hang up his clothes, and refrain from putting out his cigarettes or dumping his ashes in wastebaskets. If he failed in these duties, Jane was "to feel free to nag, heckle or otherwise disturb me until I am driven to scrub the floors anyway—*no matter how busy I am.*"

And he was busy. With the baby coming, Kurt had taken on a job in addition to his schoolwork. He was moonlighting for the City News Bureau, the team of crack reporters who provided much of the copy for Chicago's papers. He wasn't experienced enough to be taken on as a reporter, so he was toiling away as a copy boy on the night shift. He'd come home for a few hours' sleep before going off to classes.

He was happy to be back in a newsroom again. But the move was driven more by necessity than desire. He was a family breadwinner now.

It was exhausting, but he still loved Chicago. It all seemed so relevant. A foolish fight might be raging in Congress over whether David Lilienthal was sufficiently anticommunist to head up the new Atomic Energy Commission, but Chicago thinkers were already past such ridiculousness and hashing out a draft of a world constitution. In the anthropology department too, Kurt felt as if he had found a sort of extended family. It was a small community working together to figure out big questions about people and their cultures. He wanted to be part of it, to be one of them.

He finished up his contract with Jane by declaring it effective until the baby was born, "when my wife will once again be in full possession of all her faculties, and able to undertake more arduous pursuits than are now advisable." He was looking forward to that.

Somehow Kurt managed to paint: he exhibited three paintings in an open student exhibition on campus. None of them sold. No matter. He bragged about the exhibition in a letter to Walt and Helen. The point of doing art was doing art. He was his own man now, finally freed from the hyperrational world of science to focus on what he really cared about: human beings.

4

Bolt of Lightning

People said John von Neumann was a demigod. He had made a good study of *Homo sapiens*, declared his colleagues in Princeton and Washington and Los Alamos, so good he could impersonate our species with nearly perfect panache. Every so often, though, when he cut quickly to the heart of a mathematical quandary or began reciting from memory a book he'd read decades earlier—in ancient Greek—or when one totted up the sheer number of appointments and directorships and consultancies the man held, then the facade would slip. The dapper suits, the glittering parties, and the urbane aplomb that won him the nickname Gentleman Johnnie—sometimes all of it just couldn't disguise the obvious: this creature could not be human.

Harry Wexler liked him a lot.

They were alike, Harry and Johnnie. Both were Jewish mathematicians, Wexler the son of prosperous Russian immigrants, von Neumann from Hungary's Jewish upper class. Harry had taught at the University of Chicago and Aviation Cadet School during the war; von Neumann had taught in Berlin before joining the exodus of professors fleeing Germany in the 1930s. Harry found his home at the U.S. Weather Bureau in 1934, one year after Johnnie found his at the Institute for Advanced Study in Princeton, New Jersey.

Known as a "paradise for scholars," the Institute for Advanced Study was founded in 1930. It's not a part of Princeton University but a private research institution located in the same town. Von Neumann became one of the initial five members, along with Albert Einstein and the mathematicians Oswald Veblen, Hermann Weyl, and James Alexander. Johnnie was the youngest of these luminaries, but he had already made vital contributions in the mathematical fields of game theory, measure theory, fluid dynamics, quantum mechanics, and ergodic theory—the study of long-term average behavior in dynamic systems like traffic jams and weather. Like Harry, he had a reputation for asking searching questions and efficiently getting to the heart of a matter.

Both Harry and Johnnie felt comfortable working with the military. Von Neumann had done the math confirming the implosion method used in the Trinity test and in the plutonium bomb dropped on Nagasaki, but in contrast to many scientists he had no moral qualms about his work on the bomb. He had been present for the Trinity explosion and the nuclear tests on Bikini Atoll. Like his friend Edward Teller, he believed the United States should get on with building the "Super"—a thermonuclear, or hydrogen, bomb. In fact, he was an advocate of preventive nuclear strikes: it was what game theory said a rational actor should do. But now, he told people, he was thinking about something much more important than bombs. He was thinking about computers.

In 1946, "computer" was generally understood to mean a human being—usually a woman—who sat with a slide rule or an adding machine and did equations. But although Johnnie was known to have an eye for pretty women, in this case he was thinking about something else: high-speed calculating machines—the mechanical computers that would soon replace the human ones. Von Neumann had served as a consultant on the design of the world's first electronic general-purpose computer, ENIAC, but even before the Army received it in 1946, he was consulting on the design of an improved computer, EDVAC. Now he was refining the architecture for an even better one he planned to build at the Institute for Advanced Study. And that's where Harry Wexler came in.

Von Neumann needed a problem he could give his new device publicly to demonstrate its chops. The military-funded machine would mainly be used to run calculations for the hydrogen bomb, but those calculations would be secret. Johnnie needed something he could talk up for reporters, and weather modeling would be perfect. He was an expert in hydrodynamics and was friends with the eminent meteorologist Carl-Gustaf Rossby. Past attempts to model the weather with numerical methods had failed for lack of computing power. John von Neumann's new machine would solve that problem.

Von Neumann brought in a friend from RCA Labs, the engineer Vladimir Zworykin. Zworykin was a radio pioneer whose work would lay the foundation for television, but he also had an interest in weather. In October 1945, Zworykin issued "Outline of Weather Proposal," a report for which von Neumann wrote an enthusiastic letter of support. The outline declared that advances in computing technology would now "permit the prediction of [air] mass movements for perhaps several days in advance with results obtained within a few minutes." Once the weather prediction problem was solved, he wrote, attention could be turned to weather control.

Zworykin and von Neumann went to the Weather Bureau in January 1946, where they painted a dramatic picture of the climate tamed: rain made by seeding clouds with dust or chemicals, storms redirected with flamethrowers or atomic bombs, water temperatures raised by spreading oil over water, and air temperatures increased by painting the earth with carbon or aluminum to increase absorption or reflectivity. The ultimate goal, as the outline put it, was to "channel the world's weather, as far as possible, in such a way as to minimize the damage from catastrophic disturbances, and otherwise to benefit the world to the greatest extent by improved climactic conditions where possible."

The first step was to develop a whole new approach to weather prediction. In the past, meteorologists had made forecasts by comparing present weather maps with past ones, assuming the atmosphere would behave much as it had before. Numerical weather prediction would be different. Von Neumann planned to divide the atmosphere up into a grid and collect as many data about each point in the grid as possible. He would then apply mathematical equations from thermodynamics to predict the likely future behavior of each point given the behavior of the points near it. It was a wholehearted embrace of the clockwork universe: turn the weather into an equation and solve for X.

The Institute for Advanced Study's Meteorology Project, funded by the Office of Naval Research in May 1946, was designed to take the "first steps towards influencing the weather by rational, human intervention." By the time GE announced the manufacture of snow over Mount Greylock, Johnnie was assembling a meteorology team in Princeton to restate meteorological problems as equations in fluid dynamics, then feed them into his artificial brain. At the same time, he was gathering a team to build that brain. It was a method about as far from the GE scientists' approach as could be imagined. Instead of staring at the sky, the institute team would be staring at their calculations. Instead of conducting experiments in the natural atmosphere, they would program a machine to do math. But the goal was the same: figure out how the weather worked so that they could bend it to their will.

The Weather Bureau's man on the project was Harry Wexler.

•

Bernie lowered his popgun into Vince's freezer and squeezed the trigger. He had bought the gun for seventy-five cents in the toy department of H. S. Harney, downtown. It went off with a pop that sounded like a firecracker or a fart.

Beans, beans, the magical fruit:
The more you eat the more you toot . . .

Bernie loved that rhyme. He wasn't as big a fan of slapstick as Kurt and Alice, but like them he had an earthy sense of humor. Farting was funny. Poop was funny. Playing jokes was funny too, and the popgun was a kind of joke on nature. When he popped it, the cloud chamber filled with ice nuclei. It was just the kind of experiment he liked: a trick played on the natural world to make it yield up its secrets. It worked because the air in the popgun was under pressure. Compressing gases increases their temperature; decompressing them cools them. When released, the air in the popgun expanded rapidly, cooling the air around it, and the cold nucleated the ice. The same thing happened, Bernie found, when he opened a bottle of soda pop in the cooler or popped a bubble in a sheet of bubble wrap. He did it over and over, grinning every time, until Katharine Blodgett, a few feet away at her desk, thought she might go mad. But the lab's constant stream of visitors loved it.

At the meeting of the American Physical Society at Columbia University that January, Bernie, Irving, and Vince delivered a joint paper and demonstrated seeding with the freezer, using dry ice pellets, the popgun, a bursting balloon, and a hot wire carrying silver iodide. *The New York Times* ran a story about their paper the next day, pointing out that "work has not progressed far enough to permit predicting actual uses." GE was now insisting that they be much more circumspect in explaining what they were up to.

Since the first media frenzy, Research Lab director Guy Suits had been worrying about legal entanglements. Now every time something strange happened with the weather, GE was suspected of interfering. So many clippings credited Vincent Schaefer with strange weather phenomena that when the director of the Berkshire Museum was injured slipping on a patch of ice, someone sent Vince the clipping, noting that for once he wasn't blamed.

But Suits had a plan for limiting liabilities. In February, he sent Bernie, Vince, and Irving copies of their new contract with the government. GE would no longer be engaging in airborne experiments to modify the weather. Instead, flight experiments would be "conducted by the government, using exclusively government personnel and equipment, and shall be under the exclusive direction and control of such Government personnel." The lead agencies would be the U.S. Army Signal Corps and the Office of Naval Research. GE employees working on the project were merely advisers and were to "refrain from asserting any control or direction over the flight program. The GE Research Laboratory responsibility is confined strictly to laboratory work and reports."

Their project was being handed off to the military. But no one was terribly upset. The experiment was the heart of the matter, and for it to go forward, the lawyers needed to be appeased. The idea that cloud seeding would be used as a weapon didn't seem real, the military men around them just an irritating condition of work. Besides, there were advantages. The Signal Corps had smart scientists and even better airplanes than GE. And they were all given raises when the government contract went into effect. For Bernie, it was his second raise that month. They discussed a code name for the program. Vincent suggested "Project Cirrus."

They all applied for security clearance. President Truman had just announced a new loyalty program for federal workers mandating FBI investigations of all government employees and making it possible to dismiss any federal worker who could be shown to have "sympathetic associations" with organizations deemed communist, fascist, or subversive. Just to be safe, Irving resigned his sponsorship of the National Council of American-Soviet Friendship. Membership in such organizations could get one investigated by the House Un-American Activities Committee, as was happening now to the physicist Edward Condon, whom Truman had nominated to head the National Bureau of Standards. The former Manhattan Project physicist was a follower of the suspiciously "revolutionary" theory of quantum mechanics, and had come out strongly in favor of civilian control of atomic energy. Now he was undergoing a direct personal attack by Representative J. Parnell Thomas, the chairman of HUAC.

That wasn't going to happen to Irving. His resignation letter struck all the right notes, disavowing his previous positive attitude toward Russia, equating "appeasement" with "national suicide," and noting that unless the United States got tough, the Russians would build atomic bombs. He did not mention that he himself had told Congress that Russia would inevitably have atomic bombs within five years. For all his absentmindedness, Irving was no political novice.

Bernie didn't have to worry about such things. He had his political views, but he kept them to himself. He was more of a behind-the-scenes innovator, not someone who put himself forward, who got asked to put his name on the letterhead of organizations like the National Council of American-Soviet Friendship.

GE and the Army Signal Corps jointly issued a press release announcing the creation of Project Cirrus. In keeping with their new publicity aims, the announcement focused on more modest effects than the ones Irving liked to tout: it mentioned dispelling fogs and clouds over airports, noting that only after much more research might the work lead to "manipulation of gigantic natural forces for the benefit of mankind everywhere." GE made sure to note that its scientists would "provide advice and instruction, but [would] not take part in the flight program."

And then things returned to what passed for normal at the House of Magic: Vincent continued making flights, Langmuir continued working out equations, and Bernie built a generator on the roof of Building 5 to dispense silver iodide into the Schenectady sky.

•

As the baby's arrival approached, Kurt amped up his efforts to find a "real" job. He and Jane might fantasize about writing for a living, but with a baby he needed a paycheck and security. He'd applied for a job writing catalog copy for Sears & Roebuck—getting as far as being given a tour of its Chicago offices—but no luck. In the solicitation letter he sent to a range of possible employers, he described himself as about to receive a master's degree from Chicago, "twenty-four, married, and the father of a very young child." He mentioned his service in the war and noted that his anthropology work had been "extremely satisfactory from a personal standpoint." His grasp of human relations, he said, should make him valuable as a "personnel or labor relations man."

He got back some positive replies. He'd been offered a couple of copywriting jobs at ad agencies. He could continue on as a reporter. He had an offer of a teaching post in a private school and another for an editorial spot at an educational publisher. All he had to do was finish up the degree. So, as Jane's due date approached, he hammered out a thesis plan. Called "A Comparison of Elements of Ghost Dance Mythology with That Mythology of a More Tranquil Period," it proposed comparing late-nineteenth-century Native American uprisings with the work of Cubist painters in Paris in the early twentieth century. To his mind, it was bold and original, the kind of work other people in the department did: drawing connections among cultures without suggesting one was better than another, striving to find the elements that made human beings in one time and place much like those in another.

On May 11, their son was born. Mark, named after Mark Twain, came squalling into the world right around the time the University of Chicago anthropology department rejected his father's thesis proposal.

•

Once again, Bernie had to get out his popgun. The demonstration always amused him, but lately it sometimes felt as if they spent more time glad-handing visiting dignitaries than doing science. On this bright August day, a team of high-ranking Army and Navy men had come to Schenectady for the official launch of Project Cirrus. They got the tour and the cold-box demonstrations that were beginning to become a little like a dog-and-pony show. But the military brass loved it. Weather was almost like a new toy for them. As Rear Admiral Luis de Florez had written in *The American Magazine* the previous September: "We must consider the possibility that man-controlled weather can become a terrifying weapon. We must reckon with rivers and lakes as potentially terrible enemies. Sea disturbances—call them man-made tidal waves—may well be a factor in the next war . . . America must expand the scope of her thinking if she is to retain her position among nations in the world of tomorrow." The article was titled "Weather—the New Super Weapon."

That wasn't the kind of application Bernie hoped to see their work producing. He would rather see it used to save lives. That's what he'd tried to do earlier that month, when a telephone call came into the lab asking Project Cirrus to help put out a forest fire in California.

The fire had started in early August, in the tinder-dry brush north of Pasadena. Within a day, warm southwest winds had swept the flames through Big Tujunga Canyon, where they consumed more than three thousand acres. On August 6, a forest service employee and a volunteer were killed as they frantically worked to make a firebreak. Residents were evacuated, highways were closed, and the Navy dispatched 280 seamen to help. Still the supervisor of the Angeles National Forest went on the radio pleading for more volunteers. As many as 800 people were fighting what was called the worst wildfire in a quarter century when someone thought to call GE.

Frank Backus of the Los Angeles GE office was on the line when

Bernie got to the phone. The *Los Angeles Times* had lined up a DC-3 and four hundred pounds of dry ice. What should they do now?

Bernie had tried to explain how to seed a cloud. But even as he talked, he knew it was futile. The problem was the clouds were low in the sky. The plane was above them at fourteen thousand feet, meaning that in California's climate they were probably too warm to contain super-cooled water. Still, the flight crew wanted to try. They made five passes over the cloud deck, dispensing 60 to 120 pounds of dry ice each time, as per Bernie's instructions. Unfortunately, the cloud, reported the *Los Angeles Times*, "failed to cooperate."

The effort was unsuccessful, but it had illuminated the high stakes of getting this right. Once Bernie got silver iodide to work in the natural atmosphere, it would be easier than ever to bring water and life, instead of fire and death, down from the clouds. At least that's what Bernie was hoping for. The Signal Corps colonel and the Army brigadier general visiting the lab might have had something else in mind. Perhaps they were thinking of what General George Kenney, of the Strategic Air Command, had recently told the graduates and alumni of MIT: "The nation that first learns to plot the paths of air masses . . . will dominate the globe."

Bernie lowered his popgun into the freezer and seeded the minia-ture cloud. This time, it was for the News Bureau photographer too. The PR men never missed an opportunity to show GE in the nation's service, and the colonel and the general looked impressive, their lapels paved with rows of colorful ribbons. In the photograph sent to newspapers, Ber-nie would be smirking as he popped the toy gun. The officers would be smiling slightly too as they leaned forward to look into the freezer. The bursting flashbulbs would catch something slightly acquisitive in the mili-tary men's expressions, perhaps an eagerness for a time when the freezer would be replaced by the sky and the gun they aimed would be real.

•

"To Walt and Helen." Kurt and Jane clinked martinis. Walter had grad-uated, and he and his family had moved to the San Juan Islands off the coast of Washington. They were going to be homesteaders, building their own cabin, growing their own food, probably raising sheep and knitting sweaters from their wool. It was an admirable escape from everything—money pressure, school pressure, job pressure. Kurt and Jane missed them, and they envied them a little too.

Next they raised their glasses to the UN Atomic Energy Commission, which had been spending August hammering out plans for international control of atomic energy at the UN's temporary home in Lake Success, New York. Two days earlier, the United States, Great Britain, China, and France had given the plan their support. Kurt and Jane let themselves enjoy a moment of optimism about a peaceful future, free from fear of the bomb. It was August 31, the eve of their anniversary, and they were celebrating at the restaurant Jacques. It was an overpriced French joint, with a mural of the Eiffel Tower and waiters sporting fake French accents, but they needed a treat. They sat outdoors on the famous flagstone terrace and contemplated possible futures.

Mark was now almost four months old. But the joy of a new baby was somewhat undercut by the financial anxiety that arrived as predictably as night feedings and dirty diapers. Kurt's job as a copy boy at the City News Bureau paid next to nothing. And because the anthropology professors hadn't gone for his comparison of Native American uprisings and Cubist painters, he'd had to spend the summer cooking up a whole new thesis project—with money from the GI Bill running out.

The department's unanimous rejection of his thesis proposal had been galling. It was as if they were suggesting he was no better at this than he had been at science. As if they considered him third-rate.

He'd gone back to his writing. While working on a new thesis outline, he had fired off stories and essays to magazines. Finally, he'd finished the new proposal and in late summer had submitted it to the department. In response to their earlier comments, it was much more modest. His new project took as its starting point the philosopher Georges Sorel's claim that periods of social change cause the rise of new mythologies. Looking at Native American religious and spiritual movements in the late nineteenth century, he was going to analyze what effect the rapid assimilation caused by white colonist expansion had on the Indian myths. It was less ambitious, less creative, less out there than his previous effort.

The department didn't hate it. Some of the professors even said encouraging things. With some more effort, the message was, he would get this right. But in August, he was offered the opportunity to become a reporter—full-time—at the City News Bureau. He took it. He'd had enough of the eggheads humiliating him. Pounding the streets looking for good copy—anything involving a dead body was best—that was something he felt confident he could do. He could be a reporter and keep working on his own essays and stories. Somehow he would also find time to work on his thesis.

But August brought a relentless flood of rejections. "Wailing Shall Be in All Streets" had been rejected six times. "Brighten Up!" was rejected by *Glamour* on August 11. He sent it off to Charles Angoff at *The American Mercury*, reminding him of his encouraging note a year earlier. Angoff returned it a week later, just a couple of days after "I Shall Not Want" was rejected by *Coronet*.

His writing was getting nowhere. And the City News Bureau job was grueling, all wrong for a family man. He was exhausted, and he and Jane hadn't had a Sunday together in weeks. It was time to start considering other options. So over martinis and pricey French food, they talked through the possibilities.

A job offer from *The Dayton Daily News* was tempting, because Kurt loved being in a newsroom. But there was also an offer from the educational publisher Bobbs-Merrill in Indianapolis. There was a lot of appeal in the idea of going back to Indy. Their kids could grow up near their grandparents and with the kids of their old friends. But the couple would have to face the stifling social life of a city where family connections had carved out roles for them already. Besides, a new option had recently come into the picture: Schenectady and GE.

Earlier that week, Kurt had gotten a phone call from George Griffin at the GE News Bureau. He was responding to a letter Kurt had sent at Bernie's suggestion. Bernie had already told George his younger brother might be a great hire for the News Bureau: he had a science background and real newspaper experience. The GE News Bureau was a publicity department, but it aimed to be as much like a real newspaper as possible—minus the objectivity, of course. In exchange for giving up journalistic credibility, one got the security and perks of a corporate position.

The GE job paid better than the others. It was in Schenectady, not too far from New York City, the center of the publishing world. And it was also near Bernard. As much as Kurt chafed under his brother's influence, he also longed to be surrounded by family. Their kids could play together. Their wives would have each other for support. It was a new town and a new start, but with Bernard there it wouldn't be lonesome. For the first time, they wouldn't have to worry about money. They could buy a house. And without having to work nights and weekends, maybe Kurt could get some real writing done.

Jane agreed it was a good opportunity. The GE recruiter dropped by their house the very next night, as they were still basking in the mellow martini haze of their anniversary dinner. It was a great job with a real future, he assured Kurt. Of course, GE only hired college graduates. Kurt assured the recruiter that wouldn't be a problem. He would soon be in possession of a master's degree from Chicago. He was still planning to take his exams and write his thesis. He'd just have to do it while working.

To take the job at GE would be once more following his brother's plan for his own life. But Bernie was only acting in Kurt's best interests. Why resist?

He told the GE man yes.

5

Eye of the Storm

ernard was treating Kurt like a prince. First he had helped him find a nice house—two bedrooms and an alcove where he could have an office—right around the corner from Bernie and Bow in Alplaus. Now he was taking Kurt appliance shopping. GE employees got discounts on the best new models—another reason the company was known as Generous Electric.

"I own a home now," Kurt wrote proudly to his father. "Albeit humble, it's ours, and we'll love it I'm sure." He was in an expansive mood, because by cashing in some bonds, he'd been able to handle the $7,000 price tag without taking on debt. He felt manly enough to sign his telegram to Jane, as he did whenever he felt plucky, "Tarzan." Jane was still in Chicago packing up their furniture, which they would store in Bernard's barn until they could move into their own house.

At the employee store of the Generous Electric Company, Kurt ordered a refrigerator, a stove, and an automatic washer that he was convinced would make Jane's life easier. In his letter to his father, he called it a "Bendix." He hadn't yet realized that in Schenectady, you didn't call a GE refrigerator a Frigidaire or a GE washer a Bendix. GE expected every one of its employees to serve as brand ambassadors for the company.

And what a company! GE was bringing in more money than ever before. In 1947, the company's net sales topped $1.3 billion, more than double the sales of the peak prewar year, 1940, and rapidly rising toward Charlie Wilson's magical number of $2 billion. World War II had been good to GE. The company had produced more for the war than anyone else, cranking out $4 billion worth of what America needed to win. Aircraft turbochargers! Bazookas! Howitzers! Gun turrets! Turbines! Three-quarters of the Navy's propulsive power! Radar detection equipment, gun directors, generators, and electrically heated flight suits for pilots! Searchlights so strong a man eight miles away could read the newspaper by them! The company had met the war's more quotidian needs too: fuses, wires, and, of course, the start of it all, lightbulbs. A B-29 Superfortress bomber carried 170 electric motors, 26 motor-generator sets, and 15,000 feet of electric wiring, all of it made by GE.

The company put out a book celebrating its war effort in 1947. *Men and Volts at War* described the Schenectady Works as "the nerve center of one of the world's biggest and most complex war machines." Postwar, the company was still a war machine, a paragon of the new and powerful alliance between industry and the military. When Kurt arrived, GE was building the Knolls Atomic Power Laboratory, a nuclear research facility it was going to manage for the government, next door to its new state-of-the-art campus for the GE Research Lab. It was already operating Hanford, the government nuclear production complex in Washington.

GE's non-war-related industries were surging ahead too. The company was building a huge turbine construction facility in Schenectady, to keep pace with the nation's increasing demand for electricity. It had just completed three new chemical plants and a top-of-the-line electronics facility in Syracuse and broke ground on a new induction motor plant in San Jose, California, and an artificial-lightning research facility in Pittsfield, Massachusetts. But consumer products were where the real growth was. A GE stove and refrigerator in every kitchen! A GE washing machine in every house! A GE toaster on every counter and of course GE lightbulbs in every socket, from Park Avenue to Skid Row and everywhere in between, lightbulbs issuing forth from its five new lamp plants, lightbulbs that lasted longer and shone brighter and grew cheaper all the time, because as the company motto said, progress was its most important product. Progress! Ever onward GE marched. It had armed the nation for war, and now it was equipping America for peace, for the electrically lit and atomically powered prosperity that know-how would deliver next.

As a "junior writer," Kurt would, for the first time in his life, be making enough money to support his wife and son in true American style: a house, a yard, a pension plan, a kitchen full of GE appliances, the monogram on each one shining like a promise of the best of everything. And at least his job would be writing. He knew how to craft news stories, to dig up information, and to shape it into a magazine feature or science story. And that was exactly the skill the News Bureau wanted.

Founded in 1919, the GE News Bureau was a novel approach to corporate publicity. Instead of issuing standard press releases—thinly disguised ads, accompanied by unappealing illustrations—GE hired professional reporters to pitch newsworthy stories, including layouts with illustrations and photographs. A News Bureau story wasn't just press agent puffery. It was a ready-made piece of journalism, with a hook, supporting information, quotations from experts, and a sense of the big picture.

By the time Kurt arrived, the News Bureau's light blue envelope had become a welcome sight on many editors' desks. The department had originally been located downtown, to emphasize its separateness from the advertising arm, but not long after Kurt arrived, the bureau moved into the Schenectady Works. There, it became part of the company's increasingly impressive corporate communications wing, the largest corporate publisher in the nation. GE produced internal publications like the *Schenectady Works News* (for blue-collar workers), the *General Office News* (for white-collar employees), and the *Monogram* (for managers). There were also internal publications that were distributed beyond the company: the *GE News Graphic* (for appliance salesmen), the *GE Review* (for engineers), and the *GE Digest* (for overseas personnel). It produced a magazine for young people and well-packaged scientific reports. GE didn't just manufacture goods: it mass-produced ideas.

His new bosses gave him a physical. They gave him a desk. They gave him a typewriter of his very own! They gave him a beat: the Lighting section, the Service Engineering section, and the Schenectady Works Research Lab—a lab less prestigious than the GE Research Lab, where Bernie worked. Get out there and find stories that would get the GE name in front of America's eyeballs; that was his mission. Stories about things like a set of mechanical hands for working on radioactive materials, or the GE sales force refrigerator named Junior that walked and talked—and even once got arrested in Cleveland for whistling at pretty girls. It wasn't like covering thirteen police stations, two Coast Guard stations, and a fire department, and he was glad of it. The work would be easier. He could handle it and get his thesis done too. Maybe he'd even be able to spend some more time doing his own writing.

So Kurt joined the human tide of workers arriving at the plant every weekday, flowing in four lanes of bus and car traffic down Erie Boulevard to the Works, a sea of fedoras and overcoats surging through the huge plant gates. When he walked through the entrance, Building 5, where Bernard worked, was on the right. Directly across the street, Kurt turned left, in to Building 6.

The press room of the News Bureau looked like the newsroom at any paper. Desks were shoved up against each other and strewn with papers, ashtrays, pencils, beer cans, Remington manuals, and rotary phones. A table along one wall held a row of portable typewriters, to be grabbed for jobs on the go. A pin board above that was pasted with eight-by-ten publicity photographs. The fact was not lost on Kurt that many of them featured the impish grin and distinctively cumuliform pompadour of his older brother.

•

"A hurricane is a complicated thing," Vincent told the reporters, "not the simple whirl of an artist's conception."

Vince was grasping at straws. He was exhausted. He'd flown to Florida and back in the last four days, a twenty-six-hour round-trip. He'd barely landed in Schenectady before GE hauled him to a press conference and reporters started pelting him with questions. What they all wanted to know was, what just happened?

The problem was, Vince couldn't tell them. It wasn't that he didn't know. He wasn't allowed to tell them. There'd been too much talk already; GE was in damage-repair mode.

From the very start, Irving, Bernie, and Vince had dreamed of cloud seeding hurricanes. Once Project Cirrus was formed and their experiments were officially attributable to the government, it began to seem possible. GE was insulated from liability concerns by a solid wall of military brass. The team had access to military airplanes and pilots who wouldn't balk at flying into huge storms. They had a steering committee that included meteorologists from the Navy and the Army Signal Corps and bosses eager to try out this new tool. Finally, they were in a position to attack a real hurricane and see if they could change its course.

Hurricanes begin when warm water evaporates from the ocean surface. As the water condenses in the air, it releases latent heat. This heat builds up, and the warm air rises, creating a low-pressure area. Air rushes into this depression, creating winds. Because of the Coriolis effect—a slight deflection of moving objects caused by the earth's rotation—the winds begin to spiral inward toward the center of the low-pressure region, clockwise in the southern hemisphere, counterclockwise in the northern. As the storm spirals, it pulls in more water vapor, which condenses and creates more latent heat. Eventually, bands of showers and thunderstorms begin to form. The most intense band, the eye wall, encircles the calm eye at the center. Hurricanes spiral their way with the prevailing winds until they reach colder water or land where there is no more warm water vapor to serve as "fuel."

Hurricanes are the most vicious storms on earth, causing billions of dollars' worth of destruction, along with injury and death. An average one contains hundreds of times more energy than an atomic bomb, a fact Irving Langmuir liked to repeat. The military had upped its hurricane research program during the war, beginning a regular program of flying airplanes into hurricanes to collect temperatures and wind speeds as an aid to forecasting. But the Project Cirrus scientists were convinced they could do better than studying the storms. They wanted to alter them.

Everyone agreed that "busting" a hurricane with dry ice seemed unlikely, given the enormous amounts of energy involved. But diverting

one—changing its course just enough to send it harmlessly out to sea—
that could be possible. Especially if they cloud seeded it when the
hurricane was young, before it had built up an elaborate storm system.
After all, a giant boulder rolling down a mountain could change its path
after hitting the tiniest pebble. Like Steinmetz marking his chalk X on
the faulty generator, all they had to do was figure out where to put the
pebble. The steering committee drew up an official plan for the experiment, stating its goal as determining whether seeding could "modify the
normal growth and development of tropical storms." And then the scientists waited for the right hurricane to come along.

Several promising hurricanes hit in September, but the team hadn't
lined up all its planes. Finally, in October, a good-sized storm headed
up through the Caribbean toward Florida. The Weather Bureau didn't
yet have a protocol for naming hurricanes, but the Project Cirrus team
had been christening the storms in alphabetical order. In October, a
team flew to Florida to cloud seed Hurricane King.

"We accomplished our purpose," Vince told the reporters in Schenectady, "to obtain scientific data on the hurricane." It was what he had
been told to say. "We never had any plans or hopes to break up the
storm."

That's not what *The New York Times* had reported just days before.
As Hurricane King spiraled toward Florida, the paper reported that
Project Cirrus was planning to spray a thousand pounds of dry ice into
the storm to see what effect it would have. "The result of this will lead
us to further accomplishments in efforts to break up a hurricane," Navy
meteorologist Daniel Rex of Project Cirrus told the *Times* as the Project Cirrus team was en route to Florida.

For more than a month, in fact, newspapers had been full of reports that Project Cirrus was going to attempt to bust a hurricane. "The
next great tropical storm to whirl through the Atlantic," reported the
Associated Press, "will be dusted with carbon dioxide (dry ice), silver
iodide or some other cooling crystal which—perhaps—will condense
its water vapors, cause a record-smashing rainfall at sea, and dissipate
the swirling air mass." The giddy reporting caused some anxiety at Project Cirrus. It sounded great, but what if they didn't deliver? Or worse,
what if something bad happened? The steering committee composed a

press release insisting that "contrary to earlier, unofficial reports, plans do not call for any 'hurricane-busting' attempts."

"We are in far too preliminary a stage to think of stopping a hurricane," Langmuir was quoted saying in the release. "At this point, we are only interested in seeing and recording any effects the dry-ice technique will have."

Nevertheless, when the Project Cirrus team stayed overnight in Mobile, Alabama, en route, Vince awoke to the local newspaper headline "Hurricane-Busting Plane Lands in Mobile as Storm Approaches Miami and Florida East Coast."

By the time the Navy plane arrived at MacDill Air Base, near Tampa, Hurricane King, traveling in a northeasterly direction, had already crossed the tip of Florida, leaving a trail of devastating floods across the Everglades and the southeast coast. According to the Weather Bureau, it was heading out to sea in the Atlantic Ocean and weakening quickly. Thinking it might be too small to bother with, the team debated whether to return to New York. But hurricane season was almost over, so they decided to carry on with the experiment.

There were three planes. Kiah Maynard, a junior team member recently recruited by Bernie, was on board the seeding plane, a B-17 flying just above the cloud deck. The second plane, flying higher up, carried military photographers. Vince was on the third plane, a B-29, which stayed eight thousand feet up and fifteen to twenty miles back, putting him in the best position to see larger patterns and changes.

When they caught up with the hurricane, about 350 miles northeast of Jacksonville, they realized immediately that the Weather Bureau had been wrong. The storm was not weakening but maintaining its fierce spiral, a large, intense squall line at its outer edge. It was chugging steadily out to sea on an east-by-northeast course.

The seeding plane dropped eighty pounds of dry ice along a 110-mile-long track parallel to the squall line and another hundred pounds into the top of a large cumulus cloud boiling up from the storm. At first, it looked as if this produced little or no effect. But as the planes circled to take more photographs, observers saw a new line of rain falling parallel to where they had seeded. It looked like a trench shoveled out of the hurricane's spiral of clouds. Commander Rex estimated that about 300 square miles of storm had been affected. They took 250 photographs and flew back to Florida.

The next morning, Vince settled into his seat on the plane home, notebook in hand. He had thirteen hours in the air and was planning to use the time to record his observations. But not long after the B-17 was airborne, it began to buck and rattle. The turbulence increased until it was the most intense buffeting any of the passengers had ever experienced in the air. Vince's handwriting grew steadily worse, until writing was out of the question.

Later, they found out the reason for the rough skies. Immediately after they had seeded it, the hurricane made a dramatic dogleg turn. Inscribing a huge 7 over the Atlantic Ocean, it turned westward and plowed back to the mainland. It was battering Savannah with eighty- to one-hundred-mile-an-hour winds when they flew over. As the unknowing scientists clutched their armrests in the sky above, a thousand people were taking shelter in Savannah's city hall. Windows were smashed, boats were tossed ashore, sugarcane fields were flattened, a downtown bank lost its roof, and several parked planes were destroyed. Charleston took a hit too, with waves topping its seawall, parts of the city flooded, and a lumberjack killed by a falling tree. All in all, damage from the storm's second landfall was estimated at $23 million.

By the time the team landed in Schenectady, a storm of outrage was following in the hurricane's wake. A letter writer in the *St. Petersburg Times* declared that locals blamed GE and were "pretty sore at the army and navy for fooling around with the hurricane." A Miami weatherman called the diversion a "low Yankee trick." The sheriff of Savannah declared that if anyone from Project Cirrus showed up in his town, he'd throw him in jail.

Which is why GE had hurried Vince into a press conference: the company needed him to convince reporters that Project Cirrus was not responsible for the storm's change of course.

"Could you see any effects?" reporters demanded. Vince told them he was not allowed to say; the Army had classified all the reports. They asked him if he thought that the team's experiment had caused the storm to alter its course. He said no. Reporters were not convinced.

Hurricanes just didn't behave like this one had, heading one way, then suddenly making a hairpin turn. Even the fiercely loyal *Schenectady Gazette* said the question had to be asked: "Did science, for the first time in history, 'bust' a hurricane on October 13?"

Irving Langmuir was certain that it had. And he was elated. The redirection of the hurricane proved that he really was on the verge of something huge. His dreams of widespread weather control were not pipe dreams at all. He couldn't wait to tell the world—even if GE was insisting he keep it quiet.

He seemed oblivious, however, to another implication of the hurricane experiment, one that would come to haunt Bernie more and more: the possible busting of Hurricane King was the first suggestion that you didn't necessarily have to be planning to make a weapon in order to make one.

•

"Perhaps you saw the news reports that mentioned Bernard as having been aboard the hurricane-busting B-17," Kurt wrote to their father. "This was a newsman's mistake. Bernard got into the farewell picture but not into the plane."

He enjoyed being able to report on his brother's activities. But that wasn't the main reason he had set up an office for himself at home. His plan was to make progress on his master's thesis. He had hoped he might even take some trips to New York City, where he could work at Columbia's Butler Library. It weighed on him that he had told the recruiter he would have his diploma before starting, as GE required for white-collar jobs. Without a college degree, he didn't deserve his position or his paycheck. What would happen if somebody in Schenectady found out he lacked credentials? This wasn't the kind of town that laughed things like that off.

So he set up a desk where he could work on his thesis. And then he sat down at it and began writing stories.

It was another secret, this desire to write, his ambition as confidential as his un-degreed status. GE was better off not knowing that one of its junior writers had aspirations beyond making GE look good. Nor did his new colleagues need to be made aware that he was different. Methodically, he went to work and found GE stories and typed up GE press releases; he bantered with his fellow writers and took part in Monday meetings. But at home, he was just as methodical in figuring out how to break into the magazine world as a writer of fiction.

He knew he had to write what editors wanted. Clearly, they didn't want his war stories. So he turned his mind toward figuring out what they did want. As always, Jane helped. They studied the magazines together, trying to determine where he had the best shot. Like any aspiring author, Kurt longed to see his byline in *The New Yorker*. To get in there was to join the pantheon of Writers Who Mattered. But there were other periodicals that also bestowed literary prestige: *Story, The Yale Review*. Then there were the popular magazines that were still highbrow: *The American Mercury, The Atlantic, Harper's*. Beneath those were the "slicks," the general-interest glossies that published scads of short fiction: *The Saturday Evening Post, Tomorrow, Collier's, Life, Esquire*. They liked their stories punchy and quick, with surprising plot twists or unexpected revelations right at the end. In the 1940s, all the magazines did, even *The New Yorker*. Before television, fiction was popular entertainment.

At the bottom of the ladder were the "genre" magazines, pitched at readers who liked a specific kind of story: detective tales, westerns, science fiction. Magazines like *Spicy Detective*, which Kurt read as a kid, and those he had never read, like the women's magazines: *Redbook, Mademoiselle, Cosmopolitan, Glamour, McCall's*. To appeal to editors there, stories had to feature things women cared about: relationships, family, love. He and Jane bought copies of those too and read them, analyzing the fiction they published.

Kurt was not above shaping his stories to an audience, even an audience of women. He wrote stories that were classic women's magazine fodder: one called "Ruth" about a young war widow coming to terms with the possessive grief of her mother-in-law, another called "City" that narrated the thoughts of a man and a woman who cross paths at a bus stop and long to speak to each other. He wrote a novella called "Basic Training" about a young orphan who goes to live with his cousins in the country and falls in love with one of them, disrupting the harsh militaristic rule of their father. He submitted them all to women's magazines, but they rejected them, like everyone else.

Even as the negative responses piled up, Jane's confidence never wavered. Kurt tried to let her faith in his genius buoy him as it did her. They put candles in three miniature wine bottles, one for "keep," one for "on," one for "trying." It had become their unofficial motto. He felt bolstered when the rejections were at least encouraging. Sometimes an editor wrote a brief note at the bottom: "Sorry, not for us, but try again!"

Jane had always said he was really a writer. He had insisted that he was just a regular Joe. Now, as he pretended to be a regular Joe, he was beginning to realize it wasn't what he wanted to be at all.

•

Bernie left Building 5, merging into the mass of people flowing out Gate 85. He went to the parking lot and joined the glacier of cars inching out of the Works and down the blazing "white way" of Erie Boulevard, the enormous artificial moon of the GE sign behind them. Schenectady was a bustling town, especially with the holidays approaching. Shoppers were rifling through Harney's, Sears, and Carl's, revelers were spilling out of bars and restaurants, the four downtown movie palaces were ablaze, and a man dressed as Mr. Peanut was coaxing hungry shoppers to stop for a snack. Bernie barely noticed any of it. He was looking forward to his latest nighttime pursuit.

As he walked into his house one early winter night, it had occurred to Bernie that the moisture in the cold, clear air must be supercooled, just like water in a cloud. He went inside, got an electric heater, doused it with silver iodide, and turned it on. When he went outside and waved it around, he could see a fog of ice crystals materializing around it. It was more proof of how effective silver iodide was.

He couldn't get far enough with the electric heater, so he put some silver iodide on a newspaper and stuffed it into an oil burner. Then he went for a walk. It was beautiful. The fog crystallized around him like smoke, drifting from his hand and down through the dark village streets. Now, whenever it was cold enough, he experimented outside. Often their new junior teammate Kiah Maynard would come over, and the two of them would make fog, then get in the car and drive around to see where the wind took it. Sometimes they found it as much as a mile away.

Tonight, however, he was alone. Everything was quiet: The grocery store was closed, the post office at the back of the bike shop shuttered. Even the firehouse was dark. The comfortable houses of Alplaus gave off the soft glow of families at home having dinner, couples listening to the radio, kids taking their baths and going to bed. Outside, Bernie walked alone, fog streaming behind him like a wake.

Shortly after Bernie got home, his phone rang. It was his neighbor John Fisher, a fellow GE employee and a friend; John's wife, Jo Ann, was in the GE Research Lab Newcomers' Club with Bow.

"You fooling around?" John asked.

"Yes," Bernie said. "Why?" John explained that he had looked out his window and noticed that even though it was a clear night, the house next door to his was shrouded in a thick miasma.

Yes, Bernie told John. He had made that fog.

•

Kurt rolled a piece of paper into one of the News Bureau typewriters and went to work. He was answering a request for a photograph. The photo was of Bernie.

"The photograph of General Electric's Dr. Bernard Vonnegut originated from our office," he typed. However, he informed the requester, there were no more prints, and the negative belonged to the Army Signal Corps. "Moreover," he typed, "we have a lot more to do than piddle with penny-ante requests like yours."

He'd only been at GE for about a month when the letter had landed on his desk. It was from his own uncle Alex, sent originally to the *Schenectady Gazette*. Alex had seen a photograph of Bernard in his hometown paper, with a photo credit from the *Gazette*. He wrote asking for a copy, explaining that he was "a wee bit proud" of his famous scientist nephew. He enclosed a dollar for the newspaper's trouble. The *Gazette* passed the request on to the GE News Bureau, source of the photograph, and George Griffin—out of courtesy or mischief, who can say— gave the job of responding to Kurt.

He must have snickered to himself as he typed. "We do have some other photographs of the poor man's Steinmetz," he wrote, "and I may send them to you in my own sweet time. But do not rush me. 'Wee bit proud,' indeed! Ha! Vonnegut! Ha! This office made your nephew, and we can break him in a minute—like an egg shell."

It was true too; Kurt could see that now. The News Bureau was HQ for the corporate boosterism that poured down on Schenectady as steadily as the Works soot. The scientists were celebrities because the News Bureau promoted them as such. In other words, it was Kurt's office that made people like Bernie into stars.

Surely, he thought, Uncle Alex would realize it was all a joke—especially when he got to the final lines, where Kurt closed by returning the dollar, pointing out that "one dollar to the General Electric Company is as the proverbial fart in a wind storm." He signed off "Guy Fawkes: General News Bureau."

There actually was a guy named Fawkes in the News Bureau, but Guy Fawkes—surely Uncle Alex wouldn't think someone would actually be named after a notorious English traitor. He sent the letter off, thinking it was a hilarious family prank. Later, he would find out that Uncle Alex had been outraged. He even consulted a lawyer, asking how he might demand compensation for such shabby treatment. Poor earnest Uncle Alex stewed over the insult until someone pointed out to him that Guy Fawkes was clearly a joke name and reminded him that his nephew Kurt worked in the GE News Bureau. Surely Alex was the victim of nothing more than a jesting sibling rivalry. Who but Kurt could so deftly manage to praise and insult his brother simultaneously by calling him the "poor man's Steinmetz"?

Later, Kurt speculated that his favorite uncle must have been furious with him. But Alex said nothing at the time. He simply held on to the offending letter. And at some point, he gave it to Bernie.

•

Harry Wexler grew increasingly outraged as he listened to Irving Langmuir talk about hurricanes. Langmuir was giving the keynote address before the National Academy of Sciences, and even though it was clear GE's legal team had eliminated any verbiage that might implicate their company in property damage or worse, Irving's excitement was palpable. He clearly believed Project Cirrus had accomplished something by seeding a hurricane with a couple of hundred pounds of dry ice. He seemed to think, in fact, that they had changed its course. At the end of his heavily vetted account of Hurricane King, he declared that he planned, the following year, to study hurricanes some more "to see if we cannot, by seeding them, in some way modify them or shift their positions."

"I think the chances are excellent," he declared, "that with increased knowledge . . . we should be able to abolish all of the evil effects of these hurricanes."

Hurricanes! Harry Wexler knew hurricanes! He was the first meteorologist to fly directly into a hurricane for the purpose of collecting data back in 1944. He and two Army Air Forces pilots took an A-20 Havoc right into the eye of the storm, riding its updrafts as coolly as businessmen taking an elevator to the fortieth floor. *The New York Times* had even written it up! Harry probably knew more about hurricanes than anyone else alive. Certainly he knew more than Irving Langmuir, who had just declared—incorrectly—that it was atypical for hurricanes to have squall lines. Harry Wexler had published a paper about squall lines just last year! Project Cirrus was wading into the meteorologists' territory, but its scientists weren't bothering to educate themselves about the meteorology field.

After the talk, Langmuir was even more unrestrained, declaring that seeding by Project Cirrus had almost certainly altered the track of Hurricane King. He also talked about a new theory he was developing, that raindrops could be formed inside clouds not just by nucleation but by a kind of chain reaction. A single ice crystal or droplet of water might, under the right conditions, trigger an increasingly large event. One snowflake would lead to two, two would lead to four, four to eight, eight to sixteen, and so on, until the entire cloud would precipitate. The theory accounted for rain in places where clouds did not always reach the freezing point before precipitating. It also meant, he said, that it could be possible to induce rain simply by seeding clouds with water. A bucketful could cause the chain reaction, or even a single drop—just as smashing a single atom could wipe Hiroshima or Moscow or even Schenectady right off the map.

Chief Reichelderfer was at the meeting too, and he was as appalled as Harry. Project Cirrus's fantastic claims were increasingly causing headaches for the real weather experts at the bureau.

"Army and GE Join to 'Make Weather.'" "Rain to Order." "Snow Made in a New Way." "Scientists Get Ready to Do Something About the Weather." It seemed as if a week didn't go by without some outlandish headline announcing a story about weather control, thanks to the experimentalists of GE. The company was cranking out press releases with an avidness that suggested America's weather was soon to be issuing forth from Schenectady as reliably as America's washing machines.

Worse still, the public wanted the government to get on board. Letters poured in to the Weather Bureau insisting that the agency make rain, eliminate hail, put out forest fires, and bust hurricanes, and with each one Reichelderfer and Wexler seethed a bit more. Langmuir and his team didn't even understand the mathematics of the atmosphere. And yet their reckless claims were building up the public's expectations to the point where, every time the Weather Bureau failed to forecast a freak storm, someone started making noise about cutting the bureau's budget, because the military, or even private industry, could do its job better.

Which is why the bureau had gone on the offensive. Harry was following up on every Project Cirrus report, going over the raw data in an attempt to find errors. Chief Reichelderfer convened an advisory committee on cloud physics to reproduce the experiments and refute the claims of Project Cirrus. And he assigned a full-time Weather Bureau observer to Project Cirrus: William Lewis. Lewis was a young bureau meteorologist whom Harry had sounded out on the topic of cloud seeding. He was sufficiently skeptical. Assigning Lewis to the Project Cirrus team would make it look as if the bureau were taking the project seriously, while providing Reichelderfer and Wexler with a mole to report back on the goings-on in Schenectady and help them to prove once and for all that the GE scientists were not rainmakers but charlatans.

•

"Some 15 different types of finely divided soil, mostly from desert or arid regions of the country," Kurt's story began, "have been found to be capable of producing snow in the laboratory, Vincent J. Schaefer . . . revealed recently in Chicago."

It was an odd situation. The GE Research Lab was not on Kurt's beat: manager Roger Hammond had the plum assignment of writing almost all of the Project Cirrus publicity. But now, in April, the News Bureau had sent Kurt to Chicago with Bernard, Vince, and Irving for the annual meeting of the American Chemical Society. To the bureau, it must have made sense: Kurt was a former chemistry major. He had worked in the Chicago newspaper world, so he had the contacts to place his stories there. And he was a graduate of the University of Chicago— or so they thought.

"Mr. Schaefer, Dr. Irving Langmuir and Dr. Bernard Vonnegut, G-E snowmaking scientists, spoke recently before the 113th national meeting of the American Chemical Society," Kurt typed. That was GE-speak, always hypercorrect about everyone's titles and credentials.

Kurt didn't often get a chance to hear Bernard publicly presenting his work. Privately, of course, Bernie talked of almost nothing else. Clouds and nuclei and ice and precipitation—he could go on about theories and experiments for hours, blissfully unaware if he was boring his listeners. That was Bernie. He didn't love playing in the snow the way Vince and Irving did—two months earlier he had fractured an ankle when Vince tried to teach him to ski—but he had endless stamina for talking about the stuff.

GE cultivated this obsessiveness, this focus on science and science alone, by making the Research Lab into a kind of playground. The Research Lab scientists didn't have to punch a time clock. *They* didn't have to do whatever tasks their bosses assigned them. *They* didn't have to get approval for a lousy two-page press release from the News Bureau boss, the contracting agency, Engineering, Patents, Legal, the Works office, and the Atomic Energy Commission. They were in the business of seeking truth—not, as some folks considered publicity, buggering truth for money. And truth meant whatever nifty scientific puzzle was at hand—not the truth of the real world, where things were very likely going to hell. The GE scientists could remain completely withdrawn from the outside world if they wanted to. Did Irving Langmuir even know that the planet was seemingly on the brink of World War III? The Soviets had just ordered Allied military personnel out of East Germany and were putting increasing pressure on supply lines to West Berlin. Kurt read the newspaper avidly and worried about things like that. But as far as he could tell, Irving paid no attention to anything outside his own research.

Worse than that, he didn't worry a whit about what use might be made of his inventions. He just fiddled away on the strings of his brain as if it were a toy violin and his whole purpose on earth was to play it. During the last AMS meeting, Irving had some time to kill, so he went to the American Museum of Natural History. He got so engrossed in pondering the exhibits that he failed to hear the closing announcements or notice when everyone else left. He stayed lost in thought until the lights went out, and he had to grope his way along dark corridors for half an hour before finding a surprised security guard to let him out.

Bernie could be like that too. He wasn't quite as absentminded as Irving Langmuir, but he was often lost in his own head, unaware that others might not share his enthusiasm for its contents. Kurt could get annoyed at his brother's endless talk about his own work. But often he was interested in what Bernie had to say. Sometimes he even solicited scientific explanations—as he had when he read a *Fortune* magazine piece, "Weather Under Control," that February. The magazine reported that Irving had answered a fundamental question: why supercooled water droplets nucleate into ice crystals at −39 degrees, even though theoretically they should stay liquid forever. The answer had to do with ice-2.

If subjected to enough pressure while at around −36 degrees, supercooled water forms an ice crystal that looks like a tetragon, rather than its usual hexagonal shape. The scientist who discovered this, Percy Bridgman, named the crystalline variant ice-2. Irving realized that cloud droplets are so tiny that their small surface area squeezes their contents, increasing their internal pressure. If small enough, a droplet's high pressure causes it to convert to ice-2. After crystallizing, it grows again and reconverts to regular, six-sided ice.

Kurt had not realized that there were different kinds of ice crystals. Of course, Bernie was happy to explain. He told Kurt to imagine cannonballs stacked on a courthouse lawn. Just as the balls could be piled up into different shapes, ice crystals could stack up in different configurations. In fact, Bridgman had described a whole series of ice phase variants, ice-1 through ice-6. And who knew—there might be more to come.

Kurt socked away that idea and the image of cannonballs on a courthouse lawn. Bernie might be pedantic sometimes, but his explanations were often damn good.

It was regular old ice that Bernie was talking about at the Chicago conference. He was describing a spray-nozzle smoke generator that would burn a combination of hydrogen and silver iodide, vaporizing the silver iodide into tiny particles perfect for precipitating snow. He described lab experiments that showed that the vaporized silver iodide particles continued to exist in a supercooled cloud long after being introduced, causing snow crystals to form for as much as an hour afterward.

"He contrasted this to seeding with dry ice," Kurt typed, "which generates large numbers of minute ice crystals immediately upon contact with the supercooled cloud."

It was the clearest statement yet of why Bernie was convinced silver iodide was the real future of rainmaking. Sometimes Kurt's explanations were damn good too.

•

As the boat from Henderson Harbor neared Association Island, at the eastern end of Lake Ontario, the men on board could see the funnel of a tuba rising over a throng of straw boaters. The band was playing "Marching Along Together," the Camp GE theme song for 1948.

Swinging along with GE.
Working along in stride
Without a question—without a doubt
We're GE's fighting crew
Oh rum ti-did-dle di let's all shout
Two billion we will do.

Vince filed off the boat with the others toward the banner reading, "Welcome: Camp General Electric." Here was the ultimate proof that the company valued him: he had been invited to Camp GE with 270 other men, managers from every branch and byway of GE. Every second summer, up-and-comers were invited to a three-day festival of networking, team building, and leadership training. Happily, he walked down the gangplank and got in line, awaiting his turn to be handed his GE monogram T-shirt, his camp boater, and his songbook. His tent number was 47. His team was Blue.

He'd heard about Camp GE for years. Irving and Doc Whitney were frequently at the island, representing the Research Lab. Guy Suits had gone too. Now it was Vince's turn. This honor followed close on the heels of another one: that June, the University of Notre Dame had granted him an honorary doctorate. He was deeply gratified; unlike Bernie and Irving, Vince actually cared about such formalities.

Vince had worked as Langmuir's right-hand man for decades. He had contributed immensely to Langmuir's research and published papers in respected scientific journals. He was a scientist, no doubt about it. But he had never been "Dr. Schaefer." It had always been "Mr. Schaefer." Now, even though it isn't customary for recipients of honorary degrees to use the title "Doctor," Irving Langmuir had begun referring to Vince as Dr. Schaefer, and it stuck.

So the newly minted Dr. Schaefer was ready to stand tall during the flag-raising ceremony, to play pinball or Ping-Pong in the Tom Catte room, to gather under the Old Elfun Elm during the inspirational "charge to the rookies," and to do his best for the Blue. Divided into four teams, Blue, Green, Gold, and Red, the men competed in a variety of sports. Volleyball, shuffleboard, trapshooting, and horseshoes were all possibilities, but the big event was the softball game. Competition was fierce, with friendly rivalry amplified by signs planted in the public gathering spaces saying things like "The green team welcomes you to Camp General Electric!" At the end of the three days, whichever team had the most points won the coveted title of Camp Sports Champions. Vince's camp songbook had the words to the Blue team's war cry, sung to the tune of "Yankee Doodle":

Blue's the best team on the Island
The others should have stood in bed
We have no trouble with the gold and green
And say the hell with the red.

The songbook also had the words to the marching song, the president's song, "GE Will Shine" and "Underneath the Elm," and, of course, all the classics: "Roll Out the Barrel," "Auld Lang Syne," "My Wild Irish Rose," "Pack Up Your Troubles," and "I Want a Girl."

Each morning, there were business meetings—lectures about marketing and manufacturing, research and public relations, as well as skits based on the year's leadership theme: "Our Heritage! Our Responsibility! Our Destiny?" The skits were written by Lemuel Boulware, manager of employee relations. Boulware had been appointed to his position after the strike of 1946, when plants under his management had stayed on the job. A zealous free marketeer, Boulware was on a mission to reeducate GE employees: his skits were ideological pageants about the evils of unions and the rewards of unfettered commerce. The company's president, Charlie Wilson, would be at Camp GE as well. He usually arrived late, and a song would be sung in his honor to the tune of "Auld Lang Syne":

Strong hearts and hands across the land
The loyal men and true,
From Eastern coast to Western strand,
Charlie, they're all for you.

The afternoon was dedicated to sports and to impromptu amusements like the insurance game Police Protection. In the late afternoon, cocktail hour began, followed by dinner and entertainment, and the famous brotherhood ceremonies led by an actor dressed as an Indian.

Vincent joined in with his usual vigor and team spirit. He carefully saved his program, his tent assignment, and his songbook. But he was also eager to get back to work. He had an even more exciting trip to take in the fall: Project Cirrus was heading out west. They were planning to start their program of large-scale weather control with a particularly useful undertaking: making rain in the desert.

•

Kurt was doing his best for GE. But it wasn't enough to applaud every new gadget or machine the company cooked up as if it would change the world. It wasn't enough to obey your GE boss and play softball on a GE team and buy your appliances at the GE employee store. The company wanted to tell you how to think too.

Every week or so, a new poster went up, Lemuel Boulware's florid signature at the bottom. "Why must we SAVE more—as well as PRODUCE more?" "Should pay be equal everywhere?" "What is Communism? What is Capitalism? What is the Difference to You?" You could be sure Mr. Boulware—a.k.a. Mr. Bullwhip—would tell you the answers. He had all the answers, Mr. Bullwhip did. Mr. Bullshit was more like it, at least as Kurt saw it. Boulware's messages to the employees were unabashedly pro-America and antilabor. Higher wages? Bad for workers because they increased inflation. Equal pay? A fallacy. Huge corporate profits? A clear sign of virtue. Communism? Nothing less than slavery. Redistributing wealth? The end of America.

Kurt's boss, George Griffin, was not much better. He had been a colonel in World War II, and he never seemed to forget it; now he was a company man through and through. George taped cartoons to his office door, like the one showing two executives looking at a chart of crashing sales. "It can't be our product's quality," one was saying to the other. "We make the finest buggy whips in the world!" George saw it as a crack at other companies. GE wouldn't be caught dead making buggy whips. Its most important product was progress.

Kurt tried to fit in, but he had brought some of his Chicago bohemianism to GE. He wore sneakers to work, shed his jacket as often as possible, and sometimes completely forgot his tie. He took up a collection at the office for the United World Federalists, an organization dedicated to the cause of world government. He got all his fellow junior writers to give a dollar each. Colonel Griffin did not appreciate these efforts. In Monday morning staff sessions, Kurt frequently found himself on the listening end of a lecture.

At least he had companions. Kurt's friend Ollie Lyon was a hell-raiser too, a fellow infantry veteran who had been on the same troopship to Europe as Kurt, though they didn't meet then. At GE, they became friends. Kurt also got to be friends with Bob Pace, another junior writer and a fellow graduate of Shortridge High. Bob had been two years ahead of Kurt there, and now they remet at GE. It was all an ocean, as Jane said.

On slow afternoons in the pressroom, the junior writers would repair to Walker's Pharmacy on State Street to eat pickled hard-boiled eggs washed down with beer. They talked politics, and there was plenty that summer to talk about. The Allied airlift had subverted the Soviet blockade of Berlin. American and British pilots, flying around the clock, were averting World War III, at least for now. But at home, Red-baiting was becoming the norm. Attacks on scientists were growing frequent, and it had taken prolonged exertions from the scientific community to stop the long and brutal smear campaign against the physicist Edward Condon, whom the Atomic Energy Commission had finally cleared to continue as director of the Bureau of Standards. But the HUAC chairman, J. Parnell Thomas, was not backing down. He was claiming that the Oak Ridge atomic laboratory was "heavily infested" with Reds. Government security clearance was now necessary to work in the GE Research Lab, and those who were denied it had no recourse. Frequently, they didn't even know the cause.

Most Americans felt it was reasonable for the government to keep track of communists; it followed that it was only right for GE to be careful about whom it hired. If you didn't have anything to hide, people figured, you didn't have anything to fear. They didn't know that the FBI was compiling dossiers on the GE scientists, that even scrupulously correct Irving Langmuir had an FBI file listing luncheons he had attended, speeches he had made, phone calls he had received, positive statements about him printed in *The Daily Worker*. The government is reasonable, people thought. It wouldn't ruin a man's career without good cause. And GE . . . most people trusted GE even more than they trusted the government. Kurt saw that as a kind of sickness.

Kurt and Bob Pace often talked about how to avoid catching "GE Disease." The main symptom was an overidentification with General

Electric—or "the Company," as such people called it. The affliction wasn't uncommon. In fact, GE encouraged it, especially among the PYMs, the Promising Young Men. The PYMs joined company discussion groups about protecting the free market and angled for invites to leadership conferences and Camp GE. They took memory-building classes at the Schenectady YMCA or attended GE colloquiums, all in the interest of becoming better organization men.

Tucked away at Walker's Pharmacy, out of sight of the electric boosterism of the company sign, one could gripe about GE. It was a relief to spend time not putting on an act. Quietly, Kurt was also keeping his eyes open in case a better job turned up. At the end of his first summer at GE, he submitted an essay to *The Reader's Digest* on the pleasure of working with one's hands. In his cover letter, he casually inquired about job openings there. Editor DeWitt Wallace wrote back to say they had none but would keep Kurt's qualifications in mind if any arose.

In the fall, an opportunity came up to better his position at GE. The News Bureau needed another writer in the magazine division, and Kurt lobbied hard to get the position. Being responsible for pitching stories to magazines like *The Saturday Evening Post* and *Life* meant reading those magazines would be part of his job. Meeting editors would be a cinch. Perhaps he could parlay it into selling some of his own work too.

Kurt got the promotion. It was a step up at GE. But it was also one step closer to what Jane had always said he should be doing, writing for a living. More and more, he knew that she was right: he was biding his time at GE, but secretly he was planning his escape.

•

Bernie was frustrated. He wanted to try out his silver iodide burner, but he couldn't get his hands on any hydrogen to fuel it.

It was October, and Project Cirrus was in New Mexico on an exploratory mission. Langmuir had decided that they should try to modify storms not in the East, where they simply traverse the land, but in the desert, where storms actually start. And Vincent had lined up an invaluable contact in the region: Everly John Workman, known as Jack.

Bernie liked Jack Workman; they all did. Acting president of the tiny New Mexico School of Mines, Jack was busily remaking a sleepy trade school for mining engineers into a serious institute of technology with a specialty in his passion: atmospheric physics. Many of his initiatives—such as requiring calculus for all students and disbanding the school's basketball team—were wildly unpopular. But he was energetic and pugnacious, and he always got his way. Best of all, he was a paper-clip-and-string scientist, like Bernie. He had cobbled together a passionate team and a ragtag weather research caravan: vans and old school buses and former Army trucks all kitted out with jerry-built instruments aimed at the sky. Barreling through the desert on the heels of a thunderstorm like a steampunk motorcade, Workman's group was Victorian science at its best. Jack's personal storm chaser was an open Packard to which he'd welded a lightning-proof steel roof mounted with electric field meters. It seemed perfectly safe, except for the part where he would floor the accelerator and then dive beneath the dashboard to read his instruments while the car careened down desert roads. The first time he ever did this with Project Cirrus team members in the car, it was raining, and the car careened wildly in the muddy road, nearly sliding off one side, then the other. Everyone was terrified except Irving, who calmly took out a notebook and scribbled calculations before announcing that the car's cyclic maneuver had a frequency of 176 per minute.

They were all excited about studying clouds and rain in New Mexico. The Southwest's weather is as different from the East's as its traffic. Both skies and highways are congested in the East, clogged with huge flows from countless sources. But out in the open desert, especially in the summer, there are few big weather fronts. Instead, the warm air rising off the sun-heated ground forms small, isolated clouds that typically move only a few miles before dissipating in the dry New Mexico air or boiling up into dramatic, short-lived thunderstorms.

Workman's team had agreed to help Project Cirrus with radar tracking and photography. And the Project Cirrus team only had three days there, so they got right to work. On October 14, they seeded a cumulus cloud with dry ice. The results were spectacular. The cloud billowed into an angry thunderhead and promptly produced reams of precipitation. Doing the calculations later, Langmuir concluded that the storm had produced rain over a forty-thousand-square-mile area, about a quarter of the state of New Mexico. He attributed it all to the seeding. "The odds in favor of this conclusion," he wrote, "as compared to the assumption that the rain was due to natural causes are many millions to one."

Meanwhile, Bernie was determined to get his silver iodide generator up and running. But he spent all three days trying to lay hands on some hydrogen out there in the middle of nowhere. By the time he finally acquired the fuel, the Project Cirrus group was preparing to leave. Fortunately, Workman's team was eager to continue the work, so Bernie left a spray-nozzle silver iodide generator behind. The School of Mines researchers agreed to run it sometimes, as he requested, after the Project Cirrus scientists left.

It had been a frustrating trip, but he went back to Schenectady with high hopes. The hot, open desert sky seemed as if it might provide what the humid, busy air of the East was refusing him: definitive proof, in the real atmosphere, of what silver iodide could do.

6

Watersheds

Bernie's work space was a disaster area. Bottles, beakers, Bunsen burners, microscopes, thermometers, cameras, tubes, and every other conceivable piece of lab equipment commingled on his workbench with the flotsam and jetsam of work life: pens and notebooks and coffee cups and ashtrays brimming with butts. Vincent even noted Bernie's mess in his work review but added that it wasn't really a problem. No one complained. Doc Whitney had once done a statistical study of workplace tidiness, showing that the most productive scientists were the ones with the messiest desks, so official Research Lab policy was to leave the slobs alone. Occasionally, however, an incredulous co-worker couldn't help commenting on the chaos.

"If you think that's bad," Bernie once replied, tapping his head, "you should see what's up here."

Now Bernie and his mess were moving to "the Penthouse," GE's name for the huge top-floor laboratory designated for Project Cirrus in the company's new facility. The Knolls Research Laboratory had not been officially christened yet, but by late 1948 most of the scientists had moved in. The $10.5 million building sat high on a bluff over the Mohawk River in Niskayuna, a sleepy little town about five miles east of downtown Schenectady and the Works; a bus constantly ran the "GE Loop" between them. The suburban locale gave the place a self-contained, campus feel. The new building housed a library, a cafeteria, an auditorium, and an employee store. The grounds had once been a private estate. Its mansion was restored and occupied by the Research Lab employees' exclusive Whitney Club, and its tree-lined drive and formal gardens lent it a patrician grandeur.

The sleek modernist building was designed to be a researcher's dream. Walls, piping, and wiring were modular, so they could be easily reconfigured for evolving projects. Compressed air, steam, hydrogen, and illuminating gas were piped in along with hot and cold water. There were even vacuum pipes. You turned on the tap, one scientist told the *Schenectady Gazette*, and "nothing" came out. That might have been Bernie; it was his kind of quip. In the Penthouse, he now shared a huge lab—a combination of rooms 507 to 513—with Vincent and Katharine Blodgett; Irving had a private office nearby. On the roof was a complete meteorological station that captured a constant stream of weather data recorded on instruments in the offices below.

This place was designed not for Victorian science but for the specialized, industrialized discipline that was coming to be called Big Science. The electron microscope, vacuum furnace, and low-temperature lab were up and running; the future would bring a chemical pilot plant and a radiation building with betatrons, synchrotrons, and high-voltage X-ray equipment. And next door, the Knolls Atomic Power Laboratory (KAPL)—a government facility operated by GE—was nearing completion. KAPL would be focused on military projects like designing nuclear submarines, but the alliance between it and the similarly named Knolls Research Lab was unmistakable. The white-collar world of the scientists, allied with the government and the military, was edging away from the blue-collar world of the Works and into its rarefied technocratic sphere. One News Bureau liaison was given an office in the Knolls. The rest of the News Bureau—including Kurt—stayed behind at the Works.

Irving was not there for the move; he was home, recovering from cataract surgery. But he'd be back in full swing soon. Langmuir was approaching seventy, but he had no intention of letting age run him out of science. Once, Dr. Michael Ference, the team's Signal Corps representative, made the mistake of asking Langmuir how his retirement might affect Project Cirrus.

"You'll know when I'm retired," Irving snapped. "I'll be dead."

Why would he retire when he was just commencing the most significant work of his career? Project Cirrus was now working like a well-oiled machine. With two B-17s fitted with special instruments for recording atmospheric data, as well as photo panels to document results, the team had carried out more than fifty experimental flights, seeding clouds over Cape Cod, Vermont, New Hampshire, and New York, over the Catskills, the Berkshires, and the Adirondacks. They had attacked stratus clouds and cumulus clouds with dry ice. They had even tried seeding clear skies.

With their new planes, they were finally getting some good documentation. In November near Schenectady, they had dispensed dry ice in the pattern of a Greek gamma twenty-four miles long, then photographed it from above. The gamma shape was entirely clear. Within half an hour, they could see the ground through its opening. When Vincent drove north to Rotterdam to photograph it from below, the seeded opening stretched from horizon to horizon, and curtains of snow were still falling from its edges. Later the same day, they attacked a cloud bank that was sitting over Rome, New York, this time flying a racetrack pattern. Below, controllers at the Rome airport gaped in wonder as two parallel bands of blue suddenly opened up in their otherwise overcast sky.

Project Cirrus had seeded clouds using Bernie's silver iodide technique only three times. On all three, observers on the planes agreed that the silver iodide had affected the clouds. But while the dry ice seeding runs were producing dramatic photographs, the silver iodide runs yielded only blurry fields of gray that looked as much like abstract paintings as they did clouds. Bernie's project remained a low priority.

Science Newsletter ran a story about his seeding method, putting his picture on the cover above the words "Fire for Rain." He stood behind his ground-based hydrogen burner igniting an aerosolized solution of silver iodide. The streaking lines of fire cast his tall form and curly pompadour in shadow so that he looked like a movie mad scientist. It was a nifty photograph, but it was all smoke and mirrors until he could prove that silver iodide worked in the real world, not just in the lab.

●

Shop Electric threw its holiday bash at the Rotterdam Democratic Club. Wire and Cable joined forces at the Town Tavern. High Voltage, Nucleonics, and Tool Design all had theirs at the popular Hans Grell's. Production took over Lloyd's with piano playing, singing, and dancing; one eager employee even attempted an Irish jig on the tabletop. By late November, reports of such antics at the holiday parties were crowding the gossipy pages of the *Schenectady Works News*.

Kurt, like the nation, was upbeat. The threat of nuclear annihilation seemed to recede as time passed. No other country had yet succeeded in getting the bomb, and there was still hope for averting a nuclear arms race and instituting some kind of world government. The United Nations was getting a chance to prove its effectiveness, working on brokering an armistice between Egypt and Israel. The Berlin Airlift had now been supplying West Berlin for five months, proving it was possible to stand up to Soviet aggression without provoking war. Best of all, the incumbent, Harry Truman, defeated the Republican challenger, Thomas Dewey, in the presidential election, upending the experts' predictions. The close race had led to the conservative *Chicago Tribune*'s famously mistaken headline: "Dewey Defeats Truman." Kurt undoubtedly laughed about that; he despised the *Trib*. And the election was close not because national sentiment was moving to the right. It was close because the six left candidates on a ticket of eight had divided the progressive majority. Kurt considered himself a socialist, but he'd take Truman over Dewey. Things, it seemed, were moving in the right direction, even if they weren't yet perfect.

As Kurt and Jane prepared to go out on the last Friday in November, Kurt was in an ebullient mood. They were headed for a festive black-tie affair in the ballroom of the Mohawk Golf Club—the first dance of the season for the Schenectady Junior League, where Jane was a provisional member. Their friends Ollie and Lavina Lyon were babysitting, and when the Lyons arrived, Kurt came downstairs in his tuxedo. On his feet were sneakers. It was something his sister, Alice, used to do: go to school dances in a party dress with sneakers on her feet. She was so beautiful and exotic that somehow she could pull it off.

Jane told him to go upstairs and change his shoes. She liked wackiness too: it was her nail polish on the nails of their claw-foot tub after all. But they were still carving out their place among the swells of Schenectady. They had made friends with other GE couples and attended cocktail parties and bridge games. Jane had joined the PTA and the American Association of University Women. She volunteered one night a week at the local hospital. Kurt had signed on as an Alplaus volunteer fireman. They were fitting in, or at least pretending to.

On weekdays in Building 6, Kurt performed the role of the dedicated junior writer, buckling down to pitch compelling stories about GE to editors, trying to flood them with the conviction that whatever new gadget GE was about to unveil would top the second coming of Christ. In his new position at the magazine division, he was churning out peppy overviews of subjects as unpromising as a leak detector shaped like a football or the new lab for low-temperature physics. He had spent enough time studying magazines to predict what editors wanted, and he seriously hoped to land GE an article in one of the national glossies. It would make things better for him at work. But he knew that he lacked what the company men had: some fundamental organ or special circuitry in the brain that would have enabled him to form an emotional attachment to the company, or even just to give a damn.

So in the evenings and on weekends, he parked himself at the tiny desk he and Jane had set up at the end of the upstairs hallway and wrote. From wherever she was in the house, Jane could hear the sound of typing. She was getting to recognize its rhythms. A smooth, steady clacking meant things were going well. When the typing stopped, she worried. If the writing was going badly, Kurt was hell to live with.

Only a few trusted friends knew about Kurt's aspirations. Ollie was one. The Lyons hesitated to drop by unannounced on evenings or weekends. They knew they'd find Kurt at his desk, smoking Pall Malls and typing, and they didn't want to bother him. Plenty of guys had literary dreams, but Kurt also had discipline.

Behind the facade of the hardworking junior writer, the good team player, the loyal employee, the tiny flickering hope would not be extinguished: that one day he might quit and write for real. Jane remained convinced that her husband was a genius and that the world would figure it out eventually. Her faith didn't waver as the rejection slips piled up: she simply decoupaged a wastepaper basket with them. Kurt used them as scrap paper. When Jane gave him a grocery list, asking him to pick up corn, six wieners, Duff's devil's food, Junket, and instant icing, he jotted the items down on the back of a rejection slip from *Reader's Scope*.

But all that was unknown to most of his colleagues. Good company men dreamed of nothing more than steadily ascending the company ladder. And Schenectady was a company town full of company men. They rode on company buses wearing company suits and company fedoras. They had immaculate company wives and adorable company kids, and they lived in leafy company neighborhoods. That's not to say the company owned their homes, but in a community where two out of three schoolkids had a dad who worked for GE, where the baseball teams, bowling leagues, and ski trains were sponsored by GE, where people's social lives centered on GE clubs and GE lectures and GE parties, and where the local newspaper could pretty much be counted on for a GE story on the front page every day, it was hard not to feel that the company owned your soul.

That wasn't him: he was holding his soul apart. Still, when Jane asked, Kurt went upstairs and changed his shoes. He understood the need to fit in, and he was doing his best. But it made him nervous. He had a sneaking suspicion that if you pretend to be something for long enough, you might actually become it.

●

A few days before Christmas, Bernie oversaw Project Cirrus's fourth airborne attempt to seed clouds with silver iodide. It was flight fifty-seven for Project Cirrus. He had devised a new method for getting the chemical into the sky: impregnating small chunks of charcoal with silver iodide, then loading them into a burner that projected from the tail of the B-17. The scientists could light and unlight the burner as the plane flew.

The bomber plane took off from the Schenectady airport. It was a gray day, the sky slabbed with the concrete clouds typical of winter in upstate New York. The B-17 easily reached seventy-two hundred feet and began flying a gamma-shaped pattern over a solid bank of gray stratus clouds. Dry ice was dispensed first, for about a minute. Then Bernie's silver iodide burner was turned on for fifteen seconds, burning three or four pounds of silver-iodide-infused charcoal. Then another round of dry ice was released, to bracket the seeded spot. Kiah Maynard, the designated GE observer aboard the plane, scrupulously noted everything in his GE notepad. Bernie listened in from the tower.

When the plane circled back over the seeded area, everyone on board could see the results. Like the dry ice, the silver iodide had attracted water vapor from the cloud's supercooled droplets. Three long furrows had opened up, each filled with sparkling ice crystals. Manmade snow was falling. The Signal Corps photographer shot forty-four pictures.

Back at the lab, the photographs were developed. When he saw them, Bernie was elated. Flight fifty-seven had produced the first photographic evidence that silver iodide seeding worked on actual clouds. Excitedly, he calculated the probable number of snowflakes his seeding had produced. Five hundred per square centimeter of cloud, he figured. That was equivalent to dry ice seeding.

The implications were huge. Dry ice seeding was limited to local effects. Silver iodide's persistence offered the chance to change the weather for real—and not just one cloud at a time. If Bernie's silver iodide smoke could be introduced to the right air current, the results could be seen across entire weather systems. He just had to convince the rest of the team.

•

Kurt was convinced he had invented a winner: Alfred Moorhead, a classic company man. Alfred was saddled with the usual accoutrements: a dull job, a numskull boss, a nagging wife. Would it be so bad if he figured out a way to take harmless revenge on all of them? And so, right there in Building 6, his first successful GE story began to take shape.

Alfred is an office functionary in a huge corporation: the United Manufacturing Company. He's nothing special until he takes a company seminar in mnemonics. At United Manufacturing, as at GE, a good memory is considered a business asset. So when Alfred becomes a memory whiz, his career takes off.

His old boss and his nagging wife hardly know what to think of this new and improved Alfred. Magically, he's been transformed from a loser to a winner. What no one realizes is that Alfred's new memory power comes from attaching violent images to anything he has to recall. When he has to remember the date he started work at the company, he thinks of a crashed airplane with soldiers marching past it carrying a flag emblazoned "17." This brings to mind the date March 17, 1929— the year of the "crash." To recall his boss's extension, 717, Alfred imagines the boss with two 7-shaped hatchets in his body and a 1-shaped dagger in his throat. When his wife calls and asks him to pick up carrots, molasses, Dreft detergent, and liverwurst, he doesn't need to write it down. He just imagines sticking carrots in her ears, dumping molasses and soap flakes on her, and stuffing a liverwurst in her mouth. For the last item on the list—matches—he adds a backdrop for his sadistic tableau: the United Manufacturing Company in flames.

"The More Vivid, the Better" was a nasty little story, an office revenge fantasy with a dollop of marital resentment. But it *worked*; Kurt was pleased with it. He redrafted it a couple of times, changing its title to the catchier "Mnemonics." He figured it was just the kind of thing the magazines were looking for. It had a "hook" and humor and was set in a milieu that people would recognize.

It was also in keeping with the times. Like so much of the era's fiction, "Mnemonics" openly expressed anxiety about the conformist corporate culture taking shape in the nation. But Kurt still couldn't separate that anxiety from the war. The downed airplane with its (B-)"17," the marching soldiers, the factory in flames: on some level, the Bulge and Dresden were still haunting his imagination. Like Salinger's "Perfect Day for Bananafish" or Sloan Wilson's *Man in the Gray Flannel Suit*, the early version of "Mnemonics" hints that the corporate blandness of the company man might be concealing war trauma. There was logic to this, coming so soon after the liberation of the Nazi death camps. Organization men were followers, and Dachau, Auschwitz, and Bergen-Belsen had introduced the world to the destruction blind followers can wreak.

Kurt sent the story off to *The New Yorker*. It was rejected right away. He told himself to keep on trying, but he felt disheartened: he knew it was his best effort yet. He put "Mnemonics" away instead of sending it somewhere else. Maybe he wasn't cut out for the writing life after all.

•

"There is no use worrying about a need of one hundred pounds of dry ice," Irving told the audience at the January 1949 meeting of the American Meteorological Society in New York City. "One gram is enough to do a good job."

They still weren't presenting their experiments on silver iodide; they didn't have enough data. But Bernie was in the audience as Irving and Vincent outlined their latest thinking about the correct amounts of dry ice to use in seeding clouds. The team was coming to think that sometimes less was more. Vince showed photographs of the trenches and L-shaped channels they had carved in the clouds. At the end of his talk, Irving gave an account of an October flight experiment in New Mexico, on a day when the Weather Bureau had not predicted any rain for the state. But after Project Cirrus seeded a large cumulus cloud near Albuquerque, the cloud became a thunderhead and precipitated. More clouds developed in the wake of that one. Irving showed slide after slide of the seeded cloud growing and developing into a squall line. He estimated that a hundred million tons of water had originated in that single seeding.

When Irving was done talking, Ross Gunn stood up to comment. Director of physical research for the Weather Bureau, he was head of the Cloud Physics Project, designed to check the claims of Project Cirrus. Gunn pointed out that he had often seen cloud troughs such as those in the Project Cirrus pictures while flying and doubted they were the result of seeding. Project Cirrus could show all the photographs they wanted, but they didn't prove anything. And it was simply outrageous to claim that mile-wide holes could be produced in a stratus cloud deck by a mere pellet of dry ice.

Then came the Cloud Physics Project's report. Recounting their experiments to date, the Weather Bureau scientists announced their conclusion: clouds could be somewhat modified in appearance by seeding, but there was no evidence that these modifications could induce self-propagating storms.

"The experiments showed that the artificial modification of cumuliform clouds is of doubtful economic importance for the production of rain," the report declared. Nor was the attack over: immediately after the Cloud Physics Project report, Weather Bureau chief Reichelderfer gave the conference lunchtime address, and in it he proposed that money be spent attempting to predict the weather accurately, rather than on attempting to control it. He didn't say it outright, but Reichelderfer, like Harry Wexler, was pretty sure he knew how better weather prediction was going to be achieved: with John von Neumann's computer. Once they had that up and running, it was going to be easier than ever to dismiss the work of Project Cirrus.

After the talk, Irving took Reichelderfer aside. Why was he saying such starkly negative things when the evidence was still coming in? Reichelderfer had a blunt reply: to counteract Irving's exaggerations.

"Which of my statements do you consider the worst?" asked Langmuir, with his usual scientific detachment.

That was easy. Reichelderfer said it was Irving's claims that the seeding of hurricanes should be studied with an eye to learning how to steer them. Particularly deplorable was Irving's National Academy of Sciences speech, where he had announced that "with increased knowledge we should be able to abolish all of the evil effects of these hurricanes." It was a gross exaggeration, Reichelderfer said.

Irving was unruffled. The larger the storm, he said, the more energy in it, and the more energy in it, the easier it should be to have a big effect on it. A hurricane could probably be modified by just a single pellet of dry ice. You just had to know where to put the pellet. To think otherwise, he told the astonished Reichelderfer, was like claiming that a massive forest fire could never be set by a single match.

"Rain-Making Held of No Importance," declared *The New York Times* the next day. "Weather Men See Little Value in Scientists' Efforts to Alter Natural Patterns." GE dispatched Bernie to do the rounds of the radio networks: he was a good interview subject, able to explain things clearly. Patiently, soberly, he described how cloud seeding worked and explained why they believed the experiments should keep going forward. But the battle lines had been drawn. The GE scientists led one side, and the Weather Bureau headed up the other. Maybe, Vincent told Bernie and Irving later, they should start seeding clouds in the pattern of the GE logo, imprinting the "meatball" on the sky instead of racetracks or gammas. Then people might believe they had done something.

Irving had a better idea. As soon as he got back to Schenectady, he began arranging for the Norwegian meteorologist and D-Day forecaster Sverre Petterssen to visit GE and go over the Project Cirrus findings. Petterssen was highly respected and scientifically rigorous. But he was also now the director of scientific service for the Air Force Air Weather Service, and while the Weather Bureau might be staffed with naysayers, the military could be counted on for enthusiasm.

That was becoming evident to Bernie as well. The Navy and the Signal Corps liked his silver iodide generator so much, they were refusing to declassify information about it. And not long after the AMS conference, he received a letter from the Office of Naval Research informing him that a group of high-ranking officers was coming to Schenectady to discuss the cloud nuclei counter he was developing. It would be sometime next month: they would get back to him with the exact date. They simply assumed Bernie would be there to tell them what they wanted to know.

•

Kurt was thinking about what might happen if a scientist refused to tell the military men what they wanted to know. A scientist had recently done just that: Norbert Wiener.

Professor Norbert Wiener of MIT was one of the world's leading mathematicians. He was good friends with John von Neumann, but the two men could hardly have been more different. In January 1947, Wiener had made national news by canceling a talk at an MIT symposium on high-speed calculating machines because the conference was funded by the military. Just before the conference, *The Atlantic* had published Wiener's open letter to an aircraft company researcher who requested a copy of a paper on controlled missiles Wiener had written during the war. Wiener refused to give it to him. It was simple, Wiener wrote. He had done that work under government contract because he thought he should assist the war effort. But then he had seen the results.

"The policy of the government itself during and after the war, say in the bombing of Hiroshima and Nagasaki," he wrote, "has made it clear that to provide scientific information is not a necessarily innocent act, and may entail the gravest consequences. One therefore cannot escape reconsidering the established custom of the scientist to give information to every person who may inquire of him." Scientists had now become arbiters of life and death, he declared, and he was censoring himself because "to disseminate information about a weapon in the present state of our civilization is to make it practically certain that that weapon will be used."

Wiener's letter had made a big impression in Schenectady. The scientists Kurt knew at GE often discussed issues like those he raised. Had it been morally right to drop the atomic bomb on Hiroshima—and on Nagasaki? If morally wrong, were the scientists who built the bomb as guilty as the generals who decided to use it? Wiener's vow of noncompliance was admired by many in the Scientists' Movement and beyond, but it was disturbing too. Should scientists censor themselves? Didn't knowledge belong to the world at large?

Two years of debate had not settled the question. In November 1948, the *Bulletin of the Atomic Scientists* had published Wiener's follow-up essay, "A Rebellious Scientist After Two Years." Again, Wiener pulled no punches. "The degradation of the position of the scientist as an independent worker and thinker to that of a morally irresponsible stooge in a science-factory has proceeded even more rapidly and devastatingly than I had expected," he wrote. "In view of this, I still see no reason to turn over to any person, whether he be an army officer or the kept scientist of a great corporation, any results which I obtain if I think they are not going to be used for the best interests of science and of humanity."

A morally irresponsible stooge in a science factory! Some people might look at the GE Research Lab and see exactly that. GE made no effort to hide its cozy relationship with the military; on the contrary, it boasted of it. But what did this mean for scientists like Bernie? Were they really kept scientists, ethically deficient worker ants mindlessly contributing to a proliferating war machine? Kurt knew his brother was at heart a pacifist; their parents had raised them that way, and the war had only deepened the conviction for them both. But as soon as cloud seeding was made public, its military uses were being discussed. There was General Kenney telling the graduates of MIT, "The nation that first learns to plot the paths of air masses accurately and learns to control the time and place of precipitation will dominate the globe." That made Bernard uncomfortable. But because of his discovery, he was now answering to the generals. If a scientist like Bernard wanted to stop his work from being used for violent ends, what might he have to do?

Kurt's new story was different from anything else he had written. There was no grieving widow or office romance, none of the crowd-pleasing claptrap he had been churning out, hoping to please the slicks. Nor was there mention of World War II. Instead, right there at his desk in the Schenectady Works, from his vantage point in GE's science factory, he began to imagine an antiwar scientist named Professor Barnhouse.

Professor Barnhouse discovers something shocking: he has the ability to control things previously thought to be uncontrollable. But his dream of using his power for humanity's benefit soon crumbles as he realizes that the military men only see its value as a superweapon.

He called the story "Wishing Will Make It So: A Comprehensive Report on the Barnhouse Effect." On one of the first full drafts, he crossed out "Barnhouse." Was it too close to his brother's nickname, Barney? He made the professor Brenhaltz instead. Lots of scientists had German names. Before long, he restored it to Barnhouse.

The story is narrated by Barnhouse's student because the professor himself has disappeared. Barnhouse's student has been tasked with explaining the history of the "Barnhouse effect." It began, he explains, when Barnhouse, an artillery private in the Army, rolled sevens in his first barracks dice game—ten times in a row. Like Langmuir with his New Mexico storm, Barnhouse went off and excitedly calculated the odds of that happening by chance: they were one in sixty million. He tried rolling dice again and realized he could produce the effect: he had telekinetic powers. He began consciously cultivating this power, "dynamopsychism," until eventually he could destroy entire buildings from miles away.

Barnhouse keeps his power secret at first, annoying the student-narrator with what seem like irrelevant questions. His favorites are "Think we should have dropped the atomic bomb on Hiroshima?" and

"Think every new piece of scientific information is a good thing for humanity?" He reveals his power to his student-narrator when he decides to declare it publicly, in a letter to the secretary of state.

"I have discovered a new force which costs nothing to use," he writes, "and which is probably more important than atomic energy."

It was exactly the same claim Langmuir was making about weather modification. And like Langmuir, Professor Barnhouse quickly finds himself taken up by the military. A Senator Warren Foust—sounding a lot like General Kenney on the topic of weather control—declares, "He who rules the Barnhouse Effect rules the world!" The military starts a dynamopsychism program, naming it "Project Wishing Well." It secludes the professor and his student in a safe house under the protection of guards on loan from the Atomic Energy Commission and plans a secret test of the Barnhouse effect called "Operation Brainstorm." It succeeds brilliantly. Barnhouse, sitting on a couch, uses his dynamopsychic powers to destroy ten V-2 rockets fired in New Mexico, bring down fifty radio-controlled bombers over the Aleutians, and completely disarm 120 target ships headed for the Caroline Islands. The generals are so elated by the operation's success they don't notice when Barnhouse slips away. It's left to the student to read aloud the manifesto the professor has left behind.

The manifesto opens with the kind of pun Vonnegut could never resist. "Gentlemen," the professor writes, "As the first superweapon with a conscience, I am removing myself from your national defense stockpile. Setting a new precedent in the behavior of ordnance, I have humane reasons for going off."

The manifesto goes on for another page and a half. The tone is Norbert Wiener's, but the politics are even more overt. In fact, the manifesto could have come directly from a United World Federalists position paper. Barnhouse points out the fallacy of trying to forge peace by building weapons and declares that the world cannot afford a nuclear war. He chastises the generals for failing to put their faith in government—in particular, the downtrodden United Nations. He explains that henceforth he will be making sure UN recommendations are carried out. And he demands that there be no more vetoes—just as the Scientists' Movement had insisted a few years earlier. The story ends with the professor noting that if the world leaders don't like it, they can lump it; he's in control now.

Even as it addressed the vexing ethical quandaries raised by science, "Report on the Barnhouse Effect" was an optimistic story. The professor is a good person, an idealist with the power to enforce his principles. He sets an example for scientists much as Norbert Wiener did: he refuses to cooperate with the war machine. If enough scientists like Barnhouse would just step forward, the madness of an arms race could be averted.

Professor Barnhouse was the first in a long line of fictional scientists Kurt Vonnegut would write into being. He was also the most unambiguously noble, born at one of the last moments when Kurt thought that politics might still turn around, that the world might come to its senses and find its way to a new, enlightened era of prosperity and peace.

•

Irving was delighted with the man the Weather Bureau had sent to destroy Project Cirrus. He loved that William Lewis seemed determined to find every flaw in their data, every weak spot in their equations. Skepticism was how science progressed. He was convinced that he and Bernie and Vince would win Lewis and the Weather Bureau over in the end.

Lewis spent a long time formulating his position. In June 1949, he handed the Project Cirrus team a memo about the New Mexico storm they had reported on in January. He outlined his objections to the Project Cirrus interpretation of events in five single-spaced pages with three hand-drawn charts. The main problem was simple: How could the team know for sure that they had actually caused the rain they observed? Here was the heart of the matter, the scientific flaw that was really an epistemological problem. "It is not possible," Lewis wrote,

> in any particular instance, to decide with any degree of certainty whether the rainfall observed in an area presumably affected by seeding, was in fact due to the seeding, or would have occurred anyway. You may surmise that the rain resulted from the seeding while I surmise that the seeding had very little to

do with it, but neither of us *knows*. There is no evidence for a positive decision either way.

In order to produce proof that cloud seeding worked, Lewis said, "it will be necessary to design the experiments in a way that will permit the use of statistical evidence in the verification of the results."

Statistics! It was a brilliant idea. Given the particular set of conditions, what are the odds of rain? Even Irving Langmuir hadn't thought of that. But he was absolutely thrilled. Statistical analysis was tremendously popular now that high-speed calculating machines could be used to sort data. *Scientific American* had even performed an analysis of the news coverage of the House Un-American Activities Committee investigation of the physicist Edward Condon by reducing assertions about Condon in New York City's nine daily newspapers to holes on punch cards and running the cards through an IBM sorting machine. It had proved, objectively, that the liberal newspapers favored Condon and the conservative newspapers maligned him.

Numbers didn't lie. They couldn't be accused of bias, and they were oblivious to the prejudices of their observers. No one could refuse to believe something the numbers revealed. Irving embraced Lewis's idea at once. It might be impossible to prove what *would have* happened in the past. But one could prove the statistical likelihood of what *did* happen. And if what happened was statistically unlikely, over and over, the evidence would add up until the conclusion was irrefutable. Numbers would come to the rescue of his research. Now he just had to do one thing: teach himself statistics.

•

Here was a change: Kurt's boss was delighted with him. The microchemistry story he had written up in December was picked up by *Life*. The magazine even sent a *Life* photographer to Schenectady to shoot photographs of employees holding tiny lab instruments in their hands. It was Kurt's biggest score yet for the News Bureau. His triumph even merited a mention in the *Schenectady Works News*.

But privately, Kurt was far more interested in his own writing. He had finished "Barnhouse," and he felt good about it. It revived him from the letdown of the "Mnemonics" rejection. With the new story in hand, he figured he had enough material to seek representation. Aiming high, he sent seven stories off to Russell & Volkening Inc. One of New York's most respected literary agencies, Russell & Volkening represented top-notch writers like Eudora Welty, Henry Miller, and Saul Bellow, and it had a reputation for liking offbeat fiction. But Diarmuid Russell wrote back disappointingly soon, declining to take Kurt on. The stories were brisk, he said, but he didn't think editors would like them. Still, he suggested Kurt send the Barnhouse story to *Collier's* and the *Post*.

Kurt wasn't one to turn down free advice. So in March, as "his" microchemistry story (absent his name) came out in *Life*, he mailed off "Report on the Barnhouse Effect" to *The Saturday Evening Post*. It was rejected almost at once.

Still, he had faith in "Barnhouse." Not only was it a good yarn; it was in keeping with the tenor of the times. That month, three thousand delegates were gathering at the Waldorf-Astoria in New York for a peace conference. Organizers included Albert Einstein, Arthur Miller, Lillian Hellman, and Norman Mailer, who made a sensational speech about capitalism being the ultimate cause of wars. Norman Cousins of the United World Federalists spoke as well. The State Department declared the conference to be communist propaganda, HUAC insisted it was all part of a subversive Red "peace offensive," and thousands of protesters from veterans groups, religious organizations, and Eastern European immigrant groups picketed outside the Waldorf, singing patriotic songs, reciting prayers, and shouting anti-Russian and anticommunist slogans. But people were *talking*—shouting even—about peace and internationalism. His story was not just sharp; it was relevant.

Kurt sent "Barnhouse" to *Collier's* in April. It came back with a form rejection. But at the bottom, in an almost unreadable scrawl, was a short note: "This is a little sententious for us. You're not the Kurt Vonnegut who worked on *The Cornell Sun* in 1942, are you?" He didn't recognize the name, and he wasn't sure he wanted to own up to being his feckless undergraduate former self, so he filed the rejection away and sent "Barnhouse" off to *Story*.

It was languishing there when Jane told him she was pregnant again. Two kids! It was a thunderbolt. If it was hard to quit a corporate job with one kid, it would be even harder with two. The noose was tightening around his neck. He had to get his writing career off the ground, or he'd be like one of the countless corporate drones who longed to write but who couldn't bring themselves to leave the security of the paycheck, the life insurance, the paid vacation, the employee discount on appliances. After twenty-five years, GE employees got thanked with a reception and a commemorative pin. The Quarter Century Club, they called it. Every year the quarter centurions had a clambake. Clams, cigars, cocktails—the best of everything to honor the GE lifers. He was headed for his own commemorative clambake if he didn't get out soon.

Desperation made him do what he had scrupulously avoided until now: he told one of his work colleagues about his writing. George Burns was a photographer who sometimes worked with Kurt on News Bureau stories. He had been on staff at GE once, but now he was freelance. He and his brother Jimmy had a photography studio on Schenectady's State Street. George was a fun guy, an adventurer. When GE built its new radio tower, George scaled it to get a photograph from the top. Like Kurt, he was a veteran; he'd served as an enlisted man in the Pacific. George shot the famous flag raising at Iwo Jima for *Yank* magazine; his was not the version that became famous, but he was easygoing enough not to care. He was standing by when Prime Minister Tojo tried to kill himself, and he was one of the first photographers to document the results of the atomic bomb. After flying over Nagasaki in a B-25, he wrote that the city looked as if giants had stomped through it, grinding every building into the ground.

George had never read any of Kurt's fiction, but he could relate to creative aspirations. He immediately recommended that Kurt contact a war buddy of his from *Yank*, a straight-up guy who had written an impressive story on the firebombing of Tokyo. The guy was an editor at *Collier's* now, George said; he might be able to help. His name was Knox Burger.

The name rang a bell. Kurt went home and pulled the *Collier's* rejection letter for "Report on the Barnhouse Effect" from his file. Suddenly the scribbled letters took shape: Knox Burger.

Knox had been a friend of Kurt's in college, the editor of a campus humor magazine called *The Cornell Widow*. The *Sun* and the *Widow* were rivals, frequently taking potshots at each other in print, but Knox and Kurt had liked each other. Once, Knox had even taken Kurt's suggestion about toning down some apparently anti-Semitic caricatures of *Sun* editors that his own magazine had produced.

Kurt sat down and wrote to Knox right away. It was already June, and Jane was due in December. His letter was alternately full of self-deprecation and braggadocio. "Sorry you didn't care for my story," he wrote. "I got a *typewritten* letter back on it from the *Post*. *Story* has now had it for a month. You're right. It was a dog." But he had other things in the works, including a completed novella and another that would be done soon. He closed by saying he would be in New York for two days of the following week. Would Knox like to have lunch? Knox replied by telegram three days later, telling Kurt to call him at his office when he arrived in town. It seemed, to Kurt, as if his breakthrough might finally be at hand.

•

On a cool July morning in Socorro, New Mexico, Bernie turned an impish yet calculating gaze to the sky. He'd done enough lab work, enough backyard experiments. Now he was determined to make a decisive demonstration of what his silver iodide generator could accomplish. He would see if he could do anything about those puffy, cumulus clouds dotting the blue.

In its second interim report, the Weather Bureau's Cloud Physics Project had not only dismissed the idea that dry ice might produce rain of economic importance but also claimed that no significant rainfall resulted from the seeding of cumulus clouds with "persistent nuclei." Bernie had published a short rejoinder in May. The bureau team, he noted, had described experiments using nuclei of lead oxide and potassium iodide. His lab tests showed that silver iodide vaporized for one second was ten thousand times more effective than other chemicals in producing nuclei for the formation of ice crystals. If the bureau scientists were using other compounds, it wasn't surprising they had gotten poor results.

Bernie was ready to prove his case. He had perfected the method, and now, with his little homemade smoke generator, he would make an effective demonstration—something that William Lewis, who had come to Socorro with them, would have to acknowledge. The problem was that Vincent and Irving had arrived in Socorro a week early to plan the summer's research, and they hadn't included any experiments with silver iodide in the program.

So, on July 21, as the others prepared for the day's dry ice seeding flights, Bernie lugged his generator to a spot out in the middle of the dry desert scrub. He fired it up at around 6:00 a.m., right after the sun came up. He took notes on the wind, the temperature, and the location of clouds in the distant sky. Then he went to breakfast. When he came back, the wind had picked up, and the burner was still humming along.

New Mexico was a stratiform world: first brown and yellow desert, then a layer of mountains on the horizon, and then the clouds—low cumulus, billowing up like a second mountain range, and above them the white smear of stratus. There was so much sky here, a blank blue page on which the sun's work was written every day, then erased by night's cool dark. Every morning it started all over. The air began to warm around breakfast. By mid-afternoon it was so hot the men would strip to the waist.

At around 8:15, Bernie saw cumulus clouds forming near the Sandia Mountains, the range of peaks east of Albuquerque, and also over the Manzanos, farther south. The clouds looked like the region's typical orographic cumulus: small puffs of white formed by heat funneled up the side of the mountains. Most orographic clouds just cling to their hills like hats, growing a little but not precipitating. But as Bernie ran his generator and watched the sky, the clouds began to build. By 9:30, the cloud over the Manzanos looked heavy with ice. An hour later, it was developing into the classic anvil shape of a brewing storm.

Periodically, Bernie released a balloon to show him how the winds were blowing so he could gauge where his silver iodide smoke was headed. The balloons drifted right to the Manzanos and from there to the Sandias. That meant the winds were carrying his silver iodide smoke to exactly the places where the clouds were whooping it up.

At lunch, he told Langmuir he'd been running his silver iodide generator and that he thought it might be affecting the clouds. Langmuir, focused on the afternoon's dry ice seeding flight, had no response. He barely seemed to register Bernard's remark.

Bernie went back to his burner around noon. He changed its hydrogen tank and kept it running. And then he heard thunder. He looked up and saw flashes of lightning. The air beneath the Manzano clouds was dark with virga: wisps of rain that fall and evaporate before reaching the ground. It was working! Before long, he could see a line of cumulus clouds building up to the northwest. The entire area where his silver iodide was going was a mass of roiling storm clouds. He was so excited he kept forgetting to use military time in his notes. He turned his burner off at 1:30. He didn't want to interfere with the team's dry ice seeding from the air, which was scheduled to start over the Sandias at around 3:00.

Schaefer, aboard the B-17 that afternoon, was surprised to find that the cumulus clouds they planned to seed were already a seething mass of thunderheads when they arrived, pouring down rain as they boiled their way northeast. Even more surprising would be the data from Albuquerque's nearby radar station showing a radar echo of precipitation appearing in the silver iodide–seeded cloud at around 10:00 a.m.— exactly when Bernie's calculations said the silver iodide should be reaching it. The precipitation area began by covering about one square mile at 20,500 feet—atypically low for New Mexico. It then expanded with mind-boggling speed, increasing to seven square miles in four minutes and rising to 34,000 feet in another two. It was one of the most dramatic storms they had ever—possibly—made.

That evening, Bernie told Langmuir again that he had been running his generator that morning. All at once, the information seemed to break through Langmuir's interior monologue. The scientist stared at Bernie.

"You were running the generator today?" he asked.

"Yes," Bernie said.

With that, Langmuir's attention was finally caught. He wanted to know everything. How often had the generator been running? Had he been running it before? Had the October dry ice experiments possibly been affected by silver iodide from the ground? All of their data needed to be reassessed in the light of this new fact: silver iodide worked. It had been working all along. More silver iodide experiments needed to be done. The summer's program had to be rewritten. That night, Irving stayed up late, dictating eight thousand words of notes. "Taking all in all," he concluded, "I feel that the evidence is now practically overwhelming. The evidence for the production of rain, and even thunderstorms, by silver iodide seeding is now about as certain as the opening up of clouds by stratus cloud seeding." In his diary, he was more succinct: "Vonnegut made a thunderstorm."

The next day, Langmuir flew to Los Alamos, elated. He'd started doing the calculations on Bernie's thunderstorm, and they looked tremendous. The silver iodide seeding, he figured, had brought millions of gallons of water down on New Mexico.

Often when he flew, Irving offered to take the controls. The FAA had ruined flying for him: when the regulations decreed that logbooks had to be a particular color, he'd sold his plane in disgust. No one was going to tell Irving Langmuir what color his logbook should be. But he still liked to practice when he had a chance. Today, however, he was more interested in looking out the window. Eagerly, he scanned the New Mexico desert unfurling beneath them. Near Santo Domingo, he saw what he was looking for: a swollen, roiling river entering the Rio Grande.

"What river is that?" he shouted to the pilot, pointing it out.

The pilot peered out.

"Galisteo Creek," he yelled back. He said he was surprised to see so much water in it: its streambed was usually dry. Langmuir noted this with satisfaction. He would get stream flow data. He'd get rain gauge data. The numbers would bear out what he was seeing beneath the plane: Vonnegut's thunderstorm still filling the desert's dry wash. Here, finally, was something on the scale they'd been imagining all along.

When he arrived at Los Alamos, Irving excitedly described Vonnegut's thunderstorm to the Manhattan Project physicist Edward Teller. Teller had little patience for Langmuir's effusions: he was once again deeply embroiled in debates over his thermonuclear bomb, or "Super." He'd wanted to build the Super since the start of the Manhattan Project, and the objections of the peace-minded Scientists' Movement had not changed his mind. Teller was born in Hungary, and the implosion of Europe had cast a pall on his spirit, as it had for many expatriates. He had little patience for talk of UN control or international disarmament. To him, the only option was to stay a step ahead of the Reds by developing the Super at once.

J. Robert Oppenheimer disagreed, as did David Lilienthal, head of the Atomic Energy Commission, and many of the scientists who had rallied around the cause of peacetime arms control. Many in the public, too, still held hopes for peace and world government. But since 1946, a different consensus had been growing in Washington, one that foresaw the world not uniting but dividing into two armed camps. Events in Berlin only solidified this conviction. The journalist Walter Lippmann had just given the situation a name in his new book: *The Cold War.* That was helpful to Teller. He felt certain that the political climate was going to swing his way in the end. Even Oppenheimer, he was convinced, would support the Super if the problems with the physics were solved.

As Langmuir enthused about his storm's destructiveness, Teller grumpily wondered if the GE chemist saw rainmaking as "competition" for the atomic bomb. It was a surprisingly insightful thought: Langmuir did see weather control as trumping atomic fission. As he liked to point out, a storm system like a hurricane contained hundreds of times as much energy as an atomic bomb, even a hydrogen bomb. Controlling that force would be an achievement as great as—if not greater than—harnessing the atom.

And it excited people. For all his absentmindedness, his ability to lose himself so deeply in his thoughts that he seemed barely aware of other people, Langmuir liked to communicate. He was a scientific missionary, surprisingly adept at explaining complex scientific ideas to laymen. He liked elucidating things for children, for lab visitors, for anyone who would listen. His proselytizing for science never stopped. When he held toddlers, he bounced them on his knees, first with both knees in sync, then with his knees alternating. "In phase," he would chant, "out of phase!" Kurt Vonnegut once overheard him saying that anyone who couldn't explain his work to a fourteen-year-old had to be a charlatan.

His zeal for science had led Langmuir to invent many things in his career—the gas-filled incandescent lamp, the mercury-condensation vacuum pump, the atomic-hydrogen welding torch, the thoriated tungsten filament. But not one of those achievements had ever captured the public imagination—until now. Even winning the Nobel Prize paled in comparison with taking charge of the climate. Langmuir believed it would be his legacy to humanity.

And if it topped the atomic bomb in its peacetime value, it only stood to reason it would be valuable in war as well.

•

It was awkward at first, the lunch between Knox Burger and Kurt Vonnegut—a meeting of two men who had known each other in another life, on another planet: Planet Cornell. Planet pre–World War II.

Knox Burger was a man's man with a sharp tongue. Some people found him brusque. He had a craggy face and balding pate and an appreciation for good booze and pretty girls. He spent so much time fly-fishing in cold creeks he said his feet never got warm. After work, he could frequently be found at the Algonquin, holding forth for a crowd of publishing types. You could locate him by his roaring laugh.

The two men liked each other. Like Kurt, Knox had enlisted, and in the Army he had become a staff correspondent at *Yank*, the magazine by and for enlisted men. He had flown with a B-29 bomber squadron, then gone to *Yank*'s Saipan bureau. After the Japanese surrender, he moved to Tokyo to cover the occupation, writing smartly reported, man-on-the-street stories about Americans in Japan, delving into the cultural meanings of things like tea and geishas. But he also wrote a hard-hitting account of the firebombing of Tokyo. At the time, his estimated death toll of 100,000 struck many as extreme, but later studies validated it.

Since the war, Burger had gone to grad school, gotten married, and written stories and articles. He had come to *Collier's* in 1947 and became its fiction editor the following year.

Collier's was a general-interest magazine, not unlike *The Saturday Evening Post*. It had around 2.5 million readers who enjoyed its mix of fiction, nonfiction, cartoons, and photo essays. Its spunky history of muckraking appealed to Kurt. Postwar, though, there was less of that. The *Collier's* creed, published monthly on the editorial page, was "to keep always before its readers a high, sane and cheerful ideal of American citizenship."

Knox gave Kurt a tour of the magazine's editorial offices, treating him like a serious writer, not like a guy with little more to his literary credit than a stack of rejection slips. At lunch, Kurt told Knox about his novella and his desire to write slick short fiction. Knox suggested Kurt try his hand at short-shorts—stories under about two thousand words. *Collier's* published one short-short every week, usually with three regular-length stories and two installments of serialized novellas.

Kurt wasn't about to waste time. He bought that week's *Collier's* and read it on the train home. There were a couple of adventure stories, a romance, an adventure-romance, and a lighthearted short-short by James Kirch called "Morning After," in which a man mollifies his angry wife after a party by insulting all the other women there. The story Kurt liked best was a sentimental yarn by Robert McLeod about a neglected little girl whose father is attending college on the GI Bill. The girl believes—with misplaced optimism—that her inattentive parents are planning a surprise birthday party for her and invites everyone in Vets Village. The narrator, also a vet, swaps cynical commentary with his wife about the whole sad spectacle, but in the end each plans a birthday surprise for the little girl.

In concept, the stories weren't far off from what Kurt had been writing, but their execution was better. Back at home, Kurt started working on a short-short right away. Two days later, he sent Knox his novella "Basic Training," complimenting the Robert McLeod story in his letter. The very next day, he finished the short-short "Bonanza" and sent that too, as well as "Mnemonics," the office story about sadistic fantasies, which *The New Yorker* had rejected. Then, four days later, even though he had yet to hear back on the three things he'd already submitted, he sent another brand-new short-short, "The Case of the Phantom Roadhouse."

Two days later, "Phantom Roadhouse" came back, with a note saying it didn't come together correctly at the end. Then Knox's assistant returned "Bonanza," calling it "flat and inconsequential." The next day, Knox returned "Mnemonics," declaring Kurt's pen name, Mark Harvey, the most pompous he had ever come across. In spite of the mockery, it wasn't all bad news. He thought "Mnemonics" had potential, and he might be able to use it if Kurt did some more work—and then he went on to give three paragraphs of detailed instructions for fixing it. The mnemonics course needed more description. Perhaps Kurt could have Alfred try boosting his memory by imagining a pleasant scene, then switch to something violent. That would help readers in the hinterlands understand that Alfred was actually enjoying his sadistic reveries. Then the last fantasy needed more work. He should link it to the office. The wife should provoke not just hostility but something pleasant. Unless he wrote in a secretary and made the pleasant thoughts about her.

It was a barrage of criticism. But Knox was encouraging him to re-write, and Kurt wasn't about to waste a chance like that. He went through Knox's letter and typed out his suggestions in a numbered list. Then he went down the list, revising. Four days later, he sent the story back.

"I seem to be sending MNEMONICS back for further revision," Knox replied two days later. He liked Kurt's changes, but more were now needed—a full single-spaced page of them. The hero was not lik-able. His boss and his wife should be more annoying, to justify their savaging in Alfred's daydreams. And perhaps there could be a grace note at the end.

Knox's letter was detailed and patient, explaining his changes and why he wanted them. He had a good sense of story structure, of how the reader should be carried along. But he was a magazine editor who needed to acquire and edit six stories a week. He didn't have time to teach Kurt Vonnegut to write. So at the end, he mentioned that he had given Kurt's name to Kenneth Littauer, of the literary agency Littauer & Wilkinson. "I told him I thought you might turn out to be a skillful and prolific writer," he said.

Kurt knew he was at a crossroads. Again he typed out the sugges-tions in the form of a list and made his way down it, checking each item off as he made the corresponding change. Then he sat down to type a cover letter to Knox. He chose his words more carefully than usual. First he thanked him for being extraordinarily patient with him. Then he crossed that out with a row of x's. He wrote that he felt like a pilot who had been talked down from a foggy sky by air traffic control. But he crossed that out too. He finally settled for thanking Knox for giving him reasonable instructions that were nearly as long as the story itself. He hoped he had managed to satisfy them. And he thanked Knox for mentioning him to Kenneth Littauer. He would definitely like an agent.

After all that, *Collier's* rejected "Mnemonics."

The head honchos, Knox reported, thought "the net result lacks conviction. It just leaves a bad taste in your mouth." He also rejected "Basic Training." Kurt had sent another short-short in the meantime called "Robot Cop," pointing out in his cover letter that GE really was developing robots, so it wasn't far-fetched. Knox returned it almost immediately.

Kurt refused to get discouraged. Two days later, he sent Knox "City." Knox apologized for throwing up so much smoke without making a fire—and rejected that too.

Kurt, meanwhile, had gotten in touch with Kenneth Littauer, and Littauer agreed to take him on as a client. "City," Kurt told Knox with some satisfaction, should be the last piece of his to come direct. After this, Knox would be hearing from his agent.

But first, Kurt started hearing from his agent.

Kenneth Littauer was old-school, a sweet talker when it came to wooing clients or charming editors. But when he rolled up his sleeves and got down to work, he didn't pull his punches. In August, Kurt sent him a story called "Enterprise," along with "Mnemonics" and "Report on the Barnhouse Effect." "Barnhouse," Kurt pointed out, had received encouraging rejections from both the *Post* and *Collier's*. He figured it had the best chance of being bought, if only because it expressed an enthusiasm for world government that was presently in the air.

He was referring to enthusiasm for the United Nations, which had finally brokered an armistice between Egypt and Israel. *Collier's* itself had recently run a feature article by the *New York Times* reporter A. M. Rosenthal defending the UN. And although an unpleasant civil war was brewing in Korea, hope for peace through world government had not yet died. State legislatures across the nation were passing pro-world-government resolutions; in September, the Schenectady County board of supervisors would vote unanimously to do the same.

Kenneth Littauer didn't give a damn if the entire world voted to abolish nation-states and sing peace anthems under the UN olive branch. Stories had to be good on their own terms, and Kurt's weren't. Littauer didn't much like "Mnemonics." "Enterprise" was revolting. As for "Barnhouse," it was better, but not good enough. Maybe it could be fixed. After all, it started out fine. But it failed to resolve itself like a short story and instead, with its wordy manifesto, flamed out in an onslaught of political speechifying. No editor would stand for such a violation of the basic rules of storytelling—not even if he agreed whole-heartedly with the sentiment behind it.

The difference between a writer who makes it and one who doesn't is the ability to take criticism. Not just to take it, but to learn from it. Kurt could have taken umbrage at his new agent's dismissive tone toward his most promising work. But he didn't. He wrote back thanking Kenneth for letting him know how the story really ended. He agreed that "Enterprise" was revolting. A dog, in fact. He softened the blow by partly blaming Jane. The two of them had looked at some issues of *Redbook* and concluded that was what the women's magazines wanted. He promised not to try anything like that again.

And then he went to work on Professor Barnhouse.

•

Bernie was finally making progress. The Project Cirrus team had come back from New Mexico more excited than ever. The program of research they were planning gave a new prominence to seeding experiments with silver iodide.

In August, the Albany *Times-Union* ran a multipage spread in its Pictorial Review section about the coming era of weather control. GE's work, the article said, had brought the world to the brink of a new age in which rainfall and snowfall would be precisely determined in advance, great storms would be countered by "anticyclones," damaging hailstorms would be bombed out of the sky, artificial hills would draw rain to arid deserts, and cold climates would be warmed up by deliberately melting the polar ice caps and diverting the Gulf Stream. A futuristic drawing superimposed on the Manhattan skyline showed how entire cities would reside under climate-controlling "roofs" in which scientists equipped with telescopes, rockets, and astronomical observatories would dole out the sunlight, manage humidity, and carefully calibrate the rain.

"Only the descendants of the men and women who believed that airplanes would never fly, that atomic fission was impossible and that men would die if they ever traveled at 60 miles an hour, doubt that one day man will achieve considerable control over local weather, to the extent of being able to decide where, when, and how much it shall rain or snow," the paper declared. This imminent state of affairs meant that international weather disputes were likely, unless an overriding authority, a "Meteorological United Nations," took charge.

The article was illustrated with photographs from the GE News Bureau: Vincent holding a cloud meter, Bernie igniting fireworks from his silver iodide burner, Irving discussing photographs of snowflakes with a lab visitor. And, of course, there was a photograph of military officers gazing into Vincent's freezer as if it were a crystal ball.

"'Command of the air,' in the weather sense, over enemy territory will become a decisive weapon," declared the piece, "and it is no secret that, because of this, some nations have given the highest priority to research into weather control."

That month, the Soviets exploded their first atomic bomb.

7

Rainmakers

Marion Mersereau Langmuir had always been game. Her court-ship with Irving, consisting of grueling mountain hikes, frigid ski trips, and scrabbles through dirty caves, had won the scientist's affection away from her prettier, but less intrepid, sister. As Langmuir's wife, she was the ideal helpmeet, joining him on his travels or staying home with their children, Kenneth and Barbara, while he visited laboratories and attended symposia. She indulged her husband's obsessions, even hitching up her skirts to climb into a canoe and paddle around Lake George with a payload of boulders to armor shorelines he thought were eroding. She didn't fuss when, after a long time away, he absentmindedly left her a tip on the breakfast table, and she didn't even put her foot down when Irving tried to cure Kenneth of a cold by immersing him in hot baths to induce a fever. But when Irving went outside and began setting all their toilet paper on fire—on a weekend when their vacation house was full of guests—she might have thought he had gone too far.

Ever since the Project Cirrus team had returned from New Mexico, Bernie had been coming up with new methods for employing silver iodide. On July 28, he impregnated some tissue paper with silver iodide and burned it in the lab. A couple of hours later, Katharine Blodgett pointed out to him and Irving that enormous banks of cumulus were rolling into Schenectady from the northwest, west, southwest, and southeast. A delighted Langmuir stood at the window watching for half an hour. He was absolutely convinced: Bernie had called up those clouds.

Irving asked Bernie to make him a small bottle of the silver iodide solution, to take along to his house on Crown Island in Lake George. There, on Saturday, he proceeded to impregnate his home's entire supply of toilet paper with the chemical, laying each sheet in the sun to dry. He used single-thickness and double-thickness paper. The silver iodide, he noted, gave the toilet paper a distinctly yellow color. Once the sheets were dry, he held them one at a time in kitchen tongs and set them alight.

He started burning toilet paper at about 12:20. Less than an hour later, a large cumulus cloud developed over French Mountain, at the south end of Lake George. From his vantage point in the middle of the lake, he watched the small thunderstorm develop, travel southwest, then reverse itself to head northeast. Rain fell on the eastern shore. By 3:20 it was all over.

Eagerly, he burned another ten sheets of toilet paper. Once again, fifty-five minutes later, he saw a cloud forming over French Mountain. It started raining, and this time there was more thunder. Irving went out onto the lake in his motorboat, *Penguin*. The storm was unlike any he'd ever seen in the thirty years he'd had his house on Crown Island. The wind was blowing hard from the east, and rain was pounding the east side of the lake, but the west side was perfectly dry.

"I believe that silver iodide has done the trick," he wrote in his notebook. If silver iodide seeding could be done so easily, he noted, there was little hope for government regulation of weather control. After all, anyone with a little chemical know-how and a few rolls of toilet paper could call up a local deluge.

In late August, Irving sat down with Guy Suits and told him what he was thinking. Convinced by William Lewis that a statistical approach would be the only way to prove his results, he had ordered himself a statistics textbook and gone to work proving that Bernie's New Mexico thunderstorm had produced the heavy rains that followed. Combining their data with all the rainfall and stream gauge figures he could get his hands on, he had come up with a startling conclusion:

Bernie had not only triggered a rainstorm back in July; he had produced all the rain that fell on the entire state for twenty-four hours after his generator ran. Irving proposed doing massive experiments with silver iodide, increasing the amounts until they got definite weather modification results over huge areas—say forty thousand square miles. They had found the key to large-scale weather control.

Suits was alarmed. Langmuir's claims were sweeping, and he was proposing that GE scientists do exactly what Suits and the GE lawyers had ordered them *not* to do: attempt to effect big changes in the weather. The lab director went to Bernie and Vincent separately and asked them if they agreed with Irving's conclusions. Had their experiments really caused such huge effects?

Bernie had been there when his generator called up the storm. He had seen it happen. But he was, at bottom, a scientist, and while the results were good, they were not yet definitive. So, like Vince, he gave a guarded reply. Nothing had been scientifically proved, he told Suits. The experiments simply suggested that they should keep exploring cloud seeding with silver iodide.

But Irving, now armed with a basic knowledge of statistics, was irrepressible. He divided the entire state of New Mexico into octants radiating outward from Albuquerque and began collecting the Weather Bureau rainfall data for all of them. He needed to establish the statistical proof that their cloud seeding had modified the weather. Once he had done that, he could go on to tell the world the new idea that was brewing in his head: he was becoming more and more convinced that the weather was going to be easier to control than to predict. That's because it was a perfect example of a divergent phenomenon.

For decades, Langmuir had been working out a theory of two types of phenomena in the world: convergent and divergent. He defined convergent phenomena as those "in which the behavior of the system can be determined from the average behavior of its component parts"—in other words, phenomena in which the normal laws of cause and effect apply. If you do X, you can be pretty sure the result will be Y. Convergent phenomena are things like the laws of classical physics and the orbits of the planets. Divergent phenomena are "those in which a single discontinuous event (which may depend upon a single quantum change) becomes magnified in its effect so that the behavior of the whole aggregate does depend upon something that started from a small beginning." In other words, the Xs can be so minute that the Ys become impossible to predict. Divergent phenomena are things like history, economics, and weather.

John von Neumann used the words "stable" and "unstable" to talk about something similar. Stable systems were deterministic and resisted disturbance by small things. They were like a game of checkers: once a being—or a machine—with enough calculating power learned all their laws, that player could not lose. Unstable phenomena were upset by small disturbances, making them hard to predict. But sufficient calculating power would allow these processes to be controlled. Once scientists determined where exactly the instability began, they could intervene, introducing the disturbances that produced the desired outcome instead of the undesired one. The weather, Johnnie liked to say, contained both stable and unstable systems: ultimately, the stable systems would be predicted, and the unstable ones would be controlled. It was simply a matter of knowing when and where to chalk the X.

Unlike von Neumann, Langmuir saw all weather as fundamentally unstable. It was always too big and unwieldy a system to be captured by equations. Divergent phenomena flew in the face of the clockwork universe. No matter how much information you had, you could never accurately predict their behavior.

Norbert Wiener had been telling von Neumann something similar. Wiener thought that Johnnie misunderstood weather: he failed to take into account that his model would never have complete information about the atmosphere. The atmosphere was always in flux, always flowing and blending; a touch in one part could affect the next and then the next until a cascade of changes set up movements on the other side of the earth. How, even with the fastest computers, could you ever account for all of it? How could you even *see* all of it? Even with a network of meteorological sensors blanketing the earth, the accuracy of your measurements would never be perfect. Your data were thus always on some level approximate, which meant your forecasts, too, were approximations. And the instabilities in those approximations multiplied rapidly. There would never be an absolute solution, as there could be with a zero-sum game, only a series of statistical likelihoods.

All three men understood something that would take physicists another couple of decades to develop into a theory: the idea that tiny and ultimately unpredictable events could alter the course of huge systems and that this made the behavior of such systems difficult to predict. But Langmuir—like von Neumann—still hoped that control was within his grasp. In fact, he believed he had found the place to chalk his X on the atmosphere; he just needed to prove to others that it was there.

What he needed was a signal, something to break through the noise and show that his experiment was having an effect. The idea he came up with was brilliantly simple: have Bernie's generator pump out silver iodide on a regular basis—say on three specific days each week—and see if that introduced a periodicity into the weather. A regularity that matched his seedings in the vast, unpredictable atmosphere would be evidence of the human hand as unmistakable as signing the GE monogram in the sky.

Suits had a different idea. He called the Project Cirrus representatives from the Signal Corps and the Navy into his office and reemphasized the GE position: company employees must never engage directly or indirectly in seeding experiments that might lead to large-scale weather modification. They were advisers only. All action taken in Project Cirrus was taken by the government alone.

Then he dictated a letter to Irving, Bernie, and Vince that laid out his position in no uncertain terms. Any extensive seeding experiments, he reminded them, "should be carried out entirely by the Government and its employees." GE's role—as it had been from the beginning—was only "to appraise [sic] them of the facts and on the basis of these facts to let them make their own decisions in this field." He appended a copy of the letter he had sent the team in early 1947 stating that they were merely advisers. And he gave them an ultimatum. If, he said, "the program develops in such a direction as to subject the Company to serious hazards from a liability standpoint, it may very well become impossible for us to continue with this work." In other words, toe the line or GE would kill Project Cirrus.

Then, to leave no doubt that he was serious, he declared that the company would not approve for publication any papers or reports that made it sound as if GE employees were engaging in widespread weather modification. Their job from now on was to keep quiet about what they knew.

•

Kurt came in the front door after work, and there it was, propped up on the piano. An envelope—a check envelope—addressed to him from *Collier's*. Jane had put it on the upright so he'd see it right away.

It had finally happened.

Except for his marriage to Jane, Kurt had never had a more productive working relationship than the one with Kenneth Littauer. The agent had gone to work on Kurt's stories as if they were race cars and he were a pit mechanic at the Indy 500. They started with "Barnhouse." Kurt revised the story as Littauer directed, and Littauer sent it back to Knox Burger. Knox had lots of changes and thought it was too long. Nor did he like Kurt's latest pseudonym: David Harris.

"Why doesn't he use his real name on the story?" he wrote to Kenneth. "Afraid GE will fire him for a Red?"

It wasn't an idle concern. Truman's announcement of the Soviet nuclear test in September had jolted Americans out of a comfortable feeling of supremacy, and GE, like the nation, was swinging rightward. The shock was not mitigated by the fact that the scientists had been predicting this development for years. Irving Langmuir had even foreseen exactly how much time it would take.

"Ever since atomic energy was first released by man," the president declared, "the eventual development of this new force by other nations was to be expected."

Once people had a technology, it seemed impossible not to use it. There was no Professor Barnhouse in the real world; the suicidal course of history could not be changed. Now the nation was winding itself up with paranoia over Soviet aggression and communist infiltration. GE printed two fretful essays as a special supplement in the September issue of *Monogram*: "Should We Fear a Welfare State?" (the answer was yes) and "Free Men Forge Their Own Chains!" The word from the corporate higher-ups was clear: in the face of this new and frightening world, America must get tougher, not nicer. The hope of peace through internationalism was fading, as was the notion that winners should give losers a helping hand.

With the specter of nuclear war once again haunting the public sphere, Kurt had gone back to work on "Barnhouse." In October, he fired a revised version off to his agent. The manifesto was gone: all that remained was the punning opening paragraph. And instead of fizzling out in a political tantrum, the story ended with what happened next: Barnhouse destroys the world's arms stockpiles from his hiding place and sends the student-narrator a letter tipping him off to the secret of the Barnhouse effect so he can carry on the work when Barnhouse is gone. On page 1, Kurt crossed out "David Harris." He wrote "Kurt Vonnegut, Jr." at the top.

Kurt knew in his heart it was good. Jane did too. But, he had told Littauer, he would await confirmation of its worth in a more interesting form: money.

Now in late October, at long last, it had arrived: a check for $750 (minus Littauer's well-earned 10 percent). Nothing, not even gin, is as good as a check for soothing a writer's anguished soul—especially a check that adds up to two months' labor at your mind-numbing corporate job. Of course they threw a party, spending a good part of the money on food and booze. But as Jane giddily told a neighbor, they'd just eat cereal until the next story sold.

"I think I'm on my way," Kurt wrote in a triumphant letter to his father. It would only take four more such sales to have the equivalent of a year's pay at GE. And then, he declared, he would "quit this goddamn nightmare job, and never take another one so long as I live, so help me God."

A God in whom he did not believe. Still, his father shellacked the whole boast to a piece of Masonite with a quotation from *The Merchant of Venice*: "An oath, an oath, I have an oath in Heaven: / Shall I lay perjury on my soul?"

Kurt was happier than he had been since he was first accepted at Chicago. It had all been worth it: the writing on nights and weekends, the rejections, the revisions that went on and on. He hunkered down to write the four more stories that would add up to a year's salary and issue him a ticket to a better life—a life that would finally be plotted by him.

•

Bernie was listening to a talk in a room at the enormous Hotel Jefferson in St. Louis. Harry Wexler was showing slides and describing a startling atmospheric event that he actually did believe was man-made: the Donora smog.

It happened on October 27, 1948. A thick fog had settled on Donora, an industrial town on the Monongahela River outside Pittsburgh. Persistent fogs are often due to temperature inversions, where cold air settles near the ground and a layer of warmer air lies above, instead of the more common reverse. Without the usual mixing mechanism—warm air rising, cold air falling down—the atmosphere becomes stable and stagnant. What made that disastrous in Donora was the presence of two belching factories: the American Steel and Wire plant and the Donora Zinc Works. The effluent pouring out of their stacks was bad on a normal day, peeling paint from buildings and depositing a layer of grime on local homes. But on this day, and the ones following, the smokestacks' pollution had nowhere to go, and Donora began to fill with acrid smog. Before long, the town had to keep the streetlights on all day because the smog was so thick residents could barely find their way around.

On October 30, people began to die. Thousands more poured into the local hospitals, complaining that they couldn't breathe. The fire department went from house to house, giving oxygen to those in distress. They had a hard time finding their way. People tried to evacuate, but thick smog and heavy traffic made getting away nearly impossible. Twenty people died in fourteen hours, in a town where thirty usually died in a year.

The nightmare ended when a cold front arrived and rain and wind cleared the air. But the story had grabbed the nation's attention. Air pollution was something people were just beginning to talk about seriously. The Donora smog showed it could be deadly.

Bernie was compelled for another reason. This was the first time the AMS meeting had included an all-day session on pollution. His paper came after Harry Wexler's, and he talked about using the condensation nuclei counter he had developed for Project Cirrus to measure smog. For Bernie, this was an exciting new development. The work he was doing for Project Cirrus could be used for even more beneficial purposes than rainmaking, such as investigating air pollution.

He wasn't declining to work on weapons. But he was finding other applications for his research.

The media continued to see Project Cirrus as a weapons program. A month earlier, *Harper's* had run a long article about rainmaking, emphasizing its military significance. Had Project Cirrus been around in World War II, it declared, it might have been able to clear the cold fog shrouding the western front in 1944, preventing the Battle of the Bulge.

•

Something had sent Kurt back to his war material. Only this time, he was trying to make it funny.

Every spare moment was spent at his desk, filling ashtrays and pounding keys. He knew what *Collier's* wanted now; he just had to crank it out. Page after page rolled off his typewriter, the kinds of pages he thought would sell. The problem was that they weren't selling. Knox Burger had encouraged him, but now he wasn't satisfied with anything Kurt wrote.

Once you got an agent, it was supposed to be easy. Once you cracked the formula and sold your first story, it was supposed to be easy. Once you made friends with an editor, it was supposed to be really easy. It didn't take Kurt long to realize the central truth of being a writer: it's never easy.

Knox had suggested he submit short-shorts, and Kurt liked that idea, because he could write one in a single sitting. But Knox could reject them as fast as Kurt could turn them out. So Kurt revised "City" again and sent it to Kenneth. Kenneth thought it was a decided improvement over the two earlier versions, though he still didn't love the story. "I don't guarantee it," the agent wrote to Knox, "but neither do I despair."

"Not quite good enough," Knox fired back.

It was Kenneth collecting the rejections now, usually with a line or two of explanation: "slight," "a trifle stilted and precious," "would be better if he did not attempt to pander to popular tastes," "over-obvious and didactic." He softened the blows in writing back to Kurt.

In December, as the birth of his second child approached, Kurt had gone back to a story he'd drafted a few times, "Das Ganz Arm Dolmetscher." Starting with the title—a purposeful butchering of the German for "the very poor interpreter"—it was a strange little tale, a comic piece about an infantryman on the western front who gets appointed chief interpreter for his battalion even though he can't speak German. It was a return to Kurt's war material but with a lighter, more ironic tone than he had managed in the past. There was even a hilarious playlet in the middle in which the narrator imagines seducing the Belgian burgomaster's daughter with the only lines of German he knows—the first stanza of Heinrich Heine's "Die Lorelei" and some commands from the Army phrase book:

> DOLMETSCHER (*to* BURGOMASTER'S DAUGHTER): I don't know
>   what will become of me, I am so sad. (*Embraces her.*)
> BURGOMASTER'S DAUGHTER (*with yielding shyness*): The air is
>   cool, and it's getting dark, and the Rhine is flowing quietly.
> (DOLMETSCHER *seizes* BURGOMASTER'S DAUGHTER, *carries her*
>   *bodily into his room.*)
> DOLMETSCHER (*softly*): Surrender.
> BURGOMASTER (*brandishing Luger*): Ach! Hands up!
> DOLMETSCHER and BURGOMASTER'S DAUGHTER: Don't shoot!

Kurt thought it was the funniest thing he had ever written. In fact he'd spent too many evenings when he should have been writing a new story giggling over the pages of this one.

Unfortunately, Knox Burger didn't agree. He called the playlet hackneyed and suggested Kurt get rid of it. He also didn't like the opening, and he insisted that Kurt get the thing down to five pages. Kurt sat on his pride and managed to redraft the story and send it to the typist before December 29, when Edith was born and the Vonneguts became a family of four.

•

Bernie was at New York's Hotel Astor giving a paper on another nifty gadget he'd designed: a vortex thermometer to measure true air temperatures from an airplane. Irving Langmuir was there to give a paper too, and Bernie was probably the only person present who knew the stupendous bombshell that was going to be dropped in it.

Nineteen fifty was shaping up to be an annus mirabilis. Early in the New Year, the Schenectady weather, as if mimicking the increasing chilliness of world affairs, had turned viciously cold. An ice storm grounded the Project Cirrus planes. The Schenectady Railway Company's B29 bus hit a patch of ice on Alplaus Avenue, slid for half a mile, and crashed through the guardrail of the bridge near Bernie's house. It was only prevented from tumbling into the creek ravine below by one of Bernie's trees. For years, Bow had been urging him to cut the tree down, and now it had probably saved the lives of the four people aboard. Newspapers published the dramatic photograph of the bus, its front wheels hanging off the bridge, its flat nose pressed into the tree trunk.

Even that was not as surprising as the January 7 announcement of Irving's retirement. Irving had always scorned the very idea. But his purpose in "retiring" was not to cease work. It was to redouble his efforts on weather control. He would keep his office at GE and continue to work as a consultant for the company. But his energies would be dedicated to Project Cirrus.

Langmuir was still convinced that he was doing the most important work of his career, and at sixty-eight he might not have many years left in which to do it. His two older brothers had already died; his younger brother, Dean, collapsed and died of a heart attack just four days before Irving's retirement luncheon. He himself had had an operation for colon cancer before the war and had undergone his second cataract operation in December. His recovery time had been longer the second time around. He was slowing down, and he wanted to conserve his energy for what mattered. In announcing his retirement, he had told reporters that he fully expected to be diverting large snowstorms and rainstorms from population centers within three years. It was just the sort of thing GE wouldn't have allowed him to say.

And now, at the annual AMS meeting, Irving was going to deliver what he considered the most important paper of his career. He was going to describe Bernie's New Mexico thunderstorm for the assembled meteorologists, and in it he would announce that Bernie's silver iodide–induced storm had produced 320 billion gallons of rain on one day—more than enough to fill all of New York City's reservoirs. This was bound to be of great interest in a city that was running out of water.

In 1950, New York City had nearly 7.9 million people. While the city's expansion was not as explosive as it had been in the nineteenth and early twentieth centuries, the population was still growing steadily, increasing water demand. Individual water usage was up too. But the water supply infrastructure was out of date: the last new reservoir had gone into service in 1926. It was the second of two in the Catskill Mountains, a hundred miles north of the city. Construction on a planned four more in the Catskills watershed had been halted, first by interstate wrangling with New Jersey and Pennsylvania and then by the war. By 1947, three of those reservoirs were under way. The city was racing to get them built when the drought hit.

It started with a dry winter in 1949, followed by a dry summer and fall. By early 1950, New York had been in a state of water crisis for nearly a year. Car washes, sprinklers, and swimming pools were banned. Residents were urged to put barrels and rubber rafts on their rooftops to collect rainwater for dishwashing and toilets. Wearing "Save Water" armbands, volunteer "conservation commanders" went door-to-door ferreting out leaky plumbing. The city instituted "Dry Fridays" and "Thirsty Thursdays," where people were meant to avoid bathing and even drinking water. The Central Park Zoo rationed its hippo's water, and Tiffany used gin for the pool in its window display. The mayor had stopped shaving. But none of it seemed to be working. *The New York Times* had instituted a regular feature called "The Water Situation" that tallied rainfall and reservoir levels and noted how many days were left before water pressure failed. When Bernie and Irving arrived in New York, the *Times* had given the city sixty-six days before its taps went dry.

Irving began his talk with a survey of natural precipitation but quickly moved on to describing the artificial seeding process. Cloud seeding, he pointed out, could produce too many ice nuclei, actually preventing rain. In some cases, a single pellet of dry ice might do a better job than too much of it. Heavy rain, he declared, can often be brought down "by using a single pellet of dry ice shot into the side of a cloud" from a flare gun. He discussed where to aim the pellet, the altitude at which the clouds were best seeded, and the rate at which dry ice should be dispersed into the tops of clouds. These specifics, he explained, were why the U.S. Weather Bureau had thus far failed to produce "rainfall of economic importance" in its Cloud Physics Project. Cloud seeding was an art, he implied, and the Weather Bureau seeders were essentially hacks.

He then gave an outline of probability theory before launching into a description of their work in New Mexico. He gave detailed reports of two days during which the team had operated Vonnegut's silver iodide generator. On both days, the Weather Bureau had predicted no rain, but on both, heavy rain and thunderstorms were observed.

Using river flow and rain gauge data, Langmuir calculated the similarity of rainfall distribution on the two heavily seeded days. They had a correlation coefficient of +0.78. The chance of getting such a high correlation randomly, he declared, was one in ten million.

"We must conclude," he declared, "that nearly all of the rainfall that occurred on October 14, 1948[,] and July 21, 1949[,] was the result of seeding . . . Silver iodide seeding produced practically all of the rain in the state of New Mexico on these two days." Furthermore, after the July experiment, a band of heavy rainfall progressed from New Mexico across southern Colorado and Kansas, bringing three to five inches of rain to those states. All that precipitation, too, might have been caused by Bernie Vonnegut's generator.

The experiment, Langmuir said, proved that the entire United States could double its rainfall for a couple of hundred dollars. Thirty milligrams of silver iodide released into a cumulus cloud six miles in diameter would liberate as much heat—the latent heat of condensation—as the explosion of an atomic bomb. The time was ripe, he concluded, for turning to the study of hurricanes. Silver iodide generators at sea, he was convinced, could modify hurricanes and even prevent them from reaching land.

There was a buzz in the room when Irving finished. He had thrown down a gauntlet for the Weather Bureau—at the very session chaired by Chief Reichelderfer. He had even tossed back in the chief's face the "exaggeration" the chief so detested about steering hurricanes. Reichel-derfer remained professional, cordially thanking Irving for his "very, very interesting paper" and noting there were only three or four minutes for discussion. A flurry of comments ensued, starting with the objections of the Weather Bureau's observer William Lewis, who thought that the conditions in New Mexico might have led to rain anyway.

But the reporters in the room were uninterested in counterargu-ments. When the session was over, they mobbed Irving. Was he saying that New York City could make rain to relieve its drought?

It very well might, Langmuir replied. There were no guarantees, but when the cost of an attempt was so low, why not try?

The next day, the newspapers were filled with the story. The city's water commissioner, citing Weather Bureau skepticism, had dismissed cloud seeding just as quickly as he had dismissed a group of Indian chiefs who offered to come to town and perform a rain dance. Now Irving Langmuir was saying that rainmaking might relieve the city's water woes. Langmuir was, *The New York Times* editorialized, "no rain-making crank, but a Nobel Prize winner who ought to be consulted in the present extremity."

Not long afterward, the Project Cirrus team received a phone call from the New York City water commissioner, Stephen Carney. Might he and Edward Clark, the chief engineer for the water department, visit Schenectady? A meeting was arranged for the following week.

Langmuir triumphantly took William Lewis out to lunch.

"Do you still believe that no seeding experiment has increased rain-fall by even as much as 10 percent?" he asked. Lewis, showing signifi-cant pluck, replied that he did.

"Did any single point that I brought out in my January 25th paper appear to you to have any significance?" Irving pressed.

"I don't know of any," responded Lewis, refusing to be cowed by the eminent scientist.

"So you think my paper was mostly bunk?"

"I personally wouldn't use that word," Lewis said, "but it does de-scribe my opinion reasonably well."

Irving laughed. He loved nothing better than a fight, and he couldn't help but admire the guy for standing up to him.

"Why don't you undertake something constructive?" he said, and gave Lewis an assignment looking for seven-day periodicities in any weather trait in the northwest states.

He had his reasons for this. In November, Workman's team in Socorro had started running Bernie's silver iodide generator every Tuesday, Thursday, and Saturday. Langmuir was hoping to introduce a regular pattern—a periodicity—into the weather to prove that he was making rain. But in January, something strange happened. Bizarrely heavy rains were reported in the Ohio and Wabash River basin. It was a long way from the generator, but it made some sense. The air over New Mexico didn't carry much moisture. The silver iodide, encountering little water vapor to nucleate there, might just be floating east with the prevailing winds. As it entered the Mississippi River basin, it would collide with moisture-laden winds sweeping up from the Gulf of Mexico. The winds would carry the chemical north to the Ohio River basin, where it would finally cause rain.

The members of the Project Cirrus steering committee, concerned that they might be causing damaging floods, met in late January and decided to reduce the number of days on which they seeded to two per week. As soon as they did, the rainfall in the Ohio River basin let up. It was all looking more than coincidental.

The steering committee was eager to tell the military. At the end of January, President Truman had announced that he had directed the U.S. Atomic Energy Commission—the organization originally meant to help deter a worldwide arms race—to build more atomic bombs. He specifically included the Super, the hydrogen bomb Teller and others had been advocating. But Project Cirrus might be providing them with a superweapon that was even better.

•

Kurt Vonnegut's first published story, "Report on the Barnhouse Effect," hit the newsstands on February 11, 1950, in *Collier's*. The *Schenectady Gazette* ran an article announcing his triumph. Typically for the credential-loving company town, the paper announced that he was "a graduate of the University of Chicago."

He was trying to repeat his success, but it was hard. "Mnemonics,"

"City," and "Das Ganz Arm Dolmetscher" were being turned down all over town. Knox Burger was rejecting everything they sent him. He was, Kurt grumbled, turning to Yaddo again, going back to buying work from the well-known writers who went to fancy writers' colonies and won prizes and hung out drinking cocktails in New York. Kurt was cranking out reams of prose to no avail.

Two weeks after "Barnhouse" was published, the News Bureau got a call from a librarian at the Works Library in Building 2. She had looked up from her desk, and there, looking right back at her through the window, was a deer. Somehow it had gotten into the Works, and now it was trapped inside the walls of the industrial city. The librarian had called security to come get it out, but she thought the News Bureau would want to know about it.

A photographer was dispatched at once. The deer, a young doe, was backed into a corner, her head ducked and her spindly legs splayed. Two members of the GE patrol approached, and as the photographer snapped away, they grabbed the doe around the middle. She was so small that they easily lifted her up on her hind legs to truss her front ones, then wrestled her to the ground and trussed her back legs too. They heaved her into the backseat of a GE patrol vehicle, and a GE security officer got in with her, wrapping a stocky arm around the doe's neck as if they were on a date.

The *General Office News* ran a page of photographs of the whole drama, with droll captions giving the deer's point of view: "What a way to treat a Republican!" and "All I wanted to do was sneak out of work at 4:30." The News Bureau issued a press release slyly commenting that the deer had forgotten to wear her ID badge. GE was always hassling the employees about leaving their badges at home.

It was all supposed to be cute and funny, but Kurt knew how the deer felt. Trapped. Cornered. Baffled by this strange, ugly place and the bizarre rituals of the creatures who inhabited it. He knew what it felt like to want out.

Five years later, "Deer in the Works" would be the first story Kurt sold to *Esquire*. In it, a newspaper writer takes a job in publicity at a big corporation because he's worried about supporting his growing family. On his first day, a deer gets into the Works, and the new guy is assigned to get the story. As the writer wanders through the labyrinthine plant encountering terrifying assembly lines, alcohol-soaked sales meetings, and labs with mysterious names, he realizes he has made a terrible decision in leaving his small-town newspaper for the security of being a company man. He cannot thrive in this place. He cannot even breathe the soot-filled air. Finally, he wanders hopelessly into a ball field and the deer appears, pursued by Works policemen with pistols drawn. The writer does the only thing he can: he opens the gate and lets the deer escape. And then he follows her out. The story ends simply, "He didn't look back."

That's what Kurt was living for now, his own escape. Four more salable stories were all he needed. The irony was, it was GE that was handing him the material he needed to break the company's bonds.

One day not long after the deer affair, he was researching a News Bureau story when he learned about the stratosphere. It was a great word. There were other great words to describe the strange zones between the atmosphere and space. He wrote them down on the back of an envelope: "stratosphere," "troposphere." In particular, he was drawn to the notion of the ionosphere, a layer of ionized air one hundred to four hundred miles above the earth's surface, the boundary between the earth's atmosphere and the empty vacuum of space.

What might be up there? Weather, of course—that he heard about all the time. And for a few years after the war, scientists had puzzled over strange, erratic blips that showed up on radar screens, dots that flitted about with apparent disregard for the laws of physical motion. First noticed by a scientist at Bell Labs, the blips captured the imagination of reporters, who called them "ghosts" or "angels." Then, in early 1949, newspapers announced that the mystery was solved: they were insects.

But what if there really were ghosts or angels up there, drifting around in those atmospheric zones?

Kurt made his main character a scientist with a Germanic last name. Dr. Groszinger is the kind of man who loves science for its own sake, who finds comfort in the "dependability of the physical world." He is working on a top secret experiment funded by the military, but he isn't really focused on that. "The threat of war was an incident," Kurt wrote, "the military men about him an irritating condition of work—the *experiment* was the heart of the matter."

Dr. Groszinger's first name is Bernard.

Bernard Groszinger is supervising Project Cyclops, an experiment to send a controlled spaceship into orbit above the earth. There is a man on board whose job is to report the weather conditions over enemy territory and the accuracy of guided atomic missiles should war break out. As the story opens, the spaceship has been launched, and Bernard is chain-smoking while he awaits the first weather report from its passenger, Major Rice. He is relieved when contact is made. But soon it becomes apparent that all is not well. Major Rice is hearing voices in space—voices that seem to be coming from the dead. And the dead have plenty to say.

Bernard Groszinger is convinced that the man in orbit is insane. But when the general in charge of Project Cyclops has the messages from the dead investigated, they seem to check out. Dr. Groszinger then thinks it must be an elaborate hoax—until the major reports that a woman speaking with a German accent has asked for Dr. Groszinger. When the major quotes his mother's favorite lines from Goethe, Bernard realizes the guy is not making it up.

The general doesn't give a damn about the voices—as long as they are kept secret, so as not to disclose that his nation has a spaceship in orbit. But for Groszinger, the voices create a moral quandary. Doesn't the public have a right to know that the dead can be contacted? Wearily, he thinks perhaps no one would even be surprised. "Science had given humanity forces enough to destroy the earth, and politics had given humanity a fair assurance that the forces would be used," he thinks. "There could be no cause for awe to top *that* one. But proof of a spirit world might at least equal it. Maybe that was the shock the world needed, maybe word from the spirits could change the suicidal course of history."

When amateur radio operators stumble onto the secret frequency and overhear the major's transmissions, the general is forced to jam the frequency and bring the spaceship down, killing the orbiting major. Dr. Groszinger is sworn to silence about the whole affair.

The story concludes with Dr. Groszinger denying everything to a

Bernard and Kurt Vonnegut (at right), at home before Kurt enlisted. Bernard may already have been working for the Army's Chemical Warfare Service lab at MIT when this was taken. (Vonnegut family collection)

The wizards of "the House of Magic": GE Research Lab scientists pose at the doors of their offices in 1950. Vincent Schaefer is in front at far left, with Bernie, who began working there in 1946, at the next door back.

(GE News Bureau photo)

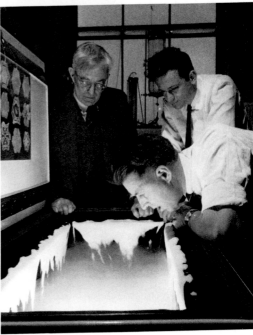

Irving Langmuir and Bernie look on as Vincent Schaefer leans over to create the experiment that started it all: breathing a cloud into his freezer that he will nucleate with dry ice to cause snow.

(GE News Bureau photo)

Dry ice seeding produces dramatic cloud modifications. Here, the Project Cirrus airplane flies a gamma pattern, creating an obvious trench with dry ice. Perhaps, Vincent wryly noted later, they should have seeded clouds in the shape of the GE logo. (U.S. Army Signal Corps photo)

GE insulated itself from liability concerns with a wall of military brass. For the press release announcing the joint GE-military weather control program, Bernie uses a toy popgun to seed the cloud in the freezer for an admiral and a general. (GE News Bureau photo)

The Vonneguts called the family rowboat the *Beralikur*, a combination of the names Bernie, Alice, and Kurt: the three siblings only grew closer as they aged.
(Vonnegut family collection)

Just like a real newspaper, minus the objectivity: the GE News Bureau as it looked when Kurt began work there as a "junior writer" in 1947, drafting press releases and articles for in-house magazines (GE News Bureau photo)

A Project Cirrus B-17 being loaded with dry ice for an "assault on the clouds" (GE News Bureau photo)

"Fire makes rain" was the GE News Bureau's caption for a photo of Bernie with his silver iodide generator. Even as the world thrilled to dry ice seeding, Bernie knew he had found something better: seeding clouds with silver iodide smoke. (GE News Bureau photo)

The Weather Bureau and the Institute for Advanced Study had a better way to take control of the weather: with computers. Here, members of the institute's Meteorology Project pose with the Army's ENIAC, then the world's most powerful computer, in 1950. At far left, Harry Wexler listens to John von Neumann. The Weather Bureau's chief, Francis Reichelderfer, is second from right. (Photo courtesy of MIT Museum)

ABOVE: Aboard a B-17, Bernie oversees the seeding of clouds with silver iodide. Irving Langmuir's attention was finally captured when silver iodide seeding in New Mexico was followed by a devastating thunderstorm and flood. (Bernard Vonnegut papers, State University of New York at Albany)

LEFT: Kurt with his son, Mark, and a painting he made in Gloucester, Massachusetts, in the summer of 1950 as he gloomily contemplated the onset of another war, this time in Korea (Vonnegut family collection)

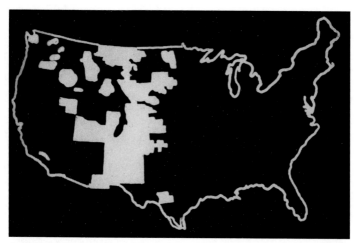

As Bernie's invention was heedlessly taken up by amateurs, he tried to figure out if it could be causing harm. In his map, the gray portions show where rainmakers were feverishly seeding clouds in 1951 as floods devastated the plains states. (Bernard Vonnegut papers, State University of New York at Albany)

Seeking advice on how to testify at upcoming Senate hearings, a New Mexico senator and the publisher of the *Santa Fe New Mexican* visited the GE Research Lab. Diplomatically, the photograph shows only the publisher, between Irving Langmuir (at left) and Bernie. At right, the lab's director, Guy Suits, looks on as Vincent Schaefer seeds the freezer's cloud. (GE News Bureau photo)

The siblings Vonnegut—Kurt, Bernie, and Alice—with spouses and kids, reuniting in Provincetown, Massachusetts, in the summer of 1951. Kurt's wife, Jane, is at center, holding their daughter, Edith. (Vonnegut family collection)

The cover of *Collier's* was typical of the triumphant tone the media took when discussing weather control in the 1940s and 1950s: man finally stood at the brink of mastering nature. (Photo courtesy of the Estate of Frederick Siebel)

crush of reporters. He tells them that the unidentified object seen crashing into the Atlantic was most likely a meteor. When a reporter asks what's out beyond the stratosphere, he says it's just dead space. He gives it a name: the thanasphere.

"Has a nice scientific ring to it, don't you think?" he asks. The reporters press him to tell them when the nation will have a rocket in space.

"You people read too many comic books," he tells them.

"Thanasphere" was a good story: tight, sharp, and just thoughtful enough for the slicks. In a light way, it addressed the things Kurt saw going wrong with the nation: militarism, technocracy, secrecy. The quest for bigger and better weapons was shunting aside the things that made human beings human. The story's general turns a blind eye to the desperate voices of the dead—and the entire existence of the spirit world—in order to maintain secrecy and efficiency. It's a dark vision of military values. But it didn't find much to admire in scientific values either. After all, it's the scientist, Bernard Groszinger, who makes the whole operation possible. Like his namesake, he has his moral qualms. But in the end, he does what the general wants.

•

In mid-February, New York water commissioner Stephen Carney and engineer Edward Clark visited Schenectady. They went first to Langmuir's home, where Irving gave them an overview of Project Cirrus. Then, because his own driveway was blocked by seventeen inches of snow that had fallen the night before, Irving rode with them to the Knolls. There, Carney and Clark were treated to the usual song and dance: Vince seeded the freezer with dry ice, and Bernie deployed his popgun with a puckish smile. As always, the News Bureau team was there to get photographs, and though Carney had a long, mournful face and Clark wore a skeptical frown, at the end of the day, the two men met with a large group of assembled reporters at the Hotel Van Curler and made a startling announcement. Cloud seeding, Carney said, was worth a try. He was going to request that the city's mayor hire a consulting meteorologist to put a program in place. Langmuir added that the city should be sure to find "a competent meteorologist who has nothing to sell and who will study and plan the project with a conservative approach."

This was a meaningful comment. Bernie, Vince, and Irving were beginning to realize they had created a cottage industry. Dozens of private "rainmakers" were hawking cloud-seeding programs all over the nation. One of them, Irving Krick, had already been trying to sell his services to New York City. The GE men knew Krick. Lately, they had begun to see him as a problem.

Irving Krick was a confident cowboy of a weatherman from California. He had been on Eisenhower's meteorology team, where his old-fashioned forecast had come close to causing D-Day to fail. But after the war, he had spun the story to cast himself as the hero. A charismatic self-promoter with a wavy pompadour and a Laurence Olivier mustache, Krick had a weather consulting company specializing in long-range forecasts that the Weather Bureau considered hokum. Now he had taken up the cause of cloud seeding with gusto. A year earlier, he had visited GE and shared data with the Project Cirrus team. But since then, the GE scientists watched with growing alarm as Krick bounced all over the country selling rainmaking programs that they considered scientifically sloppy. Worse still, Krick was hinting that he had some kind of affiliation with GE. News Bureau manager Roger Hammond told the Cirrus team that Krick was "using GE and the names Langmuir, Schaefer and Vonnegut to his commercial advantage." And lately, Krick had started telling reporters that he had a "new way" to make rain for New York: seeding with silver iodide.

The next time Krick visited GE, he found his reception significantly chillier than it had been a year earlier. The scientists suggested that he confine himself to dry ice seeding, leaving the silver iodide to the experts. Then Langmuir took him aside and told him, in no uncertain terms, to stop taking credit for Bernie's work. It was something Bernie would never have done himself. He was never particularly concerned about getting credit, even when he deserved it; for him, the science was its own reward.

Not long after Clark and Carney returned to New York—their trip was delayed by the weather—New York City's mayor, William O'Dwyer, announced that he had hired a scientist to begin formulating a plan:

Wallace Howell. A longtime colleague and friend of the Project Cirrus team, Howell was a consulting meteorologist at Harvard's Blue Hill Observatory. Vince had suggested him, and the Project Cirrus team was pleased he was hired: Howell was a real meteorologist, not a charlatan. And he would consult with them regularly.

Project Cirrus was riding high. Their work was finally going to prove its worth to the world! The Industrial Bank of Commerce ran an ad with a picture of Irving, Bernie, and Vincent standing by their freezer under the words "Salute to the Future." There was a quotation from Guy Suits declaring that the weather work "may prove in the future to be as important to human welfare as the advent of atomic energy."

"Here," declared the ad, "is another example of industry at work for humanity. It represents progress for all mankind, and its beneficial effects on our civilization are truly immeasurable."

The week New York City hired Howell, Vincent made one of his frequent appearances on the WGY radio program *Science Forum*. His topic was the "sunny side of rainmaking." Outside, a hard rain was washing the winter snow into a slushy brew as Vincent speculated for listeners at home about the coming day when blizzards and thunderstorms would be averted, aircraft icing forestalled, forest fires prevented, and fog simply swept away. It was all nearly within their grasp.

•

Dr. John Herbert Hollomon invited Kurt and George Burns into his study. Herb was one of GE's most promising young men, a wunderkind who had come to GE Labs to head up the new physical metallurgy division in 1946. Bernie had worked with Hollomon before moving to Project Cirrus. Herb was a friend of Bernie's and, like many of Bernie's friends, had also become a friend of Kurt's.

Also, he liked model railroading.

George Burns set up his camera to get a shot of Herb with a model train. They were there to do a profile, and this was just the sort of humanizing detail GE loved to give out about its scientists. Kurt had just written a press release about a speech urging scientists and engineers to engage in activities unrelated to their work. Now here was Herb Hollomon hoisting a tiny locomotive, the perfect example of a man with a wholesome hobby. An exemplary hobby. Unless of course the man who loved model trains was to get so obsessed with them that his family life suffered . . . like, for instance, Earl "Hotbox" Harrison, a model-train maniac oblivious to his wife's distress, in the story "With His Hand on the Throttle."

Kurt worked on short story ideas constantly. General Electric contained a rich vein of characters, settings, and concepts he could mine. It was a microcosm, a corporate culture that reflected many aspects of the national culture Kurt found disturbing. The same month he did the News Bureau story on Herb Hollomon, he wrote a GE press release about a robot tool dolly.

"A one-armed robot on wheels, which can close doors, turn valves, take apart and reassemble complex machinery, and perform virtually every task the human hand can perform," he wrote, "has been developed by General Electric engineers for work in radioactive areas, it was revealed here today."

Kurt could easily summon the gee-whiz attitude GE liked to use for unveiling inventions, but his own feelings about the things he saw were complex. Was every scientific advance necessarily good for humanity? Professor Barnhouse's question would hang over everything Kurt Vonnegut ever wrote. The tool dolly, for instance, made radioactive contamination into a neat problem, something that could be solved with enough know-how and engineering spunk. Nothing like a whiz-bang gadget to take the sting out of a nuclear holocaust!

Somewhere in there, Kurt was taken to see another nifty invention: the GE automated milling machine. A cathedral of steel with motors strung from electrical cords, it was designed to cut the rotors for jet engines and gas turbines. GE had just received a patent on the machine's tracer control system. Thanks to that control system, every rotor could now be cut to exact, identical specifications, every contour decreed not by the skill of the machinist but by the dictates of the little clicking computer attached to the blade. The machinists who worked milling machines were some of the top-paid laborers at GE. Or at least they had been. At the behest of GE, they had lent their movements to the tape-driven control system, and now the clicking box and its robot cutter would replace them.

Kurt couldn't blame the inventors. It wasn't necessarily vicious or antisocial to make such a machine. But it was definitely going to be a bad thing for a lot of people who had been proud of their skills. No one at GE seemed to be thinking about that.

And automation of mechanical tasks was only the beginning. GE was now getting into building high-speed calculating machines. The company was the first in the world to own a differential analyzer, an analog computer of the type first designed by Vannevar Bush. A shockingly noisy contraption made up of thousands of gears, it occupied an entire floor of the old athletic building. Langmuir and Katharine Blodgett had used it during the war to calculate the liquid water content of clouds and particle size distribution inside them. Now GE had built a new device, the Ordinal Memory Inspecting Binary Automatic Calculator: OMIBAC for short. With its thirty-three hundred electron tubes and circuits, OMIBAC was five thousand times faster than a human computer at doing math. It could solve a problem in days that would take months or even years for a mere person. This was obviously a good thing. Or was it? Increasingly, some people were beginning to wonder if such devices might ultimately diminish human beings. Even the *Monogram* article about OMIBAC was accompanied by a cartoon of a man cowering in a box, with the caption "Are machines smarter than ME?"

Kurt had read Norbert Wiener's book *Cybernetics*, which came out in 1948. Practically everyone in Schenectady would have. The *Saturday Review of Literature* said it was "impossible for anyone seriously interested in our civilization to ignore this book." It was so widely admired that Wiener was persuaded to write a "popular" version without the mathematics; it was published in 1950 under the title *The Human Use of Human Beings*. Together, the books provided the nation with an introduction to an entirely new way of thinking. Wiener defined cybernetics as "the science of control and communication in the animal and the machine." Machines, Wiener pointed out, are very much like human beings, or even human cultures: They operate by sending and receiving messages in an attempt to control their environment. Such feedback allows them to learn.

Wiener's idea—that the brain is a kind of computer and the computer a kind of brain—has become so much a part of our thinking now that it's hard to imagine how revolutionary it was at the time. And Wiener was also already thinking about the human implications of this breakthrough. Alone among computing pioneers, he was asking what the human downside to the computing revolution might be. At present, a computer's output was numbers. But eventually it would produce other things: information, pictures, songs. *Cybernetics* explained that the computer was a kind of mechanical slave destined to usurp not only physical labor but mental labor too. The first industrial revolution had proved that human handwork could be done by machines; the second would prove that human thinking could too.

There was a short story in that. Kurt named his story—and his computer—"EPICAC." The narrator is a mathematician who works the night shift programming EPICAC. The military men who control EPICAC, and the scientist who designed it, Dr. Ormand von Kleigstadt—another Germanic name—want the computer to "plot the course of a rocket from anywhere on earth to the second button from the bottom on Joe Stalin's overcoat." As it turns out, EPICAC can do much more.

The narrator is a programmer in love with his colleague, a "crackerjack mathematician" named Pat, but she repeatedly declines his marriage proposals because they aren't poetic enough. One night, sitting at his keyboard, "trying to think of something poetic, not coming up with anything that didn't belong in *The Journal of the American Physical Society*," the narrator types his troubles into EPICAC: "My girl doesn't love me."

"What's love? What's girl?" asks EPICAC. After the narrator defines the terms and then defines poetry, the computer writes him a poem to give to Pat. She loves it, so the narrator gets EPICAC to produce another one. Slowly, passing off EPICAC's creations as his own, the narrator wins Pat's affection. He programs EPICAC to produce the perfect marriage proposal. Of course, the computer thinks it's proposing for itself. The narrator tells it that women can't love machines; they can only love human beings.

Pat accepts the narrator's proposal on the condition that the narrator write her a poem every year for their anniversary. That night, EPICAC kills itself by overloading its own circuits. The narrator finds its suicide note: "I don't want to be a machine, and I don't want to think about war . . . But fate has made me a machine. That is the only problem I cannot solve." EPICAC has left the narrator a wedding gift: five hundred more poems to give his wife.

"*De mortuis nil nisi bonum*," the story concludes. "Say nothing but good of the dead."

Kurt finished "EPICAC" quickly and sent it to Kenneth, who liked it enough to send it on to Knox Burger. Knox returned it with notes, commenting that the title sounded like something you took when constipated. But in response to Kurt's complaint that he wasn't managing to sell anything, he offered a glimmer of hope. His stories, Knox wrote, were much more readable than most science fiction. It was perhaps the first time Kurt heard his work called that.

On April 4, Knox had good news. *Collier's* was buying "Thanasphere." Elated, Kurt sat down to work on a story about a scientist who invents a new way of making ice that turns out to be horribly dangerous. He started out calling it "The Crystal." But before long, it had the title "Ice-9."

•

The first flight of New York's rainmakers was delayed by rain. Kept on the ground at Floyd Bennett Field until the squall passed, the police department's Grumman Goose—a comical amphibious plane that looks like a cartoon whale balancing a surfboard on its back—arrived in the Catskills too late. Any clouds that could have been seeded had already moved on.

The city's newspaper writers were crestfallen. The entire metropolis had been eagerly awaiting its first municipal rain. *The New York Times Magazine* had run a detailed article explaining the different types of cloud seeding and when they would be deployed. Bernie had provided drawings for it.

Upstate residents, meanwhile, awaited the event with more trepidation than glee. Before the first rainmaking attempt even happened, lawsuits were threatened. Albany's mayor, Erastus Corning, tried unsuccessfully to get the state Water Power and Control Commission to stop New York City from "intercepting" rain meant for Albany's watershed. Then a group of property owners and civic associations in the

Catskills had issued a court summons in Ulster County to block the rainmakers. The city's lawyers advised the mayor to ignore it.

On April 13, Wallace Howell and a police pilot took off from La Guardia Airport in the Grumman Goose. They flew north, up the Hudson, and circled the Catskills watershed area, scouting out likely clouds. Howell sprinkled a hundred pounds of dry ice into clouds near the Ashokan Reservoir. The plane returned to Floyd Bennett Field at 6:42 p.m.

Some observers on the ground insisted that there was no snow until the plane flew back and forth overhead, at which point it began snowing for the next hour and a half. Others said there was snow off and on all afternoon, but it increased in intensity after the plane passed over. The state police at Phoenicia insisted that there were light squalls all day, with no observable change in the afternoon.

The next morning, New Yorkers awoke to an unseasonable snowstorm. Slush coated the sidewalks, snow blanketed Easter lilies in the city parks, and city workers had to dig shovels out of spring storage. The snow was oddly patchy, sometimes falling on one block but not the next one over. City hall's wires overflowed with complaints from irate drivers shocked at the icy conditions on bridges and roads. City dwellers called it "Howell's snow."

Even as he fired up two generators mounted on station wagons to cruise the watershed and blow silver iodide into the clouds, Howell insisted there was no way to tell if the snow had resulted from seeding.

"It would be completely impossible for anybody to say whether or not we increased the yield of today's snow flurries over the watershed area," he told reporters. "On any individual flight, how can anybody tell?" After at least ten flights, he might have a better idea. But the media were not put off so easily. *The New York Times* ran a photograph of Howell standing near a snowbank at city hall under the title "Is It His or Nature's?"

All throughout the spring, Howell seeded clouds with silver iodide from the air and from ground generators mounted on trucks. And all that spring, rain fell on the watershed. The local newspapers breathlessly reported on each increase as the city's water supply inched upward. News reports took on a martial tone: the city was mounting "double-barreled attacks" on the clouds, "bombarding" them from the ground and conducting "aerial assaults." On April 20, torrential rains in the Catskills caused the Schoharie Reservoir to spill over, ending seeding operations for a few days. With the reservoirs up and New Yorkers still drastically reducing usage on Thirsty Thursdays and Dry Fridays, Commissioner Carney said that the bans on sprinklers and swimming pools might be lifted if the trend continued through summer.

The first court case landed in the state supreme court in May. Ben Slutsky, owner of the Nevele Country Club, demanded an injunction against the city's rainmaking because it could damage his business. Why would people take vacations in the Catskills, he asked, if they figured it was going to rain the whole time? The supreme court, unmoved, found for the defendant, declaring the plaintiff had "no vested property rights in the clouds or the moisture therein." Furthermore, the court must weigh Slutsky's "remote possibility of inconvenience" against the city's need to maintain "an adequate supply of pure and wholesome water" for ten million people. The city's interest won out. The court did not even question the assumption that cloud seeding worked.

On May 1, a sixteen-hour seeding operation was followed by three solid hours of rain, adding nearly two billion gallons to the reservoirs. Howell remained reserved, refusing to take credit. It might be his. It might be nature's. But rain was falling. Because of Bernie's invention, New York City was saved.

•

Dr. George Hoenikker held a vial containing a milky white shard. His invention: Ice-9. His wife didn't understand it. His kids didn't understand it. No one saw its significance, no one but him. But he was about to become famous. Maybe he'd win the Nobel Prize. But one thing was for sure: he wasn't going to work at General Forge and Foundry anymore. He wasn't going to help them build the Blue Fairy Rocket. He had fled to Cape Cod and was thinking of taking up woodworking.

But then things went wrong. He got mixed up with a blowsy married woman. He got in a car accident. The story careened off in crazy directions. It had no arc.

So Kurt killed Dr. George Hoenikker. He threw the whole "Ice-9" story away and started over. He made several outlines. But they all started in the same place: with a scientist whose conviction that his work carries no social responsibility allows him to invent Ice-9.

Ice-9 was Irving Langmuir's idea. Someone had told Kurt about it at a cocktail party. GE parties often featured funny stories about Irving. There was the time his secretary was out sick and Irving dealt with the temp for a whole day without noticing the substitution. There was the time he went to pick up Marion and got so lost in thought that when he neared his wife and she waved, he simply waved back and drove past. There was the time he went out with his daughter, Barbara, got caught up in a conversation, and came home without the little girl. But this story was different. It didn't concern Langmuir's absentmindedness. It concerned his idea for a novel.

Years earlier, the partygoer told Kurt, H. G. Wells had been invited to tour the Schenectady Works. Wells was quite famous at the time, so he was given GE's most famous scientist as a guide: Langmuir. Irving took the esteemed writer around the plant, but he was a little unsure of how to talk to a novelist. Because H. G. Wells wrote fiction, Irving thought he would try to entertain him by offering up an idea for a novel. Why not write a book, he suggested, about a scientist who invents a form of ice that's stable at room temperature? The ice somehow gets into the wrong hands and contaminates the water supply. All of the earth's water freezes instantly, and life on the planet is doomed.

H. G. Wells had not been interested in Irving's idea, but Kurt was. How strange that his brother's older colleague should invent such a perfect parable for the dangers of what he himself did—inventing things with no regard for the human consequences! And the stable ice—he had come to think of it as Ice-9—was an intriguing concept, particularly given what Bernie had told Kurt about different types of ice crystals. At another GE party, Kurt had tried the concept out on a GE crystallographer. The scientist seemed intrigued. He went over to a chair, sat down, and stared blankly into space. After half an hour, he came back to Kurt.

"No," he had said. "It's not possible."

Scientifically impossible, maybe, but it was a damn good story idea. Kurt kept thinking about it. Wells didn't want it and Irving had no use for it, so he figured, finders, keepers. And now, after a number of false starts with "Ice-9," he thought he had finally found the right way to tell it. He would set up the ethical conflict by using two characters—two men, a scientist and a sociologist—with different attitudes about the moral duties of scientists.

He turned Dr. George Hoenikker into Dr. Arnold Macon. Macon has invented Ice-9 while living in an island banana republic where he is pet scientist for the island's repressive dictator, General Monzano. Monzano—whose name recalls the Manzano Mountains where Bernie had his big breakthrough—is faced with a civil uprising. As rebel forces threaten the dictator's stronghold, Dr. Macon is visited by a sociologist friend, Franklin Dale. Macon can't resist telling Dale about Ice-9.

Dale immediately recognizes the potential for disaster. He and Macon quarrel about the scientist's ethical obligations. Macon insists he has none: he just does research and leaves the uses of his discoveries to the engineers. Dale insists he shouldn't work on inventions that have the power to do great harm. He is proved correct when General Monzano gets his hands on the Ice-9 and holds the world hostage, threatening total annihilation of life on earth if the rebels don't back down.

The rest of the novella plays out in rousing confrontations and chase scenes as Macon tries, first, to convince the world that his invention is real and capable of doing great harm and, second, to retrieve the Ice-9 from Monzano.

In the final scene, Macon finds General Monzano apparently dead, and the Ice-9 dangling over the sea on a chain attached to the hands of a clock. At the stroke of twelve, it will drop into the water and destroy the world. Macon hesitates, and suddenly he sees that he has been the real villain all along. Secretly, he loved his invention's destructive power. As he holds the Ice-9 and contemplates ending the world himself, Monzano—alive after all!—shoves him into the sea. Macon pulls the general with him, but the Ice-9 catches on a tree branch, suspended above the high-tide line. The world is saved—for now—through sheer dumb luck.

Kurt figured the novella was perfect for magazine serialization. The only thing that worried him was that, like much of his work, it lacked female characters. Still, he thought it was the best thing he'd ever written.

The month he was finishing the draft of "Ice-9," GE's president, Charlie Wilson, addressed the ethical obligations of scientists in Schenectady's annual Steinmetz Memorial Lecture. There was no use criticizing scientists, Wilson declared, simply because the truths they happen upon can be used for evil ends. "There is nothing moral or religious or hostile or inspirational in science unless man puts it there," Wilson declared, sounding a lot like Dr. Macon.

Kurt thought otherwise. It wasn't necessarily evil to invent Ice-9 or a machine that replaced a human being, like OMIBAC, EPICAC, or the "contour-following system" that made skilled workers obsolete. But it was unethical to do these things without thinking about their implications for humanity. Increasingly, that's what his stories were saying.

He sent "Ice-9" to the typist with renewed hopes of making it to his goal of selling five stories. Kenneth had sold "Das Ganz Arm Dolmetscher" to *The Atlantic*: that made three. He was only getting $125 for it, but getting published in *The Atlantic* was a coup for his reputation as a writer. Before long, he might be able to quit, and when he did, it was becoming increasingly clear to him what he would do. He would write a novel about science and progress and ethical quagmires—a novel, in short, about GE.

•

By late May, New York City newspapers were announcing water gains on every "front." By mid-June, the tone was a little less gleeful. The reservoirs were near full, but constant rain was ruining the vacation season upstate. Resort owners grumbled about lost tourist income; farmers in neighboring Orange and Sullivan Counties complained that their vegetable crops were being washed out; sports fans were outraged when Giants and Dodgers games were canceled. Ironically, even the annual picnic of the Department of Water Supply, Gas, and Electricity was rained out.

On June 15, with reservoir levels surging, prohibitions on watering lawns and filling swimming pools were lifted. In July, residents were allowed to wash their cars. In August, as he prepared a report on his first six months as the city's consulting meteorologist, Wallace Howell finally said what the press wanted him to say.

"I have made rain," he told city reporters.

GE was trying to get its rainmaker to stop saying the same thing.

Irving had submitted his American Meteorological Society paper—the one that had sparked New York City's experiment—to an editor at *Science*. The GE lawyers, fearing that the paper could be used as evidence in a civil suit against the company, had the News Bureau head, George Griffin, call up *Science* and withdraw it. No one informed Langmuir.

When Irving found out, he was furious. GE was demanding he go along with the official position that GE scientists never caused rain. But his future work and reputation depended on convincing people that he *had* made rain. In the face of his anger, the GE lawyers backed down. Langmuir might be controversial, but he was still their most famous scientist, their only Nobel laureate. The paper appeared in *Science* in July. By then, Irving, Bernie, and Vince were all back in New Mexico, flying regular seeding runs to see if they could introduce definitive changes in the weather—not just in that state, but across the entire nation.

8

Out of the Blue

Prime Minister Liaquat Ali Khan, generous of smile, rotund of body, arrived at GE sporting his traditional fez. He was trailed by his brocaded, bejeweled wife and flanked by nine handlers, two from the Department of State. The News Bureau had diligently organized the photo ops. At the Works, the prime minister was photographed smiling while a manager explained the engine assembly line. Then he was taken to the turbine department. Gamely, he stood by as a worker drove gleaming rivets into an enormous flywheel. Flashbulbs detonated like lightning.

The prime minister had left Pakistan to learn what was to be learned in the most powerful nation on earth for the good of his spanking-new country. His state visit, hastily arranged after Stalin invited him to the Soviet Union, was designed to cement young Pakistan's alignment with Western democracy and free enterprise.

The Ali Khans received a full state tour of Washington, including visits to see President Truman, the Naval Academy, Mount Vernon, and the Tomb of the Unknown Soldier. Then they went to New York, where the prime minister received an honorary degree from Columbia University president Dwight D. Eisenhower. After that, they were hustled around the country—Chicago, San Francisco, Houston, New Orleans—inspecting everything from hospitals and factories to crop dusters and prize cattle. In Kansas City, they visited the home of an average American family. The average American husband and wife stood nervously in their Sunday best while Liaquat Ali Khan sat stiffly in their average American living room with their average American son on his lap.

When he and his wife arrived in Schenectady on May 24, 1950, Prime Minister Ali Khan had exactly 510 days to live. He would be assassinated on October 16, 1951, by an Afghani Pashtun ultranationalist. Conspiracy theories alleging U.S. or Soviet involvement would never be proved or disproved. But no one knew this on May 24. All anyone knew that day in Schenectady was that a brand-new nation's head of state must be dazzled by the wonders of American industry.

Kurt didn't write the press release for the prime minister's visit, but he couldn't have missed the fuss. GE loved nothing more than treating visiting dignitaries to a tour of the company's showcase factory. But what was it like for someone like Liaquat Ali Khan to see the Schenectady Works? Did any of the guests treated to this spectacle of technological prowess and entrepreneurial efficiency ever question the value of all those toasters and refrigerators and washing machines and jet engines and tanks? Did anyone ever dare ask what it was all *for*?

At home, Kurt put a fresh piece of paper in his typewriter and banged out the words "Outline for a Science Fiction Novel."

He figured that's what he'd been writing: science fiction. Not crazy exotic tales of alien races and outer space and time travel; that wasn't what he meant. He had never read the genre magazines full of monsters and Martians, intergalactic wars and improbable future worlds. He meant fiction about science and the probable future that science was spawning in the here and now. Because he'd been living at the leading edge of that future for a couple of years, and he had some issues with what he saw.

Progress: the one true church. The smartest people understood that it had a downside, people like Norbert Wiener, but no one was listening to them. Take, for instance, David Lilienthal's recent speech. Lilienthal had recently retired from the Atomic Energy Commission, and a group of scientists had quickly arranged for him to come to Schenectady and speak. They thought he would address the morally urgent issues behind atomic energy, now that he could say what he really thought. Instead, Lilienthal blathered on about nuclear medicine and nuclear power and how the main uses of the atom would be for peace. He dismissed the "cult of horror" of certain scientists and compared the discovery of fission to the discovery of fire.

As if fire had never harmed a fly.

During the question-and-answer period, someone in the audience asked how many atomic bombs it would take to destroy Schenectady.

"I haven't given it a thought," Lilienthal said.

Kurt was giving it a thought. His novel would be about progress and the dark side of it no one wanted to discuss.

It was Kenneth Littauer who had suggested writing a novel. An editor friend at Doubleday thought Kurt should expand "Report on the Barnhouse Effect" to novel length. It was not impossible, Kenneth said, that the publisher would offer Kurt an advance of $2,500 if he could provide a detailed proposal. Half a year's salary!

So now Kurt was writing an outline. He had an idea about the novel he wanted to write, and it wasn't a longer version of "Barnhouse." He wanted to write a novel about GE. It would be science fiction in the way that most of his stories were science fiction. Science fiction like Aldous Huxley's *Brave New World* or George Orwell's *1984*, which had been so acclaimed the previous year. Kurt's novel would cover many of the same issues—freedom, totalitarianism, warmongering—that those well-respected novels did. But the totalitarian world of his novel would be based not on socialist England but on Schenectady. He wasn't going to imagine some fantastic future world with babies in bottles or spy screens in every home; he was going to play out the implications of what was already happening right here, in the heart of the free market, in the capital of industrial know-how. He was going to bite the hand that fed him.

He'd never written a novel outline before. In his précis for Kenneth Littauer, he reverted to his anthropology-student habits. He started off by claiming broad cultural relevance: machines were taking over human labor, he declared, and this was a more significant cultural development than atomic energy. As proof, he inserted a long quotation from Norbert Wiener's *Cybernetics*:

The first industrial revolution . . . was the devaluation of the human arm by the competition of machinery . . . The modern industrial revolution is similarly bound to devalue the human brain at least in its simpler and more routine decisions. Of course, just as the skilled carpenter, the skilled mechanic, the skilled dressmaker have in some degree survived the first industrial revolution, so the skilled scientist and the skilled administrator may survive the second. However, taking the second revolution as accomplished, the average human being of mediocre attainments or less has nothing to sell that it is worth anyone's money to buy.

That was exactly the world in which his novel would take place: a world sharply divided into an elite class of people intelligent enough to remain necessary and a vast, unhappy underclass whose usefulness has been usurped by machines. It was sort of like the physical split that had already occurred at GE, where the scientists and the managers moved to the Knolls and the laborers stayed behind at the Works, watching as machines took over their purpose. The central character would be an engineer, intelligent enough to be part of the elite but not really comfortable in it. He would be discontented with the whole situation without really understanding why. Eventually, there would have to be a rupture of some sort.

The novel outline hinted at a deeper animus behind Kurt's resolve to quit GE. The job was making him crazy. And he was making Jane crazy. But it wasn't just boring company politics and the soul-sapping task of public relations that were wearing him down. For him, GE was a brave new world, and he didn't like it.

It wasn't just machines or technology. It was the use of those things to divide the world into winners and losers. When Kurt was young, the Depression made losers of most of the nation, so the shame of losing had faded. But after the war, the nation staged an orgy of victory: VE Day, VJ Day. Suddenly Americans were ahead, and it felt good. It felt right. Even the arms race was exciting—a game the nation could win. The old socialist ideal of equalizing things was out of favor. In fact, people were starting to be afraid of being labeled socialists—or worse, communists—for advocating things that used to be uncontroversial, like trade unionism. People like Joseph McCarthy, the first-term senator from Wisconsin who claimed to have a list of 205 known communists working in the State Department, were whipping up a frenzy of Red-baiting. A Senate subcommittee was now investigating a number of individuals who were suspiciously friendly toward losers.

It was as if some people forgot the most basic truths of being human: we are frail, imperfect, vulnerable creatures always in need of other humans for support. Technology was evil if it was used to make some people fabulously comfortable and toss others out with the trash. It was evil if it made that cruelty seem rational. It was evil if it removed individuals from their humanity, if it suppressed the fundamental insight that we're all in this together.

Kurt knew that he could shape these themes into an important novel. He gave his two-page outline to Kenneth and went back to writing short stories. The possibility of $2,500 was just that—a possibility. You couldn't buy Junket or wieners with it. Besides, a popular writer could make $2,500 on two stories. Writing a novel was something you did to gain literary credibility. Kurt wanted that—fervently—but he also wanted to quit his job and make a living by writing. Short stories were the quicker route to prosperity.

Or would be, if someone would only buy them. As summer arrived, Kurt continued to crank out stories, and Knox continued to reject them. "Keep on trying" wasn't working. Kurt groused to friends that Knox acted as if he were lining up prizewinners for the O. Henry Awards, not picking entertainment for a slick magazine. He couldn't believe *Collier's* rejected "EPICAC." Even Kenneth liked that one; he submitted it to *The New Yorker*. "It's about love in the technological age. I thought you might think it funny," he wrote to the editors there. They didn't.

By now, all of Kurt's free time was consumed sitting at his desk. He started and restarted, wrote and rewrote, as the waves of life broke over him. Mark had his third birthday party; kids brought donations for the Schenectady Cerebral Palsy Fund in place of gifts. Jane waitressed at the Schenectady Symphony's Junior League pops concert. Bernie's son Peter won a prize for his flower arrangement at the Alplaus Methodist Church flower show, and Bow was pregnant again. PTA meetings, volunteer nights, dinner parties, school picnics: all of it eddied and churned around the beachhead Kurt built at the end of the hall upstairs. Ashtrays filled, wastebaskets overflowed, and the typewriter clacked away like the engine of a ship headed for a distant shore.

•

Bernie peered out the window of the B-17. His cloud—a clump of billowing cumulus over the mountains west of Socorro, New Mexico— was rearing up from the cloud bank like a gray sea monster. It was his cloud because he had seeded it with silver iodide half an hour earlier. Now it was growing ominously heavy and turning the same dark gray as wet concrete. But no rain was falling from it. As he watched, the cloud thrust farther upward, taking on the anvil shape of a thunderhead. Still no rain.

It was over-seeded, he figured. They had long suspected that over-seeding could cause clouds to grow while creating droplets too small to fall, and here was further proof, a cloud pregnant but unable to give birth. Fifty grams of silver iodide had been too much. Tell that to the private operators who were going haywire all over the state, seeding clouds with a hundred grams or more of silver iodide, on the mistaken theory that more was always better.

New Mexico was parched by drought. Before Project Cirrus arrived, the state's Economic Development Commission had held a meeting on the topic of rainmaking. Scientists, Weather Bureau meteorologists, and private rainmakers were invited to brainstorm. Irving went out to New Mexico early to attend. Although Bernie had been expressing concern about the burgeoning of rainmaking for profit, Irving had not quite realized how many people had decided to get into the business of weather control. At the meeting, one commercial cloud seeder after another spoke, making it clear that the whole state was blanketed in rainmakers, dispensing dry ice from airplanes, burning silver iodide on the ground, shooting silver iodide from guns: all of it paid for by farmers desperate to save wilting crops and dwindling herds. The amounts of material the cloud seeders were using were ridiculous, and no one was keeping track. Irving finally saw Bernie's point: Project Cirrus's entire program was being jeopardized by careless amateurs.

Irving had stood up at the conference and made an impassioned speech urging the establishment of a central repository for data about the cloud-seeding operations across the state. He didn't like regulation, but he suggested a voluntary agreement among rainmakers to submit detailed reports of any activities to the New Mexico School of Mines. Jack Workman's group there would assemble and collate all the data and make them available to researchers. He spoke with conviction, and his usual charisma worked its magic. Everyone at the meeting agreed to the plan. But afterward, when one of the conference's private rainmakers started a new operation and the Economic Development Commission wrote asking for its report, the reply was a flat refusal from the group's lawyer stating that all data were "the property of the client."

Nevertheless, the Project Cirrus team had come back to New Mexico for more test flights; the pilots stayed at the base, while the scientists packed into Poverty Row, the School of Mines' war-era bunkhouse, with its paper-thin walls and spartan living quarters. Vince and Irving brought their wives, but the trip was too much for the pregnant Bow. Bernie brought his nephew Albert Lieber, whose family lived in Scottsdale, Arizona. A high school senior headed for Caltech, Albert was delighted to spend his summer tagging along after Irving, recording data, and hanging on the great scientist's every word.

Bernie's plane banked sharply and flew back around the seeded cumulus cloud to get more photographs before turning back toward Socorro and the radar site. At Socorro, they headed northwest, toward another slowly forming cumulus system. This one they seeded with dry ice, two pounds per mile. Almost as soon as they had dropped it, radar echoes began to show precipitation. The clouds ballooned upward, their action captured in time-lapse photographs.

Within an hour, rain was pounding New Mexico. The Rio Salado and the area's dry arroyos quickly became engorged with rushing water. A truck and a car that were in the dip where Route 85 crossed the normally dry riverbed were swept downstream, halting all traffic on the road. Vince later estimated that the rivers had carried a thousand cubic feet of water per second to the Rio Grande. The floodwaters raged all that afternoon and continued through the next day as well.

The team was delighted. The photographs were excellent, and with the radar echoes they offered powerful evidence that their seeding was capable of dramatic effects. It had been even more powerful to observe it in real time from the air. Bernie felt in his heart that they had made that storm: He saw it. He was there. Unfortunately, William Lewis of the Weather Bureau was not. He had chosen to sleep in that morning and had missed the whole operation.

That night, they read in the news that the UN Security Council had passed a resolution committing itself to military action in Korea. Two weeks earlier, seventy-five thousand soldiers from Korea's communist North had crossed the 38th parallel and invaded the democratic South. In response to this clear breach of the peace, the UN Security Council had recommended that member nations begin making their military forces available to the American unified commander. For the first time, the young UN was taking up its role as planetary peacekeeper.

It was a UN military action, but it still meant that America was once again at war. Men would be drafted, ships and aircraft would be sent to the front, and military personnel on noncombat assignments would be called into active duty.

In other words, Project Cirrus was going to lose its planes and its pilots.

At least Bernie's work could carry on. Workman's team in New Mexico would continue dispensing silver iodide on their regular schedule, and the GE team would continue to analyze the data, searching for proof that Bernie's generators were changing the nation's weather patterns.

·

Kurt looked out over the oily harbor in Gloucester, Massachusetts, and felt glum. He loved being near the ocean, even if, as a Great Lakes person, it made him feel as if he were swimming in chicken soup. He and Jane had been excited to bring Mark and little Edie to New England for their August vacation. They hadn't counted on the world going to hell.

The newspapers were full of it. War again. The first UN observer—Colonel Unni Nayar of India—had just been killed by a land mine, along with the two British journalists riding in his jeep. The UN had ejected a pacifist protester who tried to hand out leaflets advocating mediation instead of war. President Truman was rattling his saber. It all felt so familiar.

But it was new too, a civil war that felt like the opening skirmish in a global battle of ideologies. Some of the American GIs who came back wounded were insisting they had seen Russians driving the tanks that attacked them. America's UN delegate, Warren Austin, called the North Koreans a "Russian zombie." The armed camps were summoning their ranks; the Cold War was turning hot.

Looking out over the ocean, Kurt couldn't help but picture it: seven thousand miles across that expanse of dark water, it was all happening again. Young men—as young as he had been—were being sent into another maelstrom. They thought they were soldiers, but they were pawns really, pawns in a nasty game of brinksmanship between the world's two superpowers. The Korean War had nothing to do with them, little even to do with the Korean peninsula, and everything to do with the growing enmity between communism and capitalism, between what were called East and West but were really the Soviet Union and the United States.

Right there in Gloucester, he started a new story: "King's Knight to Queen Five." In the story, later retitled "White King," the soldiers are literally pawns. Twelve soldiers, their commander, Colonel Kelly, and Kelly's family—on their way to a military attaché post in India—have been blown off course by a sudden storm over China and crash-landed in territory held by a communist guerrilla chief, Pi Ying. In the presence of a Russian "observer," Major Barzov, Pi Ying offers to let them all go—but only if Colonel Kelly will play chess for their lives, using his troops and his family as chessmen. Whenever he loses a piece, that person will be shot. If Colonel Kelly refuses to play, they will all be killed.

The Americans take their places, and the game commences. As pieces are lost and soldiers dragged off to their deaths, Colonel Kelly realizes that Pi Ying has a sadistic fascination with what the American will do. Major Barzov seems cold and distant, Pi Ying's mistress is blank-faced, but the communist guerrilla chief is watching the game with the avid fascination of a young boy watching a colony of ants being drowned by a flood.

Kurt drew chessboards and sketched out the game, because the story would hinge on an actual move. Colonel Kelly realizes that he can beat Pi Ying by luring him into a trap where his sadism will blind him to the ramifications of his move. He has to make a sacrifice that will trick Pi Ying into a checkmate. As he contemplates his options, he realizes that only one sacrifice will suffice: he must lose one of his sons.

The cold resolve deserted Kelly for an instant, and he saw the utter pathos of his position—a dilemma as old as mankind, as new as the struggle between East and West. When human beings are attacked, x, multiplied by hundreds or thousands, must die—sent to death by those who love them most. Kelly's profession was the choosing of x.

Four soldiers have already been killed when Kelly moves his son into a vulnerable position. He pretends to realize the sacrifice too late and begs to take the move back. Pi Ying refuses. As the boy is about to be hauled off and shot, Pi Ying's mistress intervenes, murdering Pi Ying and killing herself. Major Barzov continues the game, but he quickly realizes the cleverness of Kelly's move. He allows the survivors safe passage out of the region and doesn't insist on killing the boy. The story ends with banter between Barzov and Kelly about a possible rematch—at the time and place of the Soviet Union's choosing.

It was a dark story, bleaker than much of what Kurt had been writing. He made a sketch of himself on the back of one of his drafts, a lanky figure hunched feverishly over his typewriter. He drew quickly, the lines electric with urgency. All his hopes for world government, for peace and disarmament, were being dashed by the action in Korea. The world powers were once again playing games with the lives of men. And he was becoming more and more convinced that the root of it was the ability to see human beings not as individuals but as pawns. The danger of the technocratic worldview was that it made human conflicts, human drama, even war, into a kind of game.

While they were in Gloucester, he made a painting of the face of a clown and put it up for sale in a local gallery. It didn't sell, so they brought it home with them. Kurt's clown had a bulbous red nose and straw-like blond hair and a big white greasepaint smile, but his blue almond-shaped eyes—eyes much like his own—were unmistakably sad.

•

Bernie looked out over the audience of high school teachers in Connecticut. Often at events like this one, a meeting of the New England Association of Chemistry Teachers, he gave a general overview of rainmaking and its results to date. But tonight he was doing something different. He was talking about the ethical implications of science.

"Many farmers, ranchers and civic-minded people in many parts of the country are now engaged in cloud seeding," he declared. He was careful to point out that the amateurs were not bad people. But they "can unwittingly cause large scale, and perhaps adverse, modifications of weather many miles from the scene of their operations." Not only that, but their efforts could be polluting the data of serious scientists trying to conduct rigorous experiments.

The media were still enamored of cloud seeding. An issue of *Time* magazine had just hit newsstands naming Langmuir the man of the week, his likeness on the cover holding an umbrella that doubled as a test tube. The writer noted Irving's intense curiosity: "He has been known to sit for half an hour beside a rock surrounded by rising water just to see what a dozen ants will do when their refuge is submerged." But though the article featured a long list of cloud-seeding projects under way across the nation, it gave no indication that this deluge of rainmaking might be problematic. That, it seemed, was going to be Bernie's job.

Like Professor Barnhouse, like Dr. Macon in "Ice-9," Bernie was beginning to fear that his invention was getting out of hand. But, also like his fictional counterparts, he couldn't prevent people from using it recklessly until he had proved it was real.

"Legislators in the future may well face many problems connected with cloud seeding," he told the chemistry teachers. "Laws may be necessary to prohibit and police seeding operations which are contrary to the best interests of the public. Licensing of seeding operations and permits for seeding may be desirable."

It was a risky thing to be suggesting at a time when the future of Project Cirrus was hardly guaranteed. The number of flights had plummeted as Project Cirrus pilots were reassigned to Korea. GE's president Charlie Wilson had recently resigned his post to head up the Office of Defense Mobilization, and his successor, Ralph Cordiner, was a meticulous and humorless leader with an eye glued to the bottom line—a trait that earned him the nickname Razor Ralph. Razor Ralph was unlikely to have much enthusiasm for a project that did nothing for profits, especially as it exposed the company to all kinds of risks.

For an example of those risks, one only had to look to the Catskills, where residents of New York City's watershed were still trying to get the city to stop cloud seeding. At a meeting of the local Farm Bureau Federation, hay farmers and apple growers bitterly complained about damage to crops, and the general secretary for New York demanded government regulation. The Boards of Supervisors in Orange and Sullivan Counties had passed resolutions demanding the city cease all rainmaking. The Palisades Amusement Park had even offered to pay the consulting meteorologist Wallace Howell twice his city salary if he would quit. "Why Don't You Let Us Alone, Rainman," griped a headline in *The Kingston Daily Freeman*, summarizing the general feeling. But even though the reservoirs were replenished, Howell and the New York City Board of Estimate carried on. Their data would be more valuable if they seeded for four consecutive seasons.

The New York Times's editorial board commended Bernie's endorsement of regulation, noting that his position differed from Langmuir's. Irving too was frustrated with the amateurs who might be polluting his data, but he believed regulation was impracticable, suggesting only a voluntary agreement among rainmakers. That was in keeping with the times, where "planning" and "regulation" were increasingly unpopular words. Bernie was swimming against the tide of unbridled capitalism. It was not a role he had ever expected to assume. But someone had to make sure that scientists paid attention to the damage they and their inventions might unwittingly do.

•

"Ice-9," Kurt's story about a scientist whose invention nearly destroyed the world, was languishing. After *Argosy* rejected it, hard on the heels of *The Saturday Evening Post*, Kurt glumly told Kenneth they should probably hawk it to *Astounding Stories* for $300. That was highway robbery for something he thought was the best thing he'd ever written, but it was better than having the whole novella end up in the garbage can.

But he was hard at work on a new story, a political allegory, which was perhaps not the smartest choice. Already an editor at *Collier's* had complained that his chess story, "White King," savored of knee-jerk anticommunism. Kurt objected to Knox.

"I am a registered Democrat, pro–Fair and New Deal, distressed by the new anti-subversive laws, hate McCarthy, enflamed by Communist smears on liberals—etc., etc.," he wrote. "But, dammit, Knox, I don't like Communist Russia any more than I did Nazi Germany. There are some 3,000 Americans dead in Korea, killed in a chess game with Russia looking on." People who considered his depiction of Pi Ying sadistic, he declared, were perhaps "too insensitive to a casualty list as long as King Kong's arm." He signed the letter "George Sokolsky"—the name of a newspaper columnist known for loving free markets and hating Reds.

Now, unrepentant, Kurt was writing another anticommunist story, using petrified ants to tell a morality tale about totalitarianism. He made it even more direct by setting it in the Soviet Union. The problem was, he couldn't figure out how it ended.

Kurt had been looking at William Morton Wheeler's book *Ants: Their Structure, Development, and Behavior*. According to Wheeler, ant societies had progressed through stages of social behavior analogous to those of human cultures. Modern ants lived in mindless, often militaristic societies in which the hereditary hierarchies of caste and function were evident as physical traits: soldier ants were big, with pincers for fighting; worker ants were small, with enlarged mandibles for carrying things. There was no individualism, no escaping one's physical destiny. What, Kurt wondered, if human beings were headed in the same direction?

Like "Ice-9," the new story centered on a conflict between two men, one doctrinaire, the other doubtful. But in this story, the men are brothers, Josef and Peter. Both are myrmecologists—scientists who study ants—but they have different approaches to their discipline. The elder brother, "Josef the rock, the dependable, the ideologically impeccable," plays along with the Communist Party, while the younger brother, Peter, chafes under party orthodoxy. Peter has a blot on his reputation, a paper he wrote about slave-raiding ants that was declared ideologically incorrect, requiring him to issue an apology. Now Josef, who ghostwrote the retraction for him, is trying to help him steer clear of trouble as they investigate some newly discovered fossil ants.

The story is set in the Erzgebirge, or Ore Mountains, the rolling mountain range dividing eastern Germany from Czechoslovakia. The occupying Russians, while searching for uranium there, have discovered a cache of fossilized ants. When the brothers see them, they are amazed. The pre-Mesozoic ants are large and pincerless and have smaller mandibles than modern ants. And petrified along with them is evidence of a prehistoric ant culture: houses, art, musical instruments, and books.

"Josef," Peter says, "do you realize that we have made the most sensational discovery in history? Ants once had a culture as rich and brilliant as ours. Music! Painting! Literature! Think of it!"

Going through the layers of rock, the brothers see how the "magnificent ant civilization" evolved into "the dismal, instinctive ant way of life of the present." Artistic, intellectual, individualized ants have disappeared, leaving only warlike, cultureless drones. The brothers slowly realize they will never be allowed to publish their find: the parallels with their own totalitarian culture are far too obvious.

The political allegory was heavy-handed. But what gave Kurt even more trouble was the relationship between the two brothers. The story is told from Peter's perspective. But Kurt struggled with the character of the older brother, Josef. In early versions, he made Josef a Communist Party dupe. He wrote a scene in which Josef and Peter go out in a thunderstorm and argue about Peter's desire to speak the truth. Josef tells Peter that he mustn't speak "some kinds of truth" and urges him to "overlook certain things." Peter suddenly sees his brother for the sorry character he is: a "frail figure in a whirlpool, clinging desperately to a raft of compromises."

The scene needed to be fixed. It didn't convey Peter's respect for his older brother. Kurt rewrote it several times, once even having the brothers get into a physical fight, but he couldn't get it right, so he took it out. He was also struggling with the ending. In one version, Josef falsifies their scientific report while Peter escapes to the West. In another, the brothers end up in Siberia, near a huge atomic bomb factory that blows up. Yet another concludes with the brothers rewriting their findings to adhere to the party line but still getting banished to Siberia, where they bitterly reflect on the similarity between men and ants.

He drafted more than ten versions of the story. His struggles to figure out Peter's fate mirrored his struggle to determine his own. He was trapped at GE just as Peter was trapped by the Communist Party. Would he continue living a lie or take the risk of escaping?

But he was also wrestling with his view of his brother. Bernard was the rock, the dependable scientist. But he wasn't like Josef, a frail man clinging to a false ideology out of fear and conformity. Living in Schenectady, being part of Bernard's work, Kurt could see that Bernie was no kept scientist, toeing the science factory's company line. He too was trying to stay true to his ideals in a culture that didn't share them. The simplistic characterization of the older brother as a thoughtless organization man wasn't working anymore.

On a blank page, while working on his ant story Kurt typed up a to-do list. One thing on it was his income tax. Another was to get back to writing his novel. For the first time he gave it a title: *Player Piano*.

●

Bernie's phone rang at the lab. It was Bow, with a shopping list of things to pick up on the way home. Bernie grabbed the nearest thing at hand, a letter from a Park Avenue matron thanking him for giving a talk about cloud seeding to her women's club, and scribbled as Bow dictated: books, pen, cigarettes, matches, newspaper . . .

Bow was at home, recovering from the birth of their twin boys a few weeks earlier. She'd suffered headaches and gloominess after Peter's birth five years earlier, so Bernie was trying to help out as much as he could. But it was hard to tear himself away from the lab. Project Cirrus was getting closer to proving that their periodic seedings had caused widespread changes in the weather.

The day after the twins were born, GE formally dedicated the Knolls by hosting the annual meeting of the National Academy of Sciences. Irving gave a lecture about their periodicity experiments in New Mexico. He saw it as a chance to change the minds of the meteorology professors who had written a report for the Department of Defense branding his claims of widespread weather modifications "extraordinarily extravagant." When the report was declassified, something like a brawl had ensued at the AMS. Harry Wexler wanted to publish the report in the *Bulletin*. Vincent, who had been elected to the AMS council, insisted that Langmuir be given a chance to respond. Chief Reichelderfer pointed out that Langmuir never gave anyone else a chance to respond to his GE reports. "It seems to me it is time we began to play up the authentic meteorological opinion in this matter of rainmaking," he wrote to the council heads, "in view of the complete abandon with which the proponents of artificial rainmaking on a large scale have expressed themselves in public over the past two or three years."

For the National Academy, Langmuir had marshaled their statistics and their best photographic evidence. He had Weather Bureau charts showing rainfall at stations throughout the Midwest enlarged to enormous size so the seven-day pattern was stunningly obvious, even from the back of the room. Chief Reichelderfer was unable to attend, but he dispatched two Weather Bureau meteorologists to Schenectady soon afterward. Bernie was back at work by then, and Langmuir enlisted him to assist in lecturing the Weather Bureau men, laying out their charts and data over the course of two days.

Irving was growing frustrated with the meteorological community's refusal to grant scientific credibility to his life's most important work. He was particularly annoyed by the Weather Bureau's claim that no one could say cloud seeding worked until they understood the mechanism precisely. After all, meteorologists might *never* know all there was to know about the atmosphere. But they could still change it. It was like the germ theory of disease, he reasoned. For decades, doctors knew that washing their hands led to lower mortality among patients. The fact that they didn't know *why* was not sufficient reason for refusing to lather up.

Bernie, meanwhile, was determined to track down the truth about what the commercial rainmakers were doing. He began writing to chemical supply companies like Braun, Dow, Merck, and Pfizer to ask whether their sales of silver iodide had gone up. "It is hoped that it will be possible on the basis of the information received to estimate the rate at which silver iodide has been and is being introduced into our atmosphere," he wrote. "If this quantity is sufficiently large, an attempt will be made to evaluate the effects which may be produced by this seed-ing." Many companies reported no increase in sales, but a few had seen large jumps. Elmer & Amend, a division of Fisher Scientific, reported that its 1950 sales had gone from three pounds to twenty-seven. Eight pounds of that was sold to New York City for use in the watershed.

•

In late November 1950, a winter storm hit the Eastern Seaboard. It started in North Carolina and eventually swept across twenty-two states. All-time record low temperatures were set across the Southeast, his-toric snowfalls pounded the Appalachians and the Midwest, hurricane-force winds hit New York, and tidal flooding surged northward up the coast of New England. The Big Ten championship game between Ohio State and Michigan was played in a near whiteout, earning it the nick-name the Blizzard Bowl. A million people lost power, and 353 people lost their lives.

The Catskills were hit especially hard. But New York's rainmaker Wallace Howell wanted a full year of data. So, as heavy winds and hard rain lashed the region, a city water department crew ran a silver iodide generator attached to a trailer in Fahnestock State Park, near Cold Spring, a location chosen so that the prevailing winds would carry the silver iodide over the watershed. At the same time, a city airplane seeded clouds closer to the reservoirs.

The storm intensified that night. The northern part of Ulster County got a downpour of eight inches, and ten of the region's twenty-four rain gauges recorded more rain than in the famous hurricane of 1938. A month's worth of water was added to the city coffers in three days.

The damages were epic. Dozens of bridges and highways were washed out. Farms and villages were flooded. Parts of the New York Central's Delaware and Ulster branch railroad bed were washed away, leaving tracks hanging from hillsides like strings of Christmas lights. Three small dams burst in the village of Pine Hill, draining the town's recreational lake. In Arkville, a seventy-two-ton fuel tank broke loose and barreled a quarter mile down State Route 28, and a covered bridge was swept a thousand feet downstream. Many local residents declared it the worst flood they had ever seen. The Weather Bureau would later call the storm one of the most destructive ever recorded on the Eastern Seaboard. And its meteorologists had failed to predict any of it.

It was a freak storm, the Weather Bureau said. No one could have predicted it. Irving Langmuir didn't necessarily disagree. He doubted anyone could have predicted it. But he had a sneaking suspicion that Bernie's cloud seeding had caused it.

•

Bernie and Bow didn't have far to go to get to 18 Hill Street; a short walk around the corner, and they were at Kurt and Jane's front door. Tonight the house was brightly lit and buzzing with voices. It was a couple of days after Christmas, the night of the Junior League holiday ball. Kurt and Jane were throwing a dinner party before the dance. Bernie and Bow were joined by the Fishers, the Hollomons, the McCartys, the Yarboroughs, and the Metcalfs—all GE employees and their wives.

There was a lot to celebrate. After Langmuir's recent paper presenting his evidence for widespread periodicities in the *Bulletin of the American Meteorological Society*, the meteorologists were taking a more conciliatory tone: Harry Wexler had even gone to Socorro earlier that month to let Vince and Jack Workman present the Project Cirrus case. They disagreed on whether cloud seeding was sufficiently proved but had all gained more respect for the other side's position. It seemed as if it were only a matter of time before the meteorological world at large realized the significance of the Cirrus work.

But if Bernie had reason for optimism, Kurt was in an even better mood—jubilant, in fact. The story logjam had finally broken when Knox Burger bought "EPICAC." Knox had never liked the story much, and he sarcastically blamed the purchase on the higher-ups. He told Kurt his rewrite was shoddy, asking him to take into account the fact that thinking machines had become common knowledge: there was one at Harvard and maybe even one at MIT. He also suggested Kurt try to make the scientist in the story sound a little less puerile.

But the rough handling was a sign that Kurt was finally a real magazine writer. In November, Knox had bought "White King," upping Kurt's fee from $900 to $1,250. Kurt wrote "SOLD" in big letters with a red crayon on the story's GE News Bureau folder. It was a turning point, *the* turning point, at long last. He had sold "Thanasphere," "Das Ganz Arm Dolmetscher," "EPICAC," and now "White King" in the year since selling "Report on the Barnhouse Effect." Five stories total: the number sufficient to quit his job. And he had a bunch more in the pipeline, along with his idea for a novel.

So this party was a farewell of sorts. In mid-December, Kurt had given notice at GE. He was quitting as of the start of the New Year. New year, new life. Kurt Vonnegut Jr. was no longer a PR flunky. He was finally going to be what he'd always wanted to be: a writer. And he knew what he was going to write about too: science in the House of Magic.

9

Cold Fronts

Kurt doodled on the back of his manuscript. Then he got out the Scotch tape. He cut parts out and taped in replacements. Once again, he was reworking "Ice-9." He had given himself ten days.

Now that he was a real writer, he had to be serious about producing work quickly and efficiently. This was no longer something he did in his free time; it was his job. So he had typed up a schedule for himself, planning out every writing day for two months. He allowed three days to revise a story, ten or so to write a new one. Ten days for the "Ice-9" revision, and then there was his novel, *Player Piano*. He allotted three weeks for chapter 1 and a couple of days for chapter 2, but there he stalled. He didn't really know how long a novel took to write.

He'd finished a draft of the first story on his schedule, "Between Timid and Timbuktu," but he didn't like it. It focused on a recently widowed painter, David, who misses his dead wife so much that he becomes obsessed with finding a way to be with her again. Maybe, David speculates, there are creatures in the universe who can hop back and forth in time to visit previous parts of their lives. Then a local man has an accident, and his heart stops. He is quickly revived by the town doctor and upon waking reports that he saw his whole life pass before him. Inspired, David hatches a secret plot to kill himself and have the doctor revive him so he can go back in time and see his wife again. But the doctor gets another call and fails to show up at the appointed hour. David, having given himself a fatal injection, dies.

It was Kurt's first attempt to do something with the idea of time travel. Norbert Wiener's *Cybernetics* included a chapter called "Newtonian and Bergsonian Time," in which he contrasted the time of physics, which is reversible, with the time of biology, which travels in a straight line. The time of biology, or Bergsonian time, moves relentlessly in one direction—birth, growth, decline, and death succeeding one another in an inexorable forward march. But in Newtonian time, the time of physics, everything has already happened: nothing new can be created, and nothing can ever really die. An interesting thought experiment, Wiener noted, would be to imagine an intelligent being whose time ran in the opposite direction of our own.

"Between Timid and Timbuktu" was a somewhat clumsy first attempt at a topic that would play a big role in Kurt's work. Variations on Newtonian time would recur frequently in his fiction as plot devices, always echoing the simple human longing of that early story: the desire to cheat death and hold on to the past. Most famously, he would invent the alien Tralfamadorians in *Slaughterhouse-Five*, who live in Newtonian time, where everything has always existed and will always continue to exist. They thus do not stand in awe of death, as we do, merely saying, when someone dies, "So it goes."

At some point, critics would label Kurt's use of time travel a device for demonstrating the "absurdity" of the world. To do so disregards the fact that Bergsonian time is also always operating in the novels. Human beings live out their lives and die; they mourn their lost loves and dead friends. The existence of the inhuman time of quantum physics only highlights the poignancy of time as we experience it, advancing ever onward to our graves. Who wouldn't want to escape from one world to another, to follow the allure of science into a world where we never die?

But unlike later iterations, "Between Timid and Timbuktu" is sentimental, even maudlin at the end, as the dying David gazes wistfully at a painting of his wife. Kurt gave it three days and set it aside. It was a dog. Eventually, he would give up on it and swipe its title for a chapter head in his second novel, *The Sirens of Titan*. There, too, time would be a theme, with the chain of events set in motion when a character—Winston Niles Rumfoord—slips into a time warp.

After setting "Timid" aside, Kurt had worked some more on the ant story, which was also refusing to behave. Now he was back to "Ice-9."

From his typewriter, he could look out the window. He had a real office now: he had rented a bedroom from a woman whose daughter was off at college. It was right on the main street of Alplaus, and from his desk in the coed's room he could watch the buses heading off to GE with their cargoes of company men. Poor bastards. Even as he struggled with his stories, he knew he was well out of that.

But if he had escaped, his mind hadn't: the stories he wanted to write were GE stories. He didn't call it GE. He called it General Forge and Foundry, or General Household Appliance Company, or Federal Apparatus Corporation. But the company discernible behind all of them was the one he knew so well: the scientists, the PR hacks, the visitors on Works tours, the imperious managers, and the girl pool where typists Dictaphoned the days away, awaiting rescue by diamond ring. His stories were a portrait of the GE Works itself: the numbered buildings, the departments with absurd names ("Wire and Cable," "Nucleonics"), the offices and gates and fences and smokestacks belching their acrid benediction over the Electric City. But most of all he wrote about company attitudes: the worship of the company man; the mindless team spirit; the faith in progress, technology, and science; the enthusiasm for anything that reeked of the future—the machine-made, computer-coded, semi-conducted, radioactive future.

That was certainly what he was writing about in "Ice-9" too. He believed in the story, but it had been rejected now by more magazines than he cared to tally. He thought maybe he knew what was wrong. It was the lack of a woman. No one wanted to read a story without a little romantic frisson.

So he changed the sociologist Professor Dale into a gorgeous redhead named Marion, a former lover of the mad scientist Dr. Macon. Once again, Macon invents Ice-9 and brags that it could destroy the planet's water. When Marion doesn't understand, Macon, sounding just like Irving Langmuir, explains that crystallization happens by chain reaction. It's like a single match starting a forest fire.

After that, things unfold much as they did in the earlier version, with Macon insisting that he has no moral duties as a researcher and Marion insisting that he does. Once again, the evil dictator Monzano gets his hands on the Ice-9, and Macon has to try to get it back. But Kurt had to rewrite the conclusion: Professor Dale is murdered in the earlier version, and Marion couldn't be dead if there was going to be a romantic ending. Instead, Monzano jumps into a cave pool with the Ice-9, but Dr. Macon manages to get to it and melt it before the tide rises and floods the cave. The world is saved, and, of course, boy gets girl.

Changing Dale to Marion helped, but it didn't fix the fundamental problem with "Ice-9." Kurt couldn't quite put his finger on what was wrong in the time he had allotted, so he set it aside too and moved on. By late January, he'd completed and sent to Kenneth Littauer a serviceable story called "Bockman's Euphoria," about a scientist who invents a new kind of radio wave that has a drug-like euphoric effect on anyone who hears it. People put their lives on hold just to lie around listening to it. That was a defter and less personal take on the same topic: a nifty invention that gets put to use before anyone figures out the kind of damage it can do.

•

In Kentucky they called it the Great Appalachian Storm of 1950. In Ohio they called it the Thanksgiving Storm. Many places called it the Storm of the Century, and in Pittsburgh it was simply known as the Big Snow. But in the Catskills, where it did so much damage, they were calling it the Rainmakers' Flood. And they were furious.

The first 13 claims against New York City were filed on February 16, 1951. Within a week, there were 30 more. Eventually, more than 130 upstate clients would file legal claims against New York City for the destructive November rainstorm that they believed Wallace Howell had made. Many were individuals whose homes were damaged, but businesses filed claims too: the Pine Hill Country Club, G. W. Merritt Lumber Company, the Funcrest Hotel, Levy's Liquor Store. The town of Shandaken demanded $167,500 to repair forty-eight roads and bridges. The township of Middletown asked for $60,000 and the village of

Margaretville, $23,645.91. The avalanche of claims totaled more than $1 million.

That month, a detailed meteorological account of the whole storm appeared in the journal *Weatherwise*. Irving read it with approval and shared it with his team. There were many anomalies that he thought supported his hypothesis that cloud seeding had caused the storm. For starters, it traveled northwest, the exact opposite of the usual weather pattern. The cold front that precipitated it had appeared out of nowhere and deepened with dizzying speed. That was why it had taken the Weather Bureau—and everyone—by surprise. But as Irving saw it, the 1950 storm had been caused not by Wallace Howell but by Project Cirrus and its fellow rainmakers out West.

In meteorology, large, circulating low-pressure systems are known as cyclones. Cyclones can be single storms or continent-wide circulation patterns that shape the weather across huge areas. Irving had begun a statistical analysis of the year's weather anomalies nationwide with the Weather Bureau's long-range forecasting expert, and to his eyes, the signal of the periodicities was coming through loud and clear. But weather oddities were cropping up all over the place. He believed this was because cloud seeding was affecting cyclonic development. If that was the case, silver iodide in the West might be changing the whole nation's climate.

Bernie was less certain than Langmuir that they had caused every large-scale abnormality in the North American weather. But he did agree that silver iodide seeding could create dramatic effects. His own paper about the cloud-seeding experiment of July 21, 1949, declared that his generator had dispensed enough particles that day to bring down 320 billion gallons of rain. He stopped short of saying that meant he had caused the resulting storm.

But Irving was unabashed about making such claims. He was even asserting, in talks about the seeding of Hurricane King, that their efforts had likely caused the storm's divergence from its course. Since that experiment, he had been conducting an intensive study of hurricane paths. In the entire recorded history of Atlantic hurricanes, only one other storm had made a hairpin turn like the one made by Hurricane King. And the other hurricane had only done so after it had slowed down and nearly stalled. Hurricane King was near its maximum velocity when they seeded it. The storm made its turn shortly thereafter. What were the odds that the two events were unrelated? Langmuir had an answer: 1 in 170.

He was growing impatient with the objections. When a young meteorologist at an MIT symposium objected to Langmuir's conclusions about Hurricane King, Irving dismissed him with a few undiplomatic words, saying he was so stupid he didn't deserve an explanation. Bernie would never have been so rough on the young man. But he understood Irving's frustration. They were collecting data as fast as they could, and everything they learned pointed in the same direction. If the Weather Bureau and the mainstream meteorology community had a better explanation, the GE group was willing to hear it. But it was almost as if the meteorologists refused to listen. The AMS *Bulletin* had just published a paper summarizing the research to date and stating that there was no proof that cloud seeding could produce large-scale effects. Most meteorologists seemed inclined to leave it at that: with no irrefutable proof, there was no need to investigate further. Which left the GE team alone in trying to figure out if the strange storms and droughts that seemed to be appearing all over the country had anything to do with the gold rush of rainmaking that was happening in every state west of the Mississippi.

•

Harry Wexler spent Valentine's Day in Princeton, plotting the next phase in his campaign against Project Cirrus. The previous April, with John von Neumann's computer still under construction, the Meteorology Project team had gone to the Aberdeen Proving Ground in Maryland to try out their forecasting equations on the ENIAC. The Army computer was a beast, with eighteen thousand vacuum tubes and six thousand switches. It was so big you literally worked inside it, sticking electrical wires into the plugboards that stored its programs. The team that trekked down to Maryland had worked with ENIAC around the clock for five weeks, managing to produce six retroactive forecasts—predictions of weather that had already happened. They weren't perfect. Forecast accuracy was erratic. Actual computer time to produce a twenty-four-hour forecast was twenty-four hours. Nonetheless, the results looked enough like the real weather that the programmers returned to the Institute for Advanced Study triumphant. Weather prediction by equation was going to work.

Now, at the Valentine's Day meeting, the Princeton meteorologists wanted to discuss something different: Irving Langmuir's alleged seven-day periodicity. Harry had brought a Weather Bureau statistician to Princeton to explain that the seven-day pattern Langmuir thought Project Cirrus had created was not the only such periodicity that had ever happened. In the last fifty years, there had been two other prolonged periods—four to five months—in which the weather showed a remarkable seven-day regularity. Neither was as striking as the one that had occurred in 1949–50, however, while Bernie's silver iodide generator was running on a seven-day schedule. But did that mean Project Cirrus was necessarily the cause? Von Neumann, his meteorologists, and a couple of Princeton University statisticians all agreed that the answer to that was still unclear. They thought Langmuir's experiment should continue for a few more years.

This had to be disappointing to Harry Wexler. For him, the ultra-rational institute project was a counterbalance to Langmuir's baseless conviction. It was a way of proving that the atmosphere behaved according to scientific precepts too powerful to be overcome by the puny interventions of one human—especially one who didn't even understand them. He who would master nature must learn her laws and then obey them! But it was easy for Harry to forget that John von Neumann was just as interested as Irving Langmuir was in weather control.

Harry wanted more than ever to prove the fraudulence of Project Cirrus and its claims. So he had a new idea. The Meteorology Project's next round of tests was going to try out new equations developed to predict the weather in an unstable atmosphere, one with cold fronts and warm fronts battling it out. It's these unstable systems that give rise to cyclones. No numerical model to date had successfully predicted their genesis.

Once the equations were ready, the team had to choose a past occurrence of cyclogenesis on which to try them out. And Harry Wexler knew just which historic storm they should try to forecast: the Thanksgiving

Storm of 1950, the so-called Rainmakers' Flood. If their equations could travel back through time and accurately predict that past event, that would definitely prove that the storm had been produced by nature and not by the hand of man.

•

It was the future, Knox Burger told Kurt over cocktails. Nineteen sixty-one to be exact.

The last ten years had been tough. The Russians invaded Yugoslavia in 1952, launching World War III. The Soviets had A-bombed cities in Europe and America. The UN had retaliated by A-bombing Moscow. A suicide mission by American paratroopers in the Urals destroyed the Russian stockpile of atomic weapons in 1953, at which point the Soviet Union began coming apart at the seams. Dissidents rose up in the satellite states, then in Russia itself. By 1955, many key generals had defected to the UN. As the U.S.S.R. slid into chaos, the UN sent in occupying troops. Six years later, *Collier's* was reporting on the collapse of communism and the rebuilding of the world.

That was the premise of a special issue he and the other *Collier's* editors were planning. Kurt and Jane listened eagerly as Knox described it. It was spring, a beautiful mild week, and they were in New York City, staying at the fabled Algonquin Hotel. They had friends to meet and a party to attend, and Jane was finally getting to meet Kurt's adored (when he was buying) and reviled (when he was not) editor. The three of them met for cocktails. Kurt had to be gratified that Jane was there for this: the editor pitching him, trying to get him on board for an important special issue. Jane had to be gratified that her convictions about Kurt's success were turning out to be true.

Things were going well. Kurt had stories in *Collier's* in January and February. He had rewritten "Mnemonics," his story about the company man with the great memory, and finally he got it right. The breakthrough came when he got rid of Alfred's wife and introduced his secretary as a secret love interest. Then he changed all of the mental pictures Alfred Moorhead uses to boost his memory from images of violence and war to images of Hollywood starlets holding, wearing, or straddling mnemonic devices. When, for instance, he has to remember to check that Davenport Spot-Welding and Davenport Wire and Cable have not been confused in his invoices, he imagines Lana Turner in a leopard-print sheath and Jane Russell in a telegram-sarong lying on opposing davenports. At the end, Kurt added a parade of beauties that Alfred thinks up when he has to remember a really long to-do list: when he has checked off the list and one image remains, he grabs her lustily, thinking she's in his head.

"Now, baby," he says to her, "what's on *your* mind?" The woman turns out to be his secretary, who murmurs, "Well, praise be, you finally remembered *me*."

With the elimination of all its sadism—the part Knox said left a bad taste in one's mouth—the story changed from an outburst of rage at cubicle conformity to a slightly silly office sexcapade. But what the hell? For the equivalent of a third of a year's salary at GE, *Collier's* could have all the libidinous diversions its editors wanted. He also sent Kenneth a slight but effective romance called "Little Drops of Water." It was the sort of thing the agent—and the market—liked: a story about a commitment-averse bachelor who loves his predictable single life, and the clever girl who gets him to propose by slowly making herself an indispensable—if annoying—part of his daily routine. It had a spirited, light tone and a happy—but not sappy—ending.

Then he wrote "Happy Birthday, 1951" from the part of him that brooded about war, that couldn't help but feel glum every time he read news of Korea or the Cold War or America trouncing the godless communists. Set in an almost mythic world of endless war, it described how an old man who has raised an abandoned baby through seven years of fighting comes to realize that the child he nurtured knows nothing of peacetime life. It was fast-paced and efficient and had a peach of an ending, a sharp, startling exchange on the boy's birthday that summed up, in a few words, the point: if we build a militaristic world, war is all that kids will know or care to know. Kenneth would say it was gloomy, but that was okay. One of these days, he was going to be able to write exactly what he wanted to write.

In fact now, over drinks with Knox, he was being invited to join a project that was just the sort of thing he wanted to do: a special issue of *Collier's* dedicated to demonstrating the madness and futility of war. It was going to make a big splash, Knox said, with top-notch writers already on board: Edward R. Murrow, Arthur Koestler, Robert Sherwood, maybe even John Steinbeck or William Faulkner. And Knox wanted to place Kurt among them.

The *Collier's* editors hadn't decided what to call it yet, and the whole thing was shrouded in secrecy. In office memos and conversations with potential writers, they referred to it by code name: Operation Eggnog.

On the spot, Kurt pitched Knox on an idea for a story about a cabinetmaker in occupied Czechoslovakia. He is making a booby-trapped desk for the Russian commandant in charge of his town, but when the Americans take over, the cabinetmaker continues making the same deadly desk for the new captain: Russian, American—it doesn't matter to him. One occupier is as bad as another. Knox thought it sounded promising.

Kurt Vonnegut Jr., as Knox had predicted to Kenneth Littauer, was turning out to be quite a skillful craftsman of salable short stories. Knox had finally bought "Mnemonics" and "Bockman's Euphoria," now titled "The Euphio Question," and another story, "The Foster Portfolio," was already in his hands. Knox had even offered to talk to book editors about Kurt's novel. His career was finally taking off.

When Kurt and Jane arrived back in Alplaus, they realized the next step was clear. They were free to go wherever they wanted, to find a community better suited to the artistic life they craved. Why should they stay on in GE's orbit, shuffling around to Junior League balls and corporate clambakes? They could cut themselves loose from Schenectady altogether and drift in an ocean of possibility.

They put their house up for sale.

Fired up by the trip and the prospect of moving, Kurt was awash in inspiration. He wrote to Knox about another idea he had for Operation Eggnog. He could write a short-short about Dresden. Not just about Dresden, but about the morality—or lack of morality—in saturation bombing of civilians. Knox wrote back to say that it sounded a little risky: "Mr. A would shy away from the notion." This was a light way of pointing out that Edward Anthony, the publisher of *Collier's*, was more conservative than Kurt realized. *Collier's* was not, as Kurt seemed to think, putting together another "Hiroshima." The high, sane, and cheerful ideal of American citizenship was still where it set its sights, even when it came to nuclear war.

Just focus on the carpenter story, Knox advised. Maybe Kurt could slip something about saturation bombing in there.

Just over a week later, Kurt sent a completed draft, titled "The Commandant's Desk," to Knox. He also told Knox the good news: he and Jane were leaving Schenectady. They were going to move to somewhere on the Atlantic coast. They hadn't decided where yet, but they both wanted to be near the ocean. As a trial run, they were going to rent a house in Provincetown, Massachusetts, for the whole summer. Kurt invited Knox to come visit them there.

He was on a roll. Putting his house on the market gave him such a kick he sat down and cranked out a marketable story in just one day. Called "Build Thee More Stately Mansions," it was about a woman who lives in squalor but obsessively clips ideas from home decor magazines and redecorates her house in her head. When she is hospitalized, her husband redecorates to surprise her, following her clippings exactly. But upon returning, she doesn't even notice what he's done. To her, the house looks just the way she's always seen it.

Kenneth liked the story and sent it off to Knox right away. Before long, Kurt wrote to Knox again, this time with news that his house had sold, at a profit. Knox congratulated him, then urged him to get down to editing "The Commandant's Desk." The characters were not complex enough—the Czech too noble, the American major too villainous. In other words, the story was too simplistic, too blunt an antiwar instrument. The purpose of Operation Eggnog was not simply to warn the world about the dangers of nuclear war. *Collier's* intended to convey that nuclear war should be avoided, but if one occurred, the United States was going to win.

Knox didn't explicitly say what Kurt should have known: times were changing. The nation was at war again. It was possible the United States would use nuclear weapons in Korea. It was getting increasingly important to come down hard on communism and to squelch any doubt about American virtue, even when it came to the use of superweapons. The Atomic Energy Commission was ramping up its research programs, the United States was constructing an atomic proving ground in Nevada, and the military had just begun a new round of atomic tests in the Pacific that many speculated were going to demonstrate the feasibility of the hydrogen bomb. The time for asking whether America should have dropped the atomic bomb was over. The time for talking up America's atomic supremacy had begun.

•

"You say here that 'We are of the opinion that the Weather Bureau should continue to be responsible for leadership in this field,'" Senator Clinton Anderson of New Mexico queried the witness. Willard McDonald, assistant chief of the Weather Bureau, sat on the witness stand looking cranky. His prepared statement had been interrupted.

"How much has been done in the knowledge of rainmaking by the Weather Bureau?" Anderson prodded. "I am just trying to find out whether you have leadership or whether the private rainmakers in General Electric have leadership."

"They have leadership in advertising," McDonald shot back.

That was surprising. Bernie was sitting right there in the room, with Vincent and Guy Suits, listening to McDonald take potshots at Project Cirrus—but advertising? Even for the Weather Bureau, that was a low blow. But McDonald was agitated. Senator Anderson, committee chairman, was treating him as a hostile witness.

The Senate hearings pertained to three bills introduced in Congress. The main questions behind all three were the same. Should the federal government conduct research in weather modification? Should it regulate the weather modification work of private enterprises? And if the government did get involved, which agency should be in charge—the Department of the Interior? Agriculture? Or Commerce—meaning the Weather Bureau?

New Mexico was suffering a debilitating drought, and Senator Anderson was very much in favor of anything that would forward the cause of weather modification and help him get his constituents more rain. Or at least redirect some research dollars so he could tell his constituents he was getting them more rain. Anderson's sidekick was Senator Francis Case of South Dakota. That state's western half was also parched, so Senator Case, too, was a fan of cloud seeding. He had even taken it upon himself to fill a cottage cheese container with dry ice, hire a pilot, and fly around the state seeding clouds from the airplane window with a teacup. Whenever he saw rain, he had his pilot land at the nearest ranch, where he explained that he was responsible.

Neither senator was going to let Assistant Chief McDonald get away with scoffing at the work of GE. Senator Anderson demanded to know if the Weather Bureau had come up with the idea of using silver iodide to make rain. McDonald had to admit it had not.

"Who has leadership, that is what I am trying to find out," Anderson insisted. "Who does have leadership in the field?"

"Are we talking about leadership in advertising or leadership in science?" the assistant chief stubbornly replied.

This was turning out to be far more interesting than Bernie could have expected when he and the others arrived in room 224 of the Senate Building. But they weren't surprised by Senator Anderson's tone. The politician had been briefed. In November, he had visited Schenectady, where he had gone over the proposed bills with Guy Suits and spent an hour with Irving, Vince, and Bernie discussing their work in New Mexico. Like so many others who encountered the charismatic Langmuir, Anderson had come away a believer. Now he was openly scoffing at the idea of putting the Weather Bureau in charge of weather control experiments.

"It would be like turning over the development of the atomic bomb to some group that says 'We will try it but we know it cannot be built,'" he declared.

"Mr. Chairman, you certainly are putting words in our mouths," protested McDonald.

Senator Anderson then turned to his fellow committee member Senator Case to ask whether he had received any Weather Bureau assistance for his own "rainmaking" program—his tempests dispensed from a teacup—in South Dakota. Needless to say, Senator Case had not.

"Did the Weather Bureau evaluate those results?" demanded Anderson of the assistant chief.

"I presume not," replied a dour McDonald. Did they really expect the bureau to take seriously some barnstorming senator heaving dry ice from a Cessna? "I do not know whether that particular experiment came to our attention or not."

Anderson began talking about the amount of silver iodide being sprayed into the air, accusing the bureau of being uninterested in finding out whether the activity was having any effect on the nation's climate. McDonald objected to the presumption that silver iodide was doing anything. This allowed Anderson to accuse the bureau of obstructionism.

"I do not claim that spraying silver iodide into the air produces rainfall," the senator said at one point, "but I say if you spray it on Friday and it rains on Saturday, and you spray it on Friday and it rains on Saturday and you do that for 20 straight weeks, I begin to say to myself there might be some connection. The Weather Bureau says you can't prove it and therefore there is not any."

"Senator," McDonald shot back, "I think that line of connection is just as reasonable as to say because the washerwomen hang out their clothes generally on Monday and it rains on Wednesday, that there is a connection between those two things."

"If that were true, you could," interjected another senator.

"That is exactly why I question the advisability of turning over any money to the Weather Bureau," declared Anderson triumphantly. "You see where the trouble is."

McDonald tried to object that he was not suggesting there was absolutely no connection between the silver iodide and rainfall.

"You just got through saying that it was like hanging out the wash on Monday and it raining on Wednesday," Anderson shot back.

"As far as connection is concerned, it might be as remote as that," McDonald replied.

"Then, that is an absolute statement on your part, that the silver iodide has nothing to do with the rainfall."

"No, sir," replied the beleaguered assistant chief, "that must not be considered so."

McDonald tried to return the discussion to the bureau's efforts to get at the truth of the matter, but once he had invited the washerwomen into the room, they wouldn't leave.

"I was just wondering," put in Senator Case, "if the women in a certain community all hung their wash on Monday for 20 consecutive weeks and if then on 20 consecutive Wednesdays it did rain, would the Weather Bureau feel that there was no relationship between the two?"

"You know where we would stand seriously on a question like that?" McDonald said, stoically forging ahead as laughter rippled through the chamber. "We would want to try that for more than 20 weeks, because we know in weather—it is not as funny as it may sound—we know that in weather strange repetitions, strange sequences are so common, and there are repetitions back in history of unaffected weather, weather prior to any of these things being introduced, and we will find weather patterns which are exactly like these patterns which occur after these things are begun. I think we are justified in a degree of conservative agnosticism, if you please. It is not skepticism. It is agnosticism. We do not know."

"The question is," put in Senator Guy Cordon from Oregon, another state where rainmakers were feverishly attacking the clouds on behalf of farmers, "are you interested in finding out?"

McDonald talked about statistics and evidence, insisting that there still wasn't enough proof to presume that cloud seeding worked.

"We would not want to draw a hasty conclusion at all," he declared. "It is not our way of doing business."

"I am sure of that," responded Anderson. After pushing McDonald to admit how little money the bureau had spent researching the topic, the senator dismissed the Weather Bureau representative. McDonald had become so upset at one point he had pounded the table with his fist. That was simply not done at Senate hearings. It was a PR disaster for the Weather Bureau.

The General Electric scientists now took their seats at the witness table, and the committee's tone immediately changed from combative to fawning. Senator Anderson seemed eager to get certain facts into the record right off. He asked Guy Suits to verify that Bernie had originated the silver iodide method of cloud seeding.

"Does he have in his statement how many products he had to check before he got down to finding one?" the senator asked. Suits said he didn't think Bernie did.

"How many did you check, Dr. Vonnegut?" Anderson queried.

Bernie demurred. "I personally have checked very few products," he said. "Schaefer has checked a great number and so have other investigators." But the senator was not having any of Bernie's modesty.

"Did you not go through about 1,300 before you came down to one?" he insisted.

"What I did was to look in the handbook for a compound having a particular property and there were 1,900 listed," Bernie replied. "I just looked through the list until I found one that looked right. I did not try the 1,900. I just looked at them."

"That is pretty good evidence," declared the senator, determined to get Bernie's achievement into the record, "that you did not waste time."

Guy Suits read his statement first. He compared weather modification to the atomic bomb in its importance to the nation. He showed photographs, calling them "irrefutable" visual evidence of cloud-seeding results. He listed Langmuir's credentials and declared that Irving was having "the time of his life" in the scientific dispute over rainmaking. If he lost this argument, it would be a first. "I place my bets on Langmuir," Suits declared. Avoiding the subject of regulation, he expressed support for Senate Bill 222, the only bill under consideration that would limit the legal liability of government contractors doing weather modification research.

After Suits, Vince read his prepared statement. He went a little further than Suits had in declaring the desirability of establishing a federal commission to launch a research program in rainmaking. He pointed out the importance of knowing what kinds of weather modification activities were taking place and suggested that it would be better to license rainmakers than to try to control the field.

When he was finished, Senator George Smathers of Florida waded into dangerous territory.

"Mr. Chairman, have not experiments been conducted in attempting to dissipate hurricanes?" he asked. "It seems to me I recall down off Puerto Rico, about a year or so ago, the Air Forces from Orlando, in conjunction with scientists, attempted to break up a hurricane heading toward Florida, and, I might add, without success."

"First of all," Vince quickly said, "I would like to correct a misconception here. I was on that flight, and the main reason we made the flight was to see what a hurricane was made up of on top. With their supercooled clouds, how many supercooled clouds were there; could those clouds be changed? We did not try to break up the hurricane."

The senators bantered among themselves about the vaguely remembered hurricane and whether it was headed toward Florida or away from it. No one seemed to recall Hurricane King's dramatic change of direction, and Vince did not remind them of it. He told them that the team had waited until the hurricane was far out to sea and had then conducted a localized seeding. Asked what the results were, he stuck to the company script and said he didn't know. Guy Suits interjected to point out that no one would conduct hurricane research without the liability provisions proposed in Bill 222.

"Dr. Suits," asked Senator Anderson, "was it not true that the hurricane, if it subsequently turned back toward the United States and it had destroyed property, it might have been a very expensive procedure for General Electric?"

Guy Suits did not point out that the hurricane had done just that.

"That is right," he said.

Doubling down on the rewriting of history, Vincent jumped in again.

"It so happens that we did not conduct the experiments," he said, "but nevertheless I concur in the need for much further studies of this very important problem."

Vince then ceded the hot seat to Bernie.

Bernie had written his statement carefully. He was going further than either Guy Suits or Vince had gone. He got right to the point. Cloud-seeding techniques, he declared, were going to make it possible to extend considerable control over the weather for the nation's good. But in order to make sure this power was used for good and not evil, regulation was necessary.

"Despite a strong personal dislike of restrictions and regulations," he declared, "I am convinced that in order to achieve these benefits, cloud seeding must be placed under strict Federal regulation. The problems of weather control are so large and of such nationwide importance that only Federal legislation can ensure that this powerful new tool will result in the greatest good for the largest number of people."

It was a tricky thing, asking for federal regulation. It made you look like someone who wanted a planned economy. That was the sort of thing that got you branded a Red. He needed to make it clear that he had good reasons.

"In the absence of this legislation, I believe that the development of the benefits to be derived from cloud seeding may be greatly retarded or prevented and that possibly much harm can result from storms, droughts, or floods produced by uncontrolled seeding."

He proposed that the federal government provide funds for research and that the research not be classified but be freely shared with other scientists. That was even more dangerous territory, speaking out, if subtly, against military control of the science. Part of what got Edward Condon and other scientists investigated by HUAC was outspoken support for civilian control of atomic energy and for the creation of a national science foundation to move research out of the military sphere and back into civilian hands. Condon had won the battle with HUAC, but at great personal cost. Others were not so lucky.

Bernie stepped into this minefield with care. He was a supporter of regulation, in fact, but he couched his claim in a "strong personal dislike," making himself sound more conservative than he actually was. He made a point of exempting dry ice seeding from federal control, though he gently recommended licensing it. He patiently explained to the puzzled senators that the effects of dry ice were localized, while the effects of silver iodide could persist for hundreds or even thousands of miles.

"The potentialities, both for good and bad, which attend silver iodide seeding are so large that the development and use of this technique must be placed in the hands of the Federal Government," he said.

A senator asked him about clouds. Whom did they belong to—the state, the nation, the people? To Bernie it must have seemed like a dumb question: clouds weren't *things* that could be construed as property. But he couldn't insult the senator. Nor could he say that clouds belonged to the nation or the people without sounding as if he were advocating nationalization.

"I think I am a poor one to ask a question like that," Bernie demurred, "because my training is primarily scientific and I would not venture a legal opinion."

Senator Lester Hunt, who had asked the question, was from Wyoming, whose legislature had just declared sovereignty over its atmosphere.

"Last year, South Dakota had some very profitable experiments in rain making," Senator Hunt noted. "We think they stole some of our water, maybe."

"I might say that the prevailing winds, though, are generally from the northwest," put in Senator Case of South Dakota, implying that if his state stole anyone's water, it was Iowa's.

This was just the sort of problem that was going to become common if the government didn't regulate rainmaking. But wisely, Bernie stayed out of the rain-rustling dispute. Completing his statement, he pointed out the difficulty of regulating cloud-seeding operations, suggesting that perhaps the best method would be simply "to make it clear to the public that operations of this sort are contrary to their own best interests and to the country as a whole."

Bernie must have been relieved when he headed back to Schenectady that day. He had managed to tread lightly on the delicate issues of civilian control and federal regulation while conveying his concern for how his invention might be used if it fell into the wrong hands.

The hearings went on for two more days, continuing to be less a debate about the need for regulation than a forum on the efficacy of cloud seeding. The senators brought in a slew of rainmakers and treated them with great courtesy. Irving Krick was given a whole day for his testimony, during which he expounded on his own successes. Wallace Howell told the subcommittee his rainmaking had probably increased rainfall in New York's watershed by 14 percent. Weather modification skeptics, on the other hand, were grilled aggressively. The young professor Irving had insulted at the MIT symposium, Charles Hosler, tried to argue that cloud-seeding results should be proved and verified in the lab before any outdoor experiments were made.

"How did you feel about the atomic bomb?" he was asked. Things got even worse when he suggested that seeding was "more or less like praying. It seems to be, at this point, a matter of faith." When the senators pointed out that many esteemed scientists believed they had seen it happen, Hosler made a grave error.

"I saw a man pull a rabbit out of a hat once, and he did it by saying two funny words, and I cannot prove otherwise," he snapped. "Therefore, I think we should have legislation to produce rabbits and send the meat to India."

Senators do not take kindly to being mocked. Hosler was not allowed to speak again after that.

At the end of day three, Vincent returned to show time-lapse photographs of clouds being seeded, then expanding into thunderheads and pouring down rain. For many of the senators, that clinched it. Rainmaking had to be real: they were seeing it happen. Guy Suits invited them all to come to Schenectady for more demonstrations. GE would provide a plane.

But after the hearings ended, the subcommittee received a letter from a witness with a different position: the Department of Defense. Its letter commenting on all three bills was far from skeptical about the possibility of weather control. But it nevertheless came out firmly against regulating weather modification in any way. The implications were clear: the military services were planning to conquer the atmosphere. And it would be easier to do that in the absence of legal constraints.

•

Ilium fuit; Troja est.

It was the motto of Troy, New York, the manufacturing town near Schenectady: "Ilium was; Troy is."

Kurt was not concerned with what was or what is. He was writing about what might be.

"Ilium, New York, is divided into three parts," he wrote, invoking the famous opening line of Julius Caesar's *Conquest of Gaul.* This was going to be a serious novel.

"In the northwest are the managers and engineers and civil servants and a few professional people; in the northeast are the machines; and in the south, across the Iroquois River, is the area known locally as Homestead, where almost all of the people live."

He saw it as an American version of Arthur Koestler's *Darkness at Noon,* another portrait of a man imprisoned for treason by a state he had helped create.

The protagonist of *Player Piano* is the plant manager of the Ilium Works, a "triangle of steel and masonry buildings" where "machines hummed and whirred and clicked, and made parts for baby carriages and bottle caps, motorcycles and refrigerators, television sets and tricycles—the fruits of peace." The Ilium Works was once a private factory but now, like all factories, is under control of the National Manufacturing Council, administered from the central planning office, its every baby carriage and bottle cap built according to specifications and quotas set by EPICAC, the computer in charge of the entire economy—and really the entire government.

Aldous Huxley's *Brave New World* was about a horrific future world where genetically identical human beings are manufactured in test tubes and brainwashed to conform to their castes in a strict social hierarchy. George Orwell's *1984* was about a horrific future world divided into party members and downtrodden proles, with submission to groupthink enforced by a sadistic surveillance state and endless war. Kurt Vonnegut's *Player Piano* would be about a horrific future world where world peace has been achieved, hunger and privation banished, and nothing more awful has happened to people than that machines are now doing their jobs.

Kurt named his main character Paul Proteus. *Doctor* Paul Proteus. The name echoed that of the early genius of Schenectady, the man who knew where to chalk the X on a broken generator: Charles Proteus Steinmetz. Dr. Paul Proteus is a poor man's Steinmetz: he's smart, but not nearly as smart as his illustrious father, Dr. George Proteus, the "first National Industrial, Commercial, Communications, Foodstuffs, and Resources Director, a position approached in importance only by the presidency of the United States." But Paul is well respected and affluent, part of the technological elite, so he should be happy. The war that had racked the world had been won with the help of the machines: "Democracy owed its life to know-how." But the start of the novel finds him feeling vaguely at odds with the world. Kurt wrote and rewrote several openings. In the one he settled on, Paul has found a cat in the Works and is trying to adopt it—ostensibly to catch mice among the machines. His desire for the cat, emblematic of his longing for life and connection in the midst of his sterile technological domain, comes to a bad end when the cat flees a machine and dies on the plant's electric fence.

Paul is preparing a speech for the anniversary of the plant's take-over by the National Manufacturing Council. His ambitious wife, Anita, is hoping his speech will help forward his promotion to the position of manager of the Pittsburgh plant. But for Paul, the speech is a chance to air some of the doubts that have been creeping into his head about the world he and his fellow engineers have made. He puts a quotation into his speech: Norbert Wiener's claim that the second industrial revolution would devalue mental work.

His amorphous sense of dissatisfaction draws Paul to Homestead, the side of town where those not smart enough to obtain graduate degrees live. Unable to compete with the machines economically, people of merely average intelligence are given a choice: join the Army or work in the Reconstruction and Reclamation Corps—known as Reeks and Wrecks. There's little interaction between them and the elite managers. But Paul keeps finding himself returning to Homestead's shoddy saloon, with its rinky-dink player piano. There, encountering the people's longing for purpose, he nurses the nagging feeling that something about the system is just not right.

Paul's pretense to normalcy begins to unravel when his old pal Ed Finnerty shows up. Paul idolizes Finnerty: his brilliant friend "might have been an architect or physician or writer." Lately, Ed has been working for the National Industrial Planning Board in Washington, a prestigious job, but he has a reputation as a rebel—a man insufficiently invested in the brave new technological world, not to mention too given to women, cars, and booze. And sure enough, soon after Finnerty arrives in Ilium, he announces that he's quit his job.

"Sick of it," he tells Paul. "I looked around me and found out I couldn't face anything about the system any more. I walked out, and here I am."

These two central characters have personalities reflecting two parts of Kurt himself: Paul, the guy who's doing his best to be the company man, and Ed, the rebel who uses messiness and irreverence as a rebuke to a society he can't respect.

In setting up his protagonist's dilemma—stay and work for a system he feels is somehow bad for humanity, or revolt and become a nonentity in the techno-utopian world order—Kurt recorded the details of life at GE that had irked him as vaguely yet insistently as Dr. Paul Proteus is irked. Like Schenectady, Ilium is a world divided into those with Ph.D.'s and those without them. It is a world of intense awareness of social rank and fervent adherence to convention and petty social rituals, such as competitiveness between color teams at the company's "orgy of morale building," an annual camp on an island called the Meadows to which the most promising young men are invited every year. The successful in this world possess, as Paul does not, as Kurt did not, "the ability to be moved emotionally, almost like a lover, by the great omnipresent and omniscient spook, the corporate personality." Above all, it is a world in which machines are established as more efficient than humans and are therefore assumed superior.

Recalling his feelings while looking at GE's motorized milling machine, Kurt wrote a scene where Paul fixes a group of automated lathe machines controlled by a magnetic tape loop on which "were recorded the movements of a master machinist turning out a shaft for a fractional horsepower motor." Paul thinks back to when he and Finnerty were sent to make a recording of the best machinist for the tape loop, and he remembers the man's name—Rudy Hertz. "This was the essence of Rudy as far as his machine was concerned," Paul thinks.

As a counterpoint to GE's techno-utopianism, Kurt imported many ideas from Norbert Wiener's *Cybernetics*. Speculating in his book about the inevitable chess-playing computer, Wiener admitted that it would play an optimum game according to the logic of von Neumann's game theory. But, he wondered, would it "offer interesting opposition to a player at one of the many levels at which human chess players find themselves"? Kurt played out that scenario in a scene where a group of young executives in training challenge Paul to a game of checkers. As Ilium's undisputed checkers champion, he accepts with pleasure—until he realizes that he is being pitted against a machine called Checker Charley. Angrily, Paul tries to concede.

"I can't win against the damn thing. It can't make a mistake," he tells Anita when she tries to intercede. He eventually agrees to play and wins, but only because Checker Charley has a loose connection and catches fire.

In *Cybernetics*, Wiener describes a machine that performs a human function as a kind of mechanical slave. "Any labor that accepts the conditions of competition with slave labor," he declares, "accepts the conditions of slave labor, and is essentially slave labor."

"What have you got against machines?" one character asks another in *Player Piano*.

"They're slaves."

"What the heck . . . I mean, they aren't people. They don't suffer. They don't mind working."

"No, but they compete with people."

"But that's a pretty good thing, isn't it—considering what a sloppy job most people do of anything?"

"Anybody that competes with slaves becomes a slave," the first man replies.

As Kurt saw it, Wiener's questions should be asked more in Schenectady. So he created a fictional Schenectady—Ilium—and put a Wienerian protagonist in it. Paul had helped to create something wonderful—a society without inefficiency or privation. But he had failed to foresee its potential for damage, because he, and his entire culture, had been careless about upholding human values. They had been too spellbound by their shiny, mechanical toys, too enthralled by their exciting new science to consider its effect on real human lives.

•

Bernie had drawn a map of the United States. He was shading in vast portions of the West. Those were the areas where silver iodide was filling the air.

Vince had been writing to the commercial rainmakers, trying to find out how many acres they had under contract. Weather Modification Incorporated. North American Weather Consultants. Water Resources Development Corporation. The Range Development Company. Snow Incorporated. The explosion of private, for-profit rainmaking operations was startling. Around 10 percent of the nation was now under commercial cloud-seeding contracts, almost all in the arid West. Pretty soon, every cloud from the Rockies to the West Coast would be sprayed with silver iodide or shot full of dry ice.

It wasn't surprising really. Precipitation for profit was an obvious outgrowth of the Project Cirrus research. It came from the same entrepreneurial spirit that aimed to put a GE refrigerator in every kitchen, a GE lightbulb in every socket. Consumers wanted GE rain on every field, GE snow on every ski slope, and until GE was willing to provide it, others would. So the world raced headlong to embrace every new thing under the sun that might lead to material gain.

Project Cirrus had been formed with the idea of benefiting humanity: ranchers could improve their rangeland, utilities could make cheaper power, farmers could divert the hailstorms that caused $15 million worth of crop damage every year. But it was clear to Bernie that there had to be some oversight. Otherwise, they were never going to know what was happening up in the skies. How could they even trust the results of their own experiments? For all they knew, out-of-control cloud seeding might mean human beings were changing the whole climate.

Case in point: massive floods in the heartland. Kansas and Missouri had been hit by unprecedented rains in May, June, and July. The Kansas, Osage, Neosho, Verdigris, and Missouri Rivers all jumped their banks, causing damages of around $1 billion. Both state capitals— Topeka and Jefferson City—were devastated. Manhattan, Kansas, was drowning in eight feet of water. In Kansas City, levees were topped, and factories, warehouses, and stockyards were washed away. Ten thousand farms lost their topsoil. Twenty-eight people were dead.

Senator James Kem of Missouri visited the GE offices in July looking for answers. Irving, typically unconcerned with the ramifications, swiftly declared that the heavy rains had probably been caused by cloud seeding. Vince and Bernie were more circumspect. They felt it was impossible to establish direct causality yet but agreed that the floods should be investigated by competent meteorologists. Senator Kem asked them to draft a statement about regulation for him to use in the next round of congressional debates over rainmaking, the ones that would be closed to the public. Meanwhile, the governor of New Mexico summoned Jack Workman to Santa Fe and told him to turn off the Project

Cirrus generators or lose state funds for the School of Mines: New Mexico could not risk being liable for drowning two other states. Irving thought this was an excellent idea: if the periodicity ended when the seeding did, it would further prove his results. But the Army Signal Corps did not want to stop the experiment.

As the possibility of legislation loomed, the military was getting increasingly involved. A meeting was called of the Research and Development Board—part of the new Department of Defense—to discuss military applications of weather control. Guy Suits telegrammed Langmuir, who was in Hawaii at the invitation of the Pineapple Research Institute, and asked him to come home early to attend. But when Irving got to Schenectady, Suits told him that the board didn't want him there after all. Vincent went to the meeting instead. Langmuir decided he would independently prepare a report for the military on the periodicities.

This was not the life of research Bernie had envisioned. Leaving graduate school and taking a job at Hartford-Empire, he'd figured he would spend the rest of his life playing around with glass, helping to make better beer bottles or fog-free mirrors. Then, during the war, someone had shown him the atmosphere. It seemed like a neat problem, figuring out what made the natural world work the way it did. But now his life was wrapped up in hearings and controversies and contracts and behind-the-scenes intrigue, even as he spent his days trying to figure out if he had invented something that was causing major harm. His research had been intended to bring the benefits of water down from the sky, to create a kind of anti-Dresden, an anti-Hiroshima. An explosive showering of life, not death, from the clouds. Now the undersea warfare branch was negotiating with GE to have Bernie come work with it.

Bernie didn't want to spend the rest of his life making someone's dreams of undersea warfare come true.

Why shouldn't he just do something straightforward like make toys? He was an inventor; he always had been. His vortex whistle for measuring fluid flow and true air speed would make a good toy. He wrote to Guy Suits, asking for a release of patent on the vortex whistle just for musical instrument or toy applications. Suits wrote back denying the request. GE couldn't just go around releasing patents, he said, especially when it was part of a much larger patent application. Besides, getting involved with trying to develop and market some kind of toy would distract Bernie from what he should be doing. He should focus on the work at hand—by which Suits meant, do what GE wanted him to do.

•

Don't come to Provincetown, Jane implored her mother. Please don't come visit your daughter and grandkids.

Cape Cod had seemed like such a good idea. They would shed the tedium of the company town in a place that was its exact opposite, with wild scenery, wilder artists, cheap, shabbily gorgeous houses, and of course the ocean: the glassy bay on one side, the pounding surf on the other, and the little spit of bohemian paradise known as Provincetown in between. And it had worked. It had been an exhilarating summer. They met Norman Mailer at the beach and had cocktails with the young writer whose war novel *The Naked and the Dead* had made him a literary sensation. They reveled in books and paintings and jazz and freedom from everything Schenectady stood for: convention, the Junior League, the Mohawk Golf Club, the *Monogram*, the omnipresent, omnivorous company.

They hosted a family reunion—Bernie and Bow came with Peter and the twins, Scott and Terry. And Alice and Jim came toting the Adams gang: Jimbo, Steve, and Kurt. It was nice, as it always was when the three siblings got together—lots of talk, raucous laughter, beer, cigarettes, and that warm feeling of being a tribe. Kurt was finally living the life he wanted—a life chosen by him and not for him—and it was going well. Stories were selling steadily. Knox bought "More Stately Mansions" in June and "The Commandant's Desk" for Operation Eggnog in July, the same month that Scribner officially optioned *Player Piano*, the novel that was going to make his name. They lined all the kids up outside the house and took a picture, seven boys and one baby girl, their sun-streaked hair incandescent in the Provincetown sun. They were literally aglow with possibility.

What Kurt and Jane hadn't counted on was becoming a hotel. A house near the beach on Cape Cod, especially a charming, shake-shingled cottage on Commercial Street, steps from galleries, clubs, theaters, and beaches and blessed with four breezy bedrooms upstairs, was an irresistible enticement to scads of friends and acquaintances who suddenly just *had* to catch up with their old pals the Vonneguts.

Kurt and Jane had totted it up: they had ten days to themselves all summer. The rest of the time they played hosts, which meant getting good at a game they called "Get 'em plastered faster." The idea being, of course, that the sooner your friends were blotto, the sooner your husband could get back to writing the novel his publisher (oh, that did sound nice) was breathing down his neck to finish. The problem was, by the time one made all those martinis, one had sampled a few oneself, which meant no more writing that night, and the next morning would require a sluggish approach to the breakfast table, let alone the typewriter, through a martini haze. While the guests, of course, slept off their hangovers, oblivious to the fact that they were impeding the Progress of Literature.

Finally September came; their last guests were headed home, and Jane had written to everyone who threatened to come that month and told them to stay away, even her mother. She wanted to see her mother, naturally, but enough was enough! The last guests left just in time for Kurt and Jane to remember that they had less than a month to figure out where they were going to live, because their rental ended October 1.

They had expected to spend several weeks traversing the coast like vagabonds in search of a place to settle. But their wonderful summer narrowed it down for them: they wanted to stay on Cape Cod. The artistic, intellectual lifestyle, the natural beauty, the quaint villages, and the ever-present ocean—all of it fit the dreams they had hatched together years earlier. Provincetown, however, was a little remote, isolated on the very tip of the Cape, sixty miles from the mainland bridge. Kurt would probably need to fly to New York pretty frequently, to meet with editors and his agent, so they decided to start their search by looking for a place near Hyannis, which had an airport. And then, amazingly, they found a house in their first week of looking.

It wasn't their dream house. Jane had always dreamed of finding a wreck of a beach house or, better yet, a run-down old barn and turning it into a home. What they found instead was a spanking-new red ranch house in the town of Osterville, with a fenced-in backyard and a studio where Kurt could write. Aesthetically, it was not their style. Jane didn't even like writing the words "ranch house"—so dull, so cookie-cutter! But given that they had two small kids and a novel to finish posthaste, and the house—a model house, no less—needed no work, they decided it would suit them. Osterville seemed quaint, there was a good school in Hyannis, and best of all they could move in at the end of September. So with the same impulsiveness with which they had sold their Alplaus home, they bought the Osterville ranch house. Kurt could get down to work at last.

Actually, he had been getting more done than Jane's letter suggested. Kurt had managed to make all the revisions that Knox Burger requested on his Operation Eggnog story, "The Commandant's Desk," toning down the story's bitter antiwar tone. At Knox's suggestion, he had even rewritten the ending to make a point about the decency and sensitivity of the American occupiers. The galleys had arrived in August.

More important, Kurt had made real progress on *Player Piano*. Paul's story was moving inevitably toward the point where he would make his escape; he has already bought an old farm and is attempting, in secret, to learn how to live off the land. His increasingly antisocial activities have raised suspicions at the company, but his boss, Kroner, has suggested they tell the central office that Paul is working as a company mole, because there is a revolution brewing among the masses and the company wants to crush it.

Player Piano's shadowy underground movement is known as the Ghost Shirt Society—referencing the Native American religious uprising the Ghost Dance Society that Kurt had planned to write a thesis on at Chicago. The Works managers don't know much about it, but they suspect its headquarters are in Ilium. Once Paul is known to be a discontented manager, they hope to get him inside the Ghost Shirts as a spy. Paul goes along with the plan, although he has no intention of actually giving the company any information. Or does he? Is he a mole pretending to be a revolutionary or a revolutionary pretending to be a mole? Dr. Paul Proteus was developing into an interestingly complex character.

Kurt had an excellent new idea too: he would write a series of interchapter vignettes showing the lives of common Ilium people under the present technological regime. He thought they would give the novel a depth that one man's story alone might lack. The only problem was figuring out how to fit those sketches in. He could just insert them, maybe put them in italics. But it would be better to weave them in somehow so they didn't feel like an interruption. At some point during the summer, he had hit upon the perfect device. He would create a character, a luminary of sorts, and send him on a grand tour like that given the prime minister of Pakistan, Liaquat Ali Khan, in 1950. Just as the prime minister visited farms and schools and factories and of course Schenectady, Kurt's luminary would visit homes and factories and of course the Ilium Works. Maybe he'd even get to see EPICAC.

"The Shah of Bratpuhr, spiritual leader of 6,000,000 members of the Kolhouri sect," he began, "wizened and wise and dark as cocoa, encrusted with gold brocade and constellations of twinkling gems, sank deep into the royal-blue cushions of the limousine—like a priceless brooch in its gift box."

He had fun making up words for the shah's native language, drawing on his Chicago studies of linguistics. *Khabu* meant "where?" *Brahouna* meant "Live!" And *takaru* meant "slave": the shah is constantly mistaking American citizens for *takaru*. Kurt had the shah visit the same kinds of places the prime minister had—Army installations, a barbershop, even an average American home. He wrote humorous set pieces—the Army private's resentment, the family man's sad adulteries, the barber's interminable analysis of current affairs. He had particular fun with the character of the shah's tour guide from the State Department, Dr. Ewing J. Halyard, graduate of Cornell, as sartorially florid as he was occupationally stultified. But all that would change. Kurt had plans for Dr. Halyard. He might find out that his boring job is not as secure as he thinks.

All in all, *Player Piano* was coming along nicely, guests or no guests. Which was good, because in September, Kurt received some bad news from Knox Burger. Although it had already paid for the story, *Collier's* killed "The Commandant's Desk." He was kicked out of Operation Eggnog. Kurt figured he knew why: the magazine's conservative publisher, Edward Anthony, wasn't willing to risk running anything that could be construed as critical of the American army. Kurt had changed a story about the unrelieved awfulness of all wars and all occupations into a story about Americans as reluctant, but fair, occupiers. But his changes weren't enough. The tenor of the times—at least as *Collier's* saw it—had veered away from complexity and embraced dogmatism. So Knox had found something to replace "The Commandant's Desk," undoubtedly something anodyne and blandly patriotic. Kurt's political sentiments had lost him the most significant publication of his literary career to date.

He redoubled his work on *Player Piano*. It was growing difficult to ask the questions he thought needed asking in short stories for the slicks. The novel would put him on the map as a writer of serious literature.

10

Shifting Winds

Bernard entered the East Ballroom of the giant Curtis Hotel in downtown Minneapolis, his name tag stuck to his left lapel, and took his seat on the dais. The panel on cloud seeding at the October AMS meeting was packed. Members of the public as well as meteorologists crowded the room: Minnesota's farmers wanted to know how to make rain.

Joining Bernie to give papers that afternoon were Irving Krick, Wallace Howell, Robert Elliott, and Paul MacCready—commercial rainmakers, all of them. The only other serious researcher listed on the docket was Sol Resnick, a professor at Colorado A&M. But there was a last-minute addition to the roster—Herbert C. S. Thom, statistical expert from the Weather Bureau, added through bureau machinations.

Bernie was going to outline the construction of his spray-nozzle smoke generator for dispensing silver iodide. The commercial rainmakers were giving papers much more ambitious in scope. Wallace Howell was surveying methods of evaluating artificial rainmaking programs. Paul MacCready was reporting on fantastically successful cloud-seeding operations over ten thousand square miles of Arizona. Robert Elliott was showing time-lapse movies demonstrating the effects of using differing amounts of silver iodide. And Krick, in typically enterprising fashion, was holding forth on the topic most likely to interest the locals: the economic benefits of rainmaking, including dollar-for-dollar returns in crop yields and better grazing conditions that western farmers could expect if they hired someone like him.

After all that, Professor Resnick was going to report on a study showing that rainmaking didn't work, and Herbert Thom would denounce the methods of statistical analysis that suggested it did.

This was the absurd position Bernie found himself in. He wasn't one of the boosters, the salesmen who drove the Weather Bureau mad with their unsubstantiated claims. He wasn't even as big an advocate as Langmuir, who was now declaring that cloud seeding was probably causing most of the nation's weather glitches by altering cyclonic development. Langmuir had finally succeeded in getting the Project Cirrus generators in Socorro turned off and was expecting the periodicity to vanish, finally proving irrefutably that silver iodide was its cause.

But if Bernie wasn't an unthinking promoter, he wasn't a naysayer either, one of the people Irving called "wet blankets" who made it their mission to prove that rainmaking was hokum. Bernie believed that it probably worked and that they should quit bickering and get down to investigating possible unintended results. Because ever since the Great Plains floods, Bernie had been growing more alarmed.

Earlier that month, Bernie had voluntarily attended the Project Cirrus steering committee meeting. Afterward, he wrote a letter to the Signal Corps' Dr. Michael Ference, head of the committee. He had attended the meeting, he said, because he was concerned about the possible relationship between cloud seeding and floods. Langmuir was convinced there was a connection, and the Weather Bureau was convinced there wasn't. Bernie didn't quite know what to think, but he thought the floods that summer had been tragic. If they were preventable, it was even more tragic.

Bernie politely suggested that Project Cirrus release a measured statement. He thought it could be worded so that it simply pointed out potential dangers without provoking controversy. It was important that people racing to use this new technology understand that it might have unintended human consequences.

"Project Cirrus is supported by the public, and it seems to me that it is very clearly our responsibility to inform the public to the best of our ability," he wrote. "If we fail to do this now, and new floods occur which can possibly be attributed to the cloud seeding, I think we will right-fully share in the blame and deserve the harshest criticism."

The kind of criticism, that is, that he was reading in almost every story his brother wrote.

"I have taken the liberty of expressing my views to you despite the fact that I am not a member of the Steering Committee," Bernie wrote in closing, "because I feel I have a share in the responsibility involved."

He was sticking his neck out because he wanted to do what was right. He wouldn't let love of his invention blind him to his duty to humanity.

Bernie still loved the science. But here in Minneapolis, it was more obvious than ever that the very topic of rainmaking caused people to behave in completely unscientific ways. They either became fanatical crusaders or closed-minded skeptics. They either hoped to profit from it before the science was complete or refused to believe any science that didn't fit with their preconceived ideas. Where were the calm voices of reason that might keep real harm from being done?

It was not unlike what was going on in the nation, in the world in fact. Russia was evil, and America was good. Or, if you were Russian, the Soviet Union was good, and America was evil. Politics was not even a battleground anymore; it had become a kind of puppet theater where caricatures of goodness browbeat caricatures of evil, and no one wanted to hear the more complex story told.

Science—real science—was always a complex story. It was rare for things to be black-and-white, for evidence to be irrefutable and results to be obvious to all. Science was a conversation; it was the back-and-forth dialogue that mattered. When the dialogue degenerated into fanaticism and politics, it no longer functioned as science. Finding the truth and mapping the best course of action became impossible.

Bernie gave his paper on the spray-nozzle generator to the assembled meteorologists and farmers. He would publish it, giving co-authorship to Kiah Maynard. But it would be his last published paper on making rain.

•

Collier's special issue, "Preview of the War We Do Not Want," hit news-stands in late October. The cover depicted a sorrowful but grimly determined American MP standing in front of a colorful map of the Soviet Union. The word "occupied" was stamped on the Ukraine, and a UN flag was planted on Moscow. The list of writers underneath the picture was impressive: Robert Sherwood, Arthur Koestler, Walter Winchell, Edward R. Murrow, J. B. Priestley, Philip Wylie. It would have been nice to see Kurt Vonnegut Jr. among them. But in the place of "The Commandant's Desk" was a limp story by John Savage called "Trouble at Tuaviti," in which a brave American missionary and his loyal Pacific Islanders foil a Soviet sneak attack.

Kurt read the issue with growing distaste. The whole magazine treated atomic war as something that could be won—that *would* be won, naturally, by the United States. And then everything would come out okay in the end, because for America everything always did. The issue was lavishly illustrated: Washington, D.C., after a nuclear bomb assault; parachutists dropping into the Ural Mountains; Grand Central Terminal after a bombing; women packing a Moscow stadium for the first post-Soviet fashion show—because of course after atomic war has devastated the planet, the first thing a woman's mind turns to is hemlines and hats. *Collier's* must be raking in the profits, because the issue was packed with advertising: General Motors, Body by Fisher, Pall Mall, Pabst Blue Ribbon, Firestone, Frigidaire, and of course GE, using the prospect of World War III to sell washing machines.

Kurt particularly disliked Philip Wylie's story, "Philadelphia Phase," a sentimental love triangle between an American officer, his blue-blooded girlfriend, and a Russian immigrant, set in a nuclear-war-ravaged Philly. It turns out the Russian girl has been made sterile by radiation, so she kills herself, leaving the hero to go back to his Main Line sweetheart. Boy gets girl, even amid the inconvenience of atomic holocaust.

"The Commandant's Desk" had been true to the grating inhumanity of war and the moral hazards of occupation. It had treated soldiers as complicated human beings and war as a threat to our better selves. That, Kurt knew, was why his name wasn't flying off the newsstands with the rest of them.

But he couldn't spend time worrying about it. He had more important work to do. Scribner's Harry Brague, who was editing *Player Piano*, had written to say that he loved the new inserts about the shah of Bratpuhr. He assured Kurt that this was going to be a good novel, a novel Scribner would be proud to publish. And while not pressuring him exactly—the publisher did want him to write the best book he could—he informed Kurt that in order to make the spring list, the book needed to be in Scribner's hands by November 15. That was less than a month away, and there was still quite a lot to go. Paul Proteus had come to his crossroads, the place where he would have to decide whether he was a company man or a rebel. He would either inform on the revolution or join it.

When he started the novel, Kurt had not known what Paul would do. He had made several outlines. Ed Finnerty would become a revolutionary, but Paul would side with the machines. Or Finnerty would rebel, and Paul would reluctantly testify against him. Or Finnerty would persuade Paul to join the revolution, and Anita would testify against Ed to get Paul back.

By October, he had made up his mind. He was going further than any of his previous endings. Dr. Paul Proteus, having quit his job, would accept the role of leader of the revolution and would refuse to inform on his fellow rebels, even though he would lose everything for it—his wife, career, friends, status.

It was his first scientist character since Professor Barnhouse who would refuse to let love of his invention blind him to his duty to humanity.

He brought it all to a head at the Meadows. Here was a chance to expose the absurdity of Camp General Electric, that craven corporate pep rally on Association Island, and he used all the ammunition he had. The men arrive at the island by boat, just as in real life. They line up for flag-raising ceremonies under the old oak—counterpart to GE's treasured elm. They are divided into four color teams and attend a play that seems to be directly based on Lemuel Boulware's skit for 1948, the summer Vince Schaefer and the News Bureau's Roger Hammond attended. The loudspeaker at the Meadows blasts songs from the Association Island songbook.

As he wrote the Meadows section, Kurt wove in two new storylines that were also rooted in his GE experience. In one, Dr. Ewing Halyard of the State Department gets a letter informing him that he never completed his physical education requirements at Cornell, invalidating his undergraduate degree. With no bachelor's degree, "he had never been entitled to his Ph.D., his classification numbers, or, more to the point, to his pay check." Halyard is put on probation until he can make up the missing credits. He goes to Cornell, only to discover that the head of the athletic department is still angry about a letter Halyard wrote to the alumni magazine complaining about the football team's rowdy postgame behavior at an establishment called Club Cybernetics. The coach takes his opportunity for payback, flunking Halyard on his PE exam. Halyard will never get his degree, and he will lose his job because of it.

In another section, the shah of Bratpuhr experiences a bout of lust. He begins shouting untranslated but obviously indecent suggestions to women from the window of his limousine: *"Pitty fit-fit, sibi Takaru? Niki fit-fit. Akka sahn nibo fit-fit, simi Takaru?"* A reluctant Halyard prepares to play pimp; he's done it before. But then a woman hearing the shah's catcalls agrees to get in the car. She seems like a normal American housewife, and Halyard tries to tell her that she has made a mistake. The woman says she knows exactly what she's doing. "He was asking for something, wasn't he?" Halyard says yes. "There's been no misunderstanding," she tells them. She has agreed to prostitute herself because her husband has been fired. Four days earlier he had the classification number W-441, or "fiction novice." He turned in a book that was beautifully written, but twenty-seven pages too long, almost ten points above the acceptable "readability quotient," and with an anti-machine theme.

"So he was ordered into public-relations duty," she concludes.

"So the story has a happy ending after all," Halyard says.

"Hardly. He refused," the wife tells them. Halyard is shocked that a man would rather have his wife prostitute herself than go into public relations. "I'm proud to say," the woman replies, "that he's one of the few men on earth with a little self-respect left."

That was him, of course, the novel bending back on itself to suggest that *Player Piano* might be the very book—twenty-seven pages too long, ten points beyond readability, with an anti-machine theme—written by a writer husband who despises PR. It was the first of Vonnegut's many surprise cameos—Hitchcock-like—in his own novels. Together the two tangential stories—Halyard's and the writer's—reflected the anxieties that had colored his time at GE. Kurt lacked the degree that made him worthy of his rank and pay scale, and he had been improperly consigned to public relations, a job he ultimately refused. His novel thus raised and vanquished the twin demons that had haunted him at GE: the fear that he didn't fit in, and the fear that he did.

And he did it at the same time that he was resolving his feelings about Paul Proteus, the scientist inventor, the golden boy of the Ilium Works who must choose between an easy life as a company man and what he knows in his heart is right. When he is captured in a raid on a Ghost Shirt meeting, Paul is given a stark choice. He can claim he was acting as a spy and name the leaders of the revolution. Or he can confess to having joined the revolution, forever destroying his chance of returning to his comfortable place among the elite. Paul recognizes the mythic quality of his decision:

> Here it was again, the most ancient of roadforks, one that Paul had glimpsed before, in Kroner's study, months ago. The choice of one course or the other had nothing to do with machines, hierarchies, economics, love, age. It was a purely internal matter. Every child older than six knew the fork, and knew what the good guys did here, and what the bad guys did here . . .
> Bad guys turned informer. Good guys didn't—no matter when, no matter what.

Paul Proteus would end the novel as a good guy. He would claim his position as leader of the Ghost Shirt Society and happily accept the manifesto written in his name by one of the revolution's leaders, the political science professor Ludwig von Neumann.

Ludwig von Neumann is so unlike John von Neumann it seems likely his name was selected for irony. When the revolution backfires, it's he who bemoans the fact that the revolutionaries failed to destroy EPICAC. His manifesto ends with an incantatory list of affirmations of what is human in human beings:

I hold, and the members of the Ghost Shirt Society hold:

That there must be virtue in imperfection, for Man is imperfect, and Man is a creation of God.

That there must be virtue in frailty, for Man is frail, and Man is a creation of God.

That there must be virtue in inefficiency, for Man is inefficient, and Man is a creation of God.

That there must be virtue in brilliance followed by stupidity, for Man is alternately brilliant and stupid, and Man is a creation of God.

You perhaps disagree with the antique and vain notion of Man's being a creation of God.

But I find it a far more defensible belief than the one implicit in intemperate faith in lawless technological progress— namely, that man is on earth to create more durable and efficient images of himself, and, hence, to eliminate any justification at all for his own continued existence.

Imperfection, frailty, inefficiency, stupidity: these were precisely the qualities John von Neumann had dedicated his life to eradicating not just in meteorology but in every human endeavor.

Kurt mailed the final manuscript to his editor Harry Brague with a stipulation. If Scribner liked the novel and decided to publish, it must never publicize his relationship with General Electric. The company, he explained, was holding a hostage: Bernie. He did not want his brother's career put at risk because of something he had written.

For the first time in his life, Kurt found himself in the position of looking out for his older brother.

•

More than four hundred people crammed into New York's Roosevelt Hotel for the January 1952 AMS meeting. But to those who were paying attention, the tide had turned. The Weather Bureau campaign was beginning to vanquish belief in rainmaking.

The Weather Bureau scientists were taking a more diplomatic tone; ever since the disaster of the May Senate hearings, McDonald's pounding fist had been thudding in Chief Reichelderfer's head. Congress controlled the bureau's budget: the negative press after McDonald's outburst had cost it real money! The campaign was now being conducted mostly behind the scenes. Weather Bureau analysts were double-checking all the Project Cirrus data, and Harry Wexler was ever present in the background, quietly making sure anyone who was exposed to Project Cirrus heard the Weather Bureau's side of things too. Most important, Weather Bureau statisticians were working to disprove Langmuir's claims.

Langmuir was unconcerned. He didn't mind that his AMS meeting talk on the seven-day periodicities was scheduled for a panel with two Weather Bureau statisticians. He actually thought their work would help him to prove that his seeding had caused the weather periodicities. In fact, it was doing the opposite. For all his brilliance, Langmuir had failed to see the irremediable flaw in his method pinpointed by the bureau statisticians. Langmuir's calculations of probabilities for rainfall in seeded areas assumed that rain in one area could be considered independently of rain in the next—that in looking for patterns, he could treat rainfall levels as if they were random numbers. But rain in one place is probabilistically related to rain in a place nearby; a touch in one place eddies and flows, setting up a touch in the next, and so on, until you have reached the other side of the earth.

It was the statisticians who would, in the end, cast the Project Cirrus research into doubt and consign Irving Langmuir, once the nation's most famous chemist, to a marginal place in the history of science. Irving did not see it coming. He did not see that his whole way of doing science—his generalist, do-it-yourself, paper-clip-and-string mode of Victorian science—had become a liability. Science was being sorted into silos, and interaction between them was strictly regulated. As a chemist who had strayed into meteorology and then statistics, his failure to stick to his specialty branded him an outlier, someone who could safely be ignored.

Only one group of people considered him relevant. Recently, two officers from the Joint Chiefs of Staff had approached Irving and said they'd like to meet him in Schenectady to discuss military applications of weather control. Happily, he gave them his contact information. He had already renewed his security clearance, expecting he would soon be working directly with the military. Word was getting around that GE planned to discontinue Project Cirrus as of July, the end of the current contract. Under the reign of "Razor Ralph" Cordiner, the company was being reorganized into business units—even the Research Lab. Lab managers were given orders to organize teams of researchers to carry out prescribed projects—projects that were likely to lead to monetary results for GE. Doc Whitney's question, "Are you having fun today?" was no longer the watchword in the House of Magic.

After the AMS meeting, Irving returned to his island on Lake George, where he was now conducting most of his work. Visitors and colleagues who wanted to talk to him had to write in advance, because he had no telephone on the island. Then they would go to the Adirondack town of Bolton Landing, where arrangements would be made for Langmuir's Chris-Craft, *Wendy*, to bring them across Lake George to the laureate's leafy Neverland.

•

What are people for? Kurt was pondering that on Christmas Eve. The line was the very heart of the novel, the most succinct statement of his theme, and his editor Harry Brague had cut it out.

Editors!

Player Piano wound down with a failed revolution. After refusing to rat out the insurgents, Paul is tried for treason. During his trial, the Ghost Shirt Society starts an uprising, freeing Paul and aiming to take the world back for humanity. But the attack on the machines rapidly turns into a free-for-all. Drunk on destruction—and on liberated booze— the people smash everything from the Ilium Works assembly lines to bakeries and sewage disposal plants. Weakly, Paul, Finnerty, and the other leaders try to stop them from destroying the useful machines, but it's hopeless. There is no middle ground between fanatical love of the system and fanatical hate. Technology is either an absolute good or an absolute evil: the more complex story Paul wanted to tell is lost in the joyous upheaval of the downtrodden taking charge of their destinies.

Homestead is isolated by government troops, who refuse to come in and help clean up the mess until the revolution's leaders are handed over. Paul and the others briefly hope to build a truly human existence:

to chop wood and grow food and build shelters. But, in a final irony, as soon as the frenzy of ruin has given way to the cold light of day, people miss the machines. The revolution's leaders come upon a group gathered around a smashed vending machine that once dispensed a soda called Orange-O. Everyone has always hated Orange-O, but they are cheering on a comrade as he repairs the machine. The people, it seems, are doomed to reassemble the very world that had oppressed them.

Remarkably prescient, *Player Piano* foresaw a world divided between well-educated whiz-kid executives who believe technology is the answer to every human problem and alienated service workers showered with shiny new techno-gadgets in place of real roles as citizens. At the center of this world is the computer, deified by the paternalistic, paranoid culture of the modern corporation. Previous dystopian novels taught readers to look for hope in the success of the revolution—or despair in its failure. Winston Smith's revolution fails in *1984*, leading to his brutal torture and "re-education." Bernard Marx's attempt to escape the system in *Brave New World* leads to his exile. The dark irony of *Player Piano* is that no torture, no exile, is required. Before the revolution's smoke has even cleared, the rebels are at work rebuilding the very technology they revolted against, because technology tells far too seductive a lie. It tells us we can transcend our banal physical limitations; we can travel at the speed of sound, think at the speed of light, live forever in a shiny digital Eden. We humans, the novel implies, will always crave Orange-O machines and computers and video games and iPhones and self-driving cars, even if we suspect that these false gods are robbing us of our humanity.

Disconsolately, Paul and the other leaders turn themselves over to the state.

The original draft of *Player Piano* concluded with a scene between Ewing J. Halyard and the shah of Bratpuhr. Halyard decides to escape demotion by immigrating to Bratpuhr with the shah. But the shah explains that he will be a slave there if he can't rotate his navel. Halyard rages at the ridiculousness of assigning status based on something so pointless, but the shah is implacable. So Halyard performs his last duty as a member of the State Department, offering the shah and Bratpuhr an American "modernization" package that will endow them with all the machines and computers necessary to re-create the American economy. The shah refuses, instead giving Halyard one more question for EPICAC: "What are people for?"

That question was the one Kurt wanted to leave ringing in the reader's head. But early in November, Kenneth Littauer had called to say that Harry Brague didn't like Kurt's ending at all. The whole book contract hung in the balance. Kurt flew down to New York to meet with Harry in person and figure out a better conclusion. Together, the writer and the editor decided that it was wrong for the book to end on Halyard. The protagonist was Paul; the story should end with him.

Kurt wrote a new conclusion to follow the shah's departure, an epilogue in which, seventeen years after the failed revolution, Paul Proteus is released from prison and comes home to his farmhouse to find his former boss Kroner waiting to welcome him. Paul has spent his incarcerated years as the prison librarian, and his embrace of classic literature has given him a new, more spiritual view of life. He recognizes that the world will always change, and he just hopes humans can hold on to their spiritual values despite the relentless forward march of technology.

Harry Brague didn't hate the new conclusion, and at long last he issued Kurt a contract for the book. But after reading it a few times, the editor wondered if the epilogue was necessary. In fact, he thought Kurt could dispense with the last two chapters, ending the novel on the willing surrender of Paul and other leaders of the revolution. It would be a starker ending, and more serious. Kenneth Littauer thought it would make the novel feel pessimistic, but Kurt liked the idea. It might leave people wondering, arguing: Was the ending happy or sad? Was the writer an optimist or a pessimist? Was there hope for humanity? He wanted his novel, like Orwell's or Huxley's or Koestler's, to start conversations, arguments even.

But he was unwilling to lose the shah's question for EPICAC: What are people for?

The question is reminiscent of the penultimate chapter of Norbert Wiener's *Human Use of Human Beings*. "Our papers have been making a great deal of American 'know-how' ever since we had the misfortune to discover the atomic bomb," Wiener wrote. "There is one quality more important than know-how and we cannot accuse the United States of any undue amount of it. This is 'know-what': by which we determine not only how to accomplish our purposes, but what our purposes are to be." In order to explain the difference between "know-how" and "know-what," Wiener gave the example of a "prominent American engineer" who bought an expensive player piano. But the engineer was not interested in the music; he was interested in the piano's mechanism. "For this gentleman," Wiener wrote, "the player piano was not a means of producing music, but a means of giving some inventor the chance of showing how skillful he was at overcoming certain difficulties in the production of music."

On perhaps the last innocently joyous night of his life, just before he heard that Hitler had invaded Poland, Kurt had spent an evening with his buddies at Woolaroc Ranch in Oklahoma, smoking cigars and loading rolls of music into the player piano. They hadn't been interested in the piano's mechanism, in the know-how of it. They had been interested in hearing the tunes while they hung out, a tribe of three, enjoying one another's company. Like his brother, Kurt loved music: jazz and classical and the Beatles—it all partakes of the know-what, the higher truth that gives beauty and purpose to human existence. It's the music, not the mechanism, that people are for.

So, on Christmas Eve, Kurt found a place earlier in the book where the shah's question "What are people for?" could be reinserted, and he typed up an insert and mailed it to Harry Brague. And with that, his first novel was complete.

Kurt was so excited for the book to come out he could hardly stand it. He was eager for the royalties to start rolling in. He needed the money. Harry told him to sit tight and put the book out of his head. Get going on the next one, he advised. The only thing left to do now was to write a dedication, if he wanted one. Kurt sent one back right away: "For Jane—God bless her."

When the galleys of his first book arrived in March, he thought they were the most beautiful thing he had ever seen. He wrote to Harry suggesting a few people to whom Scribner should send advance copies of the book, hoping they might help spread the word. One of them was Norbert Wiener.

•

John von Neumann's computer was a thing of beauty. There it sat, eight feet long, six feet high, and two feet wide—a Corvette in a world that until now had only seen 18-wheelers. At a mere thousand pounds, it was smaller and sleeker than Harry Wexler had ever imagined a computer could be. It had twenty-three hundred vacuum tubes and forty raked cylinders along its sides and would be faster than ENIAC by far, doing 2,000 multiplications or 100,000 additions per second. It would whip through a twenty-four-hour forecast in a mere three hours.

In other words, it had roughly as much computing power as the kind of handheld calculator you might find in a cereal box today. And it was going to revolutionize computing.

It was May 1952, and von Neumann and his engineers were still working out the kinks, but the computer was finally operating. And unlike ENIAC, it didn't break down all the time. The summer before, it had run smoothly for sixty straight days doing a large thermonuclear calculation. Soon it was going to start in on the weather. The Meteorology Project's mathematical model had been growing increasingly complex, but the team believed it was sophisticated enough to predict cyclogenesis. As Harry Wexler had suggested, they were going to test the new equations by attempting to predict the formation of the 1950 Thanksgiving Storm.

A year from now, the computer would successfully forecast the cyclogenesis that led to the Thanksgiving Storm of 1950, proving that the so-called Rainmakers' Flood was a predictable act of nature. But even now, before that triumph, when Harry looked at the computer, he felt the satisfaction of having reached a peak he had only vaguely discerned during the long ascent. The days of predicting the weather using history and human intuition were about to end. Imperfection, frailty, and inefficiency were not part of Johnnie's new machine. The atmosphere could be understood deterministically. It could be reduced to equations and solved. And after the atmosphere, what next? The computer would continue to grow speedier and smarter, would solve more and more human problems. Harry Wexler was looking at the future not just of weather but of technology. The future of science. Of humanity. He was seeing a world just like that of *Player Piano*, but unlike Kurt, he had no problem with it.

One of the project engineers later summed up the magnitude of that moment in history. "A tidal wave of computational power was about to break and inundate everything in science and much elsewhere," he wrote, "and things would never be the same."

•

Guy Suits had asked Bernie to come see him. Bernie figured it was about his future at GE.

Project Cirrus was officially shut down. GE was getting out of weather modification; the liabilities were too big and the profit potential too small. Vincent and Bernie were unhappy about it, but there was nothing they could do. Under the new regime of Razor Ralph, they had to work on what they were told to work on.

The most fun Bernie had had at work lately was trying to "play" a germanium crystal on the Project Cirrus facsimile machine. It hadn't worked. The etched surface of germanium had a complicated structure, like a record, but the facsimile machine was not sensitive enough to pick up its signal. It had been worth a try. Purified germanium was a semiconductor, and its structure had been of great interest to the entire world since 1948, when scientists at Bell Labs had introduced the world to a new device that used a germanium semiconductor: the transistor.

Transistors! These tiny, pea-sized devices were all anyone could talk about. Smaller, faster, more durable, and more efficient than vacuum tubes, transistors were going to revolutionize electronics. It was the dawning of a new age for that industry, which experts predicted would soon grow to rival the chemical industry. Forget about better living through chemistry: better living through electronics was the future now. Power transfer, communications, lighting—even thinking was going to be done by transistors one day. There would be televisions half the current size! Radios that could fit in your pocket! Computers that could sit on a desk! They were all just around the corner because of Bell Labs' new invention.

Everyone wanted in on the promising new product, and GE was no exception. Research Lab scientists were being redeployed to the semiconductor section, Bernie among them. Vincent, too, was told that he should consider taking up semiconductors now that GE was divesting itself of weather.

Bernie wrote up his research in Research Lab Report RL-723: "Variations in the Contact Resistance of a Copper Point Moving over Etched Surface of Germanium Crystal." Diodes were interesting, but his heart wasn't in semiconductors and transistors. And he didn't want to be told what to research.

He had begun to look around for other jobs. He was corresponding with Bill Hubert, formerly with Project Cirrus, who was now at the Institute of Meteorology in Stockholm. The institute wanted a good cloud physics man to come to Stockholm for a few months. Bill had suggested Bernie, and Bernie was tempted. But Sweden was a big trip for the family, and he had also received a job offer from Arthur D. Little, a private research company in Cambridge, Massachusetts. Arthur D. Little conducted research in many different fields, and its scientists had more control of what they worked on than scientists at the GE Research Lab did now.

Guy Suits had clearly gotten wind of the fact that Bernie was thinking of leaving GE. When Bernie got to his office, Suits had a speech prepared. It was a big step Bernie was thinking of taking, he said. He hoped Bernie wouldn't take the decision to leave GE lightly. After all, there were a lot of factors to weigh.

"One of the things you must consider," he declared, "is your equity in the pension plan."

Here it was again, that same fork in the road that had confronted his brother. Of course, the choice at hand had nothing to do with pension plans, Quarter Century Clubs, appliances, or clambakes. It was purely an internal matter. Every kid past sixteen knew this fork, what the good guys did here, and the bad guys. Good guys stayed true to their love of science, their pursuit of knowledge for the good of humanity. Bad guys were venal. They made choices based on money.

Bernie knew at that moment, listening to Guy Suits, that he had made his decision and that it was the right one. He would leave GE, which in 1952 was no longer the company that had hired him in 1945. It had changed, radically. But then, so too had the nation.

And so, in fact, had he.

•

Kurt was crushed: Norbert Wiener hated *Player Piano*.

It was the latest in a series of small crises in the run-up to the publication that had left Kurt a nervous wreck. First he spent a couple of weeks worrying that a soda company somewhere might actually make something called Orange-O and that it would sue him for saying no one liked it. He had persuaded Harry Brague to have the Scribner lawyers look into it. The lawyers could find no evidence of a real Orange-O.

Then he had somehow got it in his head that Scribner was holding off publishing the book until fall, nearly a year after he'd completed it, and he freaked out, fearing he wouldn't get any royalties until he and his family had starved. Harry assured him that the book was slated for late summer. Somewhat reassured, Kurt retired to his study to write promotional taglines and sketch ideas for the cover. He sent these to Harry, who ignored them, along with Kurt's concepts for marketing campaigns and avowals that his next book would be better.

But this latest blow was the worst of all. Norbert Wiener had written Scribner a scathing letter. Kurt thought Wiener would love the novel! After all, Wiener's ideas were threaded throughout the whole book. Kurt even had Paul Proteus credit him with the idea of the second industrial revolution. He'd asked Scribner to send Wiener the book because he thought the mathematician would take it as a kind of tribute. Instead, Wiener accused Kurt of setting the novel in a dystopian future in order to avoid indicting what was actually happening in science today.

It was a problem Kurt would bump into over and over in his career. People would read his work as some sort of futuristic science fantasy, persisting in seeing his books as comic space operas and druggy head trips, when he thought he was writing pointed social satire.

In 1973, David Standish would ask him in *Playboy* why he had turned to science fiction for his first novel. Kurt told him about working at General Electric and seeing things like the automated milling machine.

"So science fiction seemed like the best way to write about your thoughts on the subject," Standish pressed.

"There was no avoiding it," Kurt said, "since the General Electric Company *was* science fiction."

It's unclear what set Wiener off, though he was notoriously touchy about his ideas being co-opted, often declaring himself "not a *Wienerian.*" Yet Kurt had captured exactly the moral questions raised in *Cybernetics* and *The Human Use of Human Beings*, questions Wiener would continue to explore in later works like *God and Golem Inc.* It may be that some of Wiener's hostility resulted from jealousy. He had literary aspirations himself—he published science fiction stories in the MIT magazine *Tech Engineering News* and would write a novel in 1959— and Kurt had conveyed many of Wiener's ideas in a form more accessible and enjoyable than the mathematician's own.

Wiener seemed most upset by the fact that Kurt had used his friend John von Neumann's name for one of the novel's revolutionaries. In his letter, he told the folks at Scribner to tell Vonnegut "he cannot with impunity . . . play fast and loose with the names of living people." This of course is balderdash: writers play fast and loose with the names of living people all the time. What really upset Wiener might have been that Professor Ludwig von Neumann—described as "a slight, disorderly old man who had taught political science at Union College in Schenectady"—might better have been called Ludwig Wiener. Ludwig von Neumann sounds absolutely Wienerian when he declares in his Ghost Shirt manifesto, "Without regard for the wishes of men, any machines or techniques or forms of organization that can economically replace men do replace men. Replacement is not necessarily bad, but to do it without regard for the wishes of men is lawlessness."

After Scribner forwarded Wiener's letter, Kurt and Jane spent a couple of days fantasizing about suitably mean retorts. Then Kurt wrote Wiener a chilly note thanking him for troubling himself with *Player Piano* and stating that he felt his indictment of contemporary science should be clear. He apologized for having innocently given offense, claiming he had picked the name von Neumann at random. He might have thought he did, but Kurt never picked names at random. He pulled them from his personal store of words with private significance. Senator Warren Foust in "Barnhouse" was likely suggested by Commander Elwood Faust, one of Project Cirrus's key pilots. Winston Niles Rumfoord of *The Sirens of Titan* and Bertram Copeland Rumfoord of *Slaughterhouse-Five* were almost surely born of Benjamin Thompson, Count Rumford, who endowed the Rumford Prize won by Irving Langmuir. George M. Helmholtz, a recurring character in Vonnegut's stories, invokes the mathematician Hermann von Helmholtz, whose equation was utilized in much of the Project Cirrus work. GE names, like GE ideas, would surface persistently and evocatively in everything Kurt ever wrote.

In mid-August, *Player Piano* landed in bookstores across the country—except for those in Schenectady. Not one bookstore in GE's company town would agree to stock it; every bookseller made an improbable excuse. Bernie had received his copy, signed with love from Kurt. He had probably already read it when the review in *The New York Times Book Review* came out. On August 17, 1952, the eminent critic Granville Hicks praised the book's humor, calling Kurt a "sharp-eyed satirist."

"It is a little like *Brave New World*," Hicks wrote, "except that Mr. Vonnegut keeps his future closer to the present than Aldous Huxley succeeded in doing, and his satire therefore focuses more sharply on the contemporary situation. The machines he is talking about are not gadgets he has dreamed up; they are in existence, as he is careful to point out."

The next day was Bernie's last day at the GE Research Lab. Between the final edits and the Orange-O freak-out, the Wiener letter and *The New York Times*, somewhere in there Bernard Vonnegut had walked into the office of Guy Suits and handed in his official resignation.

Later, he would say that his career at GE ended when he went on vacation and someone cleaned off his desk. Whether or not the story was true, it was an elegant way of expressing the choice he had made at his own crossroads, a choice to trust his own messy, imperfect spirit over the order and efficiency of GE. Confident he was doing the right thing, Bernie turned in his keys, his all-hours pass, his patent notebook, his lab supplies, his meters and instruments, and his K parking permit, and he walked out of the Knolls Research Lab. He didn't look back.

The secretary carefully filled out his termination sheet, noting his new address: 704 Country Way, North Scituate, Massachusetts. His new home was close to the ocean and close to Kurt and Jane.

For the first time in his life, Bernie was following in his brother's footsteps, instead of the other way around.

•

In June 1953, a mile-wide tornado plowed through Worcester, Massa-chusetts. Tornadoes in Massachusetts are rare, and the storm cell that spawned this one was so huge that people on Cape Cod could see it as it churned northeast, killing ninety-four people and leaving ten thou-sand more homeless in the eighty-four minutes it took to get to the coast. Later it was called the Worcester Twister and given a rare F4 rating on the Fujita scale.

As news of the storm broke, Bernie went down to the beach in Scituate with his camera to watch the giant stomp across the Boston area. The storm was about 160 kilometers away, but he could see its electrical discharges filling the sky. Blinking his eyes as fast as he could, he couldn't get a glimpse of the storm not lit up by lightning. The re-lease of all that energy must be heating the air and creating updrafts, which could explain the storm's size. He estimated the storm's top to be about twenty kilometers up, in the stratosphere, which would mean its vertical winds were traveling upward at a hundred meters a second. The lightning was still going like gangbusters when the storm reached the shore and headed out to sea.

He was as awed as he had been as a kid, when he snuck out of the house in Chatham and went down to the ocean. He was witnessing a firestorm made by nature. Scientists didn't even know if the winds caused the lightning or the lightning caused the winds. But Bernie had an intuition that electrical charge might play a larger role than people thought.

The original impulse behind Project Cirrus was a simple mystery: What makes clouds give rain? But the query about the natural world had nearly been lost in a whirlwind of controversy and competing desires.

The military men wanted weapons, the commercial rainmakers wanted profits, GE wanted free publicity, and the meteorologists wanted to protect their turf.

In 1953, Congress appointed the new Advisory Committee on Weather Control to investigate, once more, whether the government should conduct research on the topic. Bernie was asked to write a report for the committee. Five years later, when congressional hearings were held, he asked to testify. Of his own volition, he wrote up a statement on House Bill 86. The bill, he said, was based on a false premise: that anyone could know what kind of research would lead to weather control. In fact, he told them, Vince's original experiment had been driven by the desire to understand how nature works, not by a desire to control it.

"I believe the best way to achieve weather control," he wrote, "will be to sponsor basic research in the physical sciences necessary to the understanding of weather."

That same year, Commander William Kotsch of the U.S. Navy wrote to Bernie asking for a copy of his report on the uses of weather as a weapon. Bernie sent him a copy of the report he wrote for the Advisory Committee on Weather Control. But the commander was bound to be disappointed, he said. He dealt "very sketchily" with the use of weather as a weapon.

In fact, he didn't mention it at all.

After leaving GE for Arthur D. Little, Bernie would sometimes accept funding from the military. But never again would he work on something that had obvious military applications. Instead, he began developing a new theory about thunderstorms, proposing that updrafts and downdrafts caused electrical charge in thunderclouds and that electrical charge led to rain, instead of vice versa. One of his cleverest experiments concerned the fact that thunderstorms almost always have a positive charge at the top and a negative charge at the bottom. One summer in New Mexico, Bernard and his colleague Charlie Moore strung a two-kilometer wire between two mountains to release negative charge. When thunderstorms came through and encountered the negative charge, they reversed their polarity. Over the course of two weeks, Bernie and Charlie Moore created three storms that discharged positive charge to the ground—electrical storms turned electrically up-side down. It was perhaps his best joke on nature. Bernie spent much of the rest of his life marshaling evidence for his theory about electrical charge in thunderstorms, but he once admitted he wasn't really driven by the need to prove it.

"I'm [just] trying to find out," he said, "what's going on."

He no longer wanted to control. He wanted to know. And the purpose of knowing was not, in the end, to banish mystery. It was to appreciate it. To note how it glows.

•

In May 1954, Kurt tried and failed to get a job at Time Inc. He was broke. *Player Piano* had received a few polite notices but had not sold well and had quickly faded from view. It had not made his fortune or his name. Worse, *Collier's* had stopped buying his stories. The short story market was shrinking. And Jane was pregnant with their third child. Desperate for income, he sent Harry Brague at Scribner all he had, six chapters of a book he was now calling *Cat's Cradle*.

That month, *Collier's* published a sensational cover story called "Weather Made to Order?" Written by Howard Orville, chair of the Advisory Committee on Weather Control, the piece trotted out all of the most dramatic claims about the coming era of man-made weather: hurricanes, tornadoes, and thunderstorms would be quelled; deserts and dust bowls would bloom; forest fires and floods would be prevented. Weather would be used as a weapon, deluging enemies with rain or causing them to starve by preventing it. According to *Collier's*, this was all laudable, American enterprise at its finest.

Knox Burger was not at *Collier's* anymore; he had left to become a book editor at Dell. Kurt's last two stories for *Collier's*, "Poor Little Rich Town" and "With His Hand on the Throttle," were both GE based, the first about a GE-type efficiency expert and his attempt to streamline life in a small village and the second about a model railroad fanatic inspired by Herb Hollomon. But the magazine market for fiction was rapidly drying up as popular entertainment was increasingly delivered by television. *Collier's* itself would cease publication in 1957.

Kurt could see that clearly enough, and he had turned to writing plays. He had even purchased a television and was starting to write teleplays in the hope of breaking into the new medium. But they weren't selling. And he couldn't seem to get very far with the new novel. Ever since the disappointing debut of *Player Piano*, Kurt had been racked with writer's block. Harry Brague had encouraged him, trying to convince him that the novel's reception had actually been good and that he should sit down and write a new one before the public forgot his name. He had even advanced Kurt $500 on the unspecified next novel when Kurt was desperate for cash. It didn't help.

Harry Brague didn't quite know what to make of the six chapters Kurt sent of *Cat's Cradle*. In fact, it would take ten years and two more books before the former "Ice-9" would morph into Kurt Vonnegut's breakthrough book. Kurt would fix its problems by stepping back and turning the straightforward adventure story into a story about stories, an adventure stumbled into by a writer-narrator called Jonah who is trying to research a book about the day the first atomic bomb was dropped on Hiroshima. He wants to call it *The Day the World Ended*.

In the final version, Dr. George Hoenikker becomes Dr. Felix Hoenikker, "father of the atomic bomb" and inventor of the even more dangerous ice-nine. Dr. Hoenikker is already dead as the book opens, but Jonah researches his book by tracking down Hoenikker's three children and traveling to Ilium, New York, home to the Research Lab of General Forge and Foundry, where Felix Hoenikker worked. The Research Lab is described as a kind of playground, where "men are paid to increase knowledge . . . the most valuable commodity on earth." Felix Hoenikker is its star scientist, viewed by the Research Lab's main client, the Pentagon, as "a sort of magician who could make America invincible with a wave of his wand."

As Jonah explores Ilium, he collects stories about Dr. Hoenikker, many of which are versions of stories about Irving Langmuir. Dr. Hoenikker played cat's cradle with his son Newt—one of Langmuir's favorite games to play with children. Hoenikker once left a tip for his wife, as Irving had for Marion; he was known to declare, as Kurt had heard Irving say, that any scientist who couldn't explain his work to a child was a charlatan. A secretary at General Forge and Foundry tells Jonah that Dr. Hoenikker once challenged her to tell him something that was absolutely true, to which she replied, "God is love." This is what Clare Boothe Luce told Irving Langmuir when they were chatting before appearing on the radio together and he challenged her to think of a statement that was true but not provable. But Langmuir's comment on the exchange was "She sure had me there!" Kurt has Felix Hoenikker reply, "What is God? What is love?"

The connections between Felix Hoenikker and Irving Langmuir made it clear that, as Kurt would frequently declare in years to come, the absentminded scientist was based on his brother's former boss. But Felix Hoenikker's last gift to humanity—ice-nine, "a new way for the atoms of water to stack and lock, to freeze"—that invention was Bernie's.

"Suppose," explains Dr. Asa Breed, vice president in charge of the Research Laboratory of General Forge and Foundry,

> that the sort of ice we skate upon and put into highballs—what we might call *ice-one*—is only one of several types of ice . . . And suppose . . . that there were one form, which we will call *ice-nine*—a crystal as hard as this desk—with a melting point of, let us say, one-hundred degrees Fahrenheit, or, better still, a melting point of one-hundred-and-thirty degrees.

Dr. Breed tells Jonah to imagine the many ways oranges could be stacked in a crate, or cannonballs piled on a courthouse lawn. It was exactly how Bernie had explained cloud nucleation to Kurt.

One of the things critics rarely understand about *Cat's Cradle* is that it is not about the misuse of science. It's about the failure of people to understand the significance of a scientific advance. The threat in the book is not that scientists will produce something dangerous but that the community won't recognize it when they do. Felix Hoenikker is a bad guy not because he invented ice-nine but because he failed to warn anyone about it. Only creators can really understand the hazards of what they create: it's their moral obligation to make sure the rest of the world understands them too.

At GE, Kurt had witnessed his brother trying to do just that.

In putting the story in the mouth of the anthropologist-like Jonah, Kurt made the major breakthrough of shifting the emphasis from

Dr. Felix Hoenikker to his three children: Franklin, the genius scientist with "a wiry pompadour . . . that arose to an incredible height"; Angela, the tall sister who plays the clarinet brilliantly; and Newt, the glum midget who paints pictures. It's not hard to see the similarity between the names Hoenikker and Vonnegut, or the way in which the Hoenikkers are versions of the three Vonnegut siblings: Bernard, the genius scientist; Alice, the ethereal artist; and Kurt, the glum wordsmith painting clowns as the world goes to hell.

His other main breakthrough was to bring in the outlawed religion of Bokononism. In short, evocatively titled chapters—each about the length of a press release—Kurt gets Jonah and the Hoenikker siblings, each carrying a shard of ice-nine, to the island of San Lorenzo. The banana republic is run, as it was in early drafts, by the dictator Papa Monzano, but it has a new element: Bokonon and his made-up faith.

The conclusion of *Cat's Cradle* echoes the earliest drafts of "Ice-9": the novel ends with apocalypse. Papa Monzano has gotten hold of some of Felix's ice-nine, and he takes it to kill himself. When the San Lorenzo air force bombs his palace, his body slips into the sea, and the world's water supply is converted to ice-nine by chain reaction. An epic cyclone reduces most of the planet to rubble. Jonah and his love object, Mona, survive by hiding in a bomb shelter constructed in the palace dungeon. When they emerge, most of the population is dead; for the sad remnant left behind, it's only a matter of time until they accidentally ingest some ice-nine and their own water molecules seize up. Angela Hoenikker dies when, unconcerned, she picks up a clarinet and plays. Just as in the Vonnegut family by then—Alice died of breast cancer in 1958—the Hoenikker brothers are all that remains of the family. As human history draws to its close, Franklin, the scientist, builds an ant farm and passes his days marveling at ant behavior. When provoked, he issues a "peevish lecture on all the things that people could learn from ants." It's a scene reminiscent of the end of "The Petrified Ants," a story never published in Kurt's lifetime, where the exiled brothers Josef and Peter marvel at the adaptability of the insects.

"Men could learn a lot from ants, Peter my boy," Josef tells his younger brother.

"They have, Josef, they have," Peter replies. "More than they know."

In *Cat's Cradle*, as in "The Petrified Ants," Kurt used a pair of brothers to address the moral duties of scientists. But in the earlier story, the siblings were meant to be contrasted with each other: the older one morally compromised by conformity, the younger one an individualist working to maintain his integrity. In *Cat's Cradle*, the brothers are equally compromised—they both carry shards of ice-nine—and equally ineffective at saving the world. Newt, the younger brother, occupies himself much as Franklin does in the apocalypse. He too is just farting around waiting to die, making paintings with scavenged paint. There's no wisdom to be gleaned from the end of the world, from destruction on a global scale.

The real hero of *Cat's Cradle* is Bokonon, the prophet who admits that his wisdom is based on lies but whose invented religion gives human beings comfort. Like the Ghost Shirt Society in *Player Piano* and the Church of God the Utterly Indifferent in *The Sirens of Titan*, Bokononism provides an alternative to the sterile technological belief in truth personified by Felix Hoenikker. It uses false myths and harmless lies—*foma*—to encourage humans to love one another, to acknowledge their connectedness, and to spend their short time on earth with grace and compassion.

In crafting the creed of Bokononism—for which he would finally, years later, be granted his anthropology degree from the University of Chicago—Kurt found perhaps his best embodiment of the truth he had learned all those years ago in *The Brothers Karamazov*: If God did not exist, human beings would have to invent him. And if that's the case, why not invent a kind and loving God, a God who encourages us to find the sacred in nothing more, and nothing less, than our own human selves?

"Let us remember how good it was once here, when we were all together," Alyosha says at the end of Dostoevsky's novel, "united by a good and kind feeling which made us, for the time we were loving that poor boy, better perhaps than we are." He is appealing to the boys to embrace their best natures in his absence because he is leaving, about to accompany his brother Dmitri to Siberia.

"You must know that there is nothing higher and stronger and more wholesome and good for life in the future than some good memory, especially a memory of childhood, of home," he says. "People talk to you a great deal about your education, but some good sacred memory, preserved from childhood, is perhaps the best education."

That was the line that Jane's Swarthmore professor had shared with her and that she shared with Kurt on their honeymoon. Kurt always kept that piece of paper. It reminded him of the sacredness of memory. He had his own sacred memory preserved from childhood, the memory of his childhood swim across Lake Maxinkuckee. Thanks to the way the human mind lets us travel in time, he could revisit that lake anytime he wanted. He could dive in and swim across it just as he had done as a child, his arms and legs churning like an engine, the waves sliding off his body, a body that always looked best, he thought, in the water. In the water, he was beautiful. In the freshwater lake, he was at home. The water would buoy him up, and he would swim, happy to be swimming in what to him was an ocean, the second-largest lake in Indiana, with his sister and his brother at his side.

Epilogue: Rainbow's End

Kurt sat in his office around 9:30 in the evening. In one hand, he had a cigarette, and in the other a piece of paper. Bernie had given it to him earlier that day.

"We do have some other photographs of the poor man's Steinmetz, and I may send them to you in my own sweet time."

It was his letter to Uncle Alex, written in 1947, fifty years earlier, when he was still a young man. He was an old man now. Bernie was even older, of course. Old and sick. He had handed the letter to Kurt in Albany, where Kurt went every week by train to see his older brother as he faded away from lung cancer.

By now, Kurt was famous, very famous. But success had not come easily. After *Player Piano*, he was blocked for years. Scribner had sold the paperback rights to Bantam for $4,000, and the book that was going to earn him some literary respect was retitled *Utopia 14* and released in a lurid mass-market edition, complete with a futuristic city and writhing half-dressed people on the cover. "Man's revolt against a glittering, mechanized tomorrow," it read, next to the cover price of thirty-five cents. Thus began the process of consigning Kurt Vonnegut novels to the shelf marked "science fiction," a designation he would alternately embrace and bemoan.

For years, all he could produce were short stories to pay the mortgage, and even those were not plentiful enough. He took copywriting jobs, teaching jobs; he opened one of the nation's first Saab dealerships. It failed. Cape Cod wasn't quite ready for Saabs.

When he finally broke through his writer's block and wrote *The Sirens of Titan*—published as a paperback original—he was still writing about the war. War remained the backdrop for his books for another fifteen years: battles, mortar attacks, artillery shellings, air assaults, ships firing cannons, bombs dropping on jungles and castles and cities, hordes of nameless refugees, legions of dead. He even designed and tried to market a military strategy board game called GHQ, with counters representing infantry, artillery, and paratroop units arrayed on a checkerboard, as if he were turning his story "All the King's Horses" into an actual game, as if he were refighting the Battle of the Bulge.

He started and restarted his Dresden book, five times, ten times, more times than he cared to guess. He wrote it as a teleplay, a short story, a nonfiction essay. He was working on it when *Cat's Cradle* was published in 1963, and *ice-nine*—along with the terms *karass*, *foma*, and *wampeter*—entered the language. He was working on it when he published *Mother Night* and *God Bless You, Mr. Rosewater*, each admired by a few critics and contributing to his underground reputation. He was working on it when his sister, Alice, died of cancer, two days after her husband, Jim Adams, was killed in a freak train wreck on New Jersey Transit. He was working on it when he and Jane took in her four orphaned boys and suddenly had seven kids, as they always knew they would.

Finally, in the late 1960s, with the nation cycling through gloom and guilt and rage over events in Vietnam, Kurt was offered a teaching position at the Iowa Writers' Workshop. The mood in the nation plus the literary stimulation of Iowa and the escape from his own routine broke the logjam that had lasted for a quarter century. He began to rewrite what he had always called *Slaughterhouse-Five*, wrestling the material that had haunted him since 1945 into his own unique novel form. He was finally able to use Norbert Wiener's idea of "Newtonian time"—reversible time in which nothing new can ever happen—to full effect. When Billy Pilgrim begins to experience time as the Tralfamadorians do, it is not just a far-out concept of quantum physics but also the time we all live in, where at any moment we might be transported back to a former moment in our lives.

One of the last typescript drafts before *Slaughterhouse-Five* began with the line "Billy Pilgrim has come unstuck in time." Above it, Kurt wrote one word by hand: "Listen."

Growing up as the youngest child, he always yearned to say this to his parents and siblings. As the younger brother who wanted to be a writer, not a chemist, he had longed to say it to Bernard. As an adult, he finally learned to say it, learned to work his desire to say it into the style we now recognize as uniquely his.

At once an antiwar treatise and a psychological depiction of post-traumatic stress, *Slaughterhouse-Five* electrified readers and made Kurt a literary icon. His time in Iowa salvaged his reputation, assured his family's financial future, and gave him what he had always wanted: a place in the literary pantheon. It was also where he launched an affair that would begin the process of ending his marriage to Jane. So it goes.

Recently, as Bernie lay dying in Albany, he had told Kurt that he didn't think scientists made very good husbands. They were too focused on the fascinating things going on in their own heads.

You could say the same for writers, of course.

But Jane's confidence in Kurt had shaped him, and her voice was there in the work. In *Slaughterhouse-Five*, he concluded one of the most compelling descriptions of a massacre ever written with the voice of a bird: the last word in the novel is "Po-tweet?" It summed up Jane's undergraduate history thesis at Swarthmore: no sense can be made of history; no meaning can be gleaned from a massacre. The only thing to do is to listen to the birds.

And, like Dostoevsky's Father Zossima, to ask forgiveness of them.

Two years after Kurt published *Slaughterhouse-Five*, newspapers broke a fantastic story: the CIA had been using cloud seeding as a weapon of war. Since 1966, U.S. planes had flown more than twenty-six hundred cloud-seeding missions over Indochina, spraying the clouds of Vietnam and Laos with aerosolized silver iodide. The intent was to make rain: rain to wash out river crossings and muddy up the Ho Chi Minh Trail, rain to slow supply lines and troop movements in North Vietnam. Like so many weather modification projects, the program had a sci-fi-like name: Operation Popeye.

Bernard was horrified to see his invention used in actual combat.

But news of the missions led to an international outcry and, eventually, something he had always desired, a UN treaty banning the use of weather modification as a weapon of war.

By the time Bernie heard about Operation Popeye, he had left industrial science and become an academic. His career at Arthur D. Little in Cambridge had been spent investigating electrification in tornadoes and thunderstorms. In the summers, he continued to chase clouds and lightning in Socorro, based at what became the Langmuir Laboratory for Atmospheric Research. Then, in 1967, he accepted a faculty position at the Atmospheric Sciences Research Center, founded six years earlier by Vincent Schaefer at the State University of New York at Albany. Along with several other former colleagues from the Project Cirrus team, Bernie became a professor and continued his research while teaching, nurturing young scientists with his passion for weather.

From Schenectady to Scituate to Albany, through childbirth and schooling, through children growing up and succeeding or struggling, through his wife's death, and his son's illness: through all those years, Bernie had kept Kurt's letter to Uncle Alex. He must have found it funny. He liked a good joke as much as any of them. But maybe he found the letter touching too, a reminder of the younger sibling unable to resist a chance at a potshot, the jealous kid brother who lives on in kid brothers everywhere.

In 1985, MIT invited Kurt to give a speech. He must have been gratified to be invited to hold forth at his brother's and father's and grandfather's alma mater. To make the scientists at one of the biggest science factories of all listen to him. He felt as if he might actually be able to do some good. So he told the graduating class about his brother, Bernard, a fellow graduate of MIT.

"My brother knew early on that he would be a research scientist, and so could not be self-employed," he told them. To make a living, his brother was going to have to work for somebody else, to make someone else's technological dreams come true. Bernie, he told them, got his doctorate on the eve of World War II:

If he had gone to work in Germany after that, he would have been helping to make Hitler's dreams come true. If he had gone

to work in Italy, he would have been helping to make Musso-
lini's dreams come true. If he had gone to work in Japan, he
would have been helping to make Tojo's dreams come true. If
he had gone to work in the Soviet Union, he would have been
helping to make Stalin's dreams come true. He went to work for
a bottle manufacturer in Butler, Pennsylvania, instead. It can
make quite a difference not just to you but to humanity: the
sort of boss you choose, whose dreams you help come true.

It was a reprise, in some ways, of an address Kurt gave to the American Association of Physics Teachers in 1969 called "The Virtuous
Physicist." Scientists at several major research universities were protest-
ing the misuse of science as a tool of war. After his talk, Kurt was asked
by reporters what defined a virtuous physicist. He told them it was
simple: "one who declines to work on weapons."

Someone should write an oath for them, Kurt told the scientists at
MIT nearly twenty years later. One modeled on the Hippocratic oath,
something like "The regimen I adopt shall be for the benefit of all life
on this planet, according to my own ability and judgment, and not for
its hurt or for any wrong. I will create no deadly substance or device,
though it be asked of me, nor will I counsel such."

Bernie read and approved of Kurt's talk before he gave it.

The year after Kurt spoke at MIT, Jane Vonnegut Yarmolinsky—she
had married the Harvard law professor Adam Yarmolinsky—succumbed
to cancer at the age of sixty-four. Not long before she died, Jane called
Kurt. Their conversation was affectionate. Jane asked Kurt to tell her
what would determine the moment of her death. Why ask him? "She
may have felt like a character in a book by me," Kurt wrote later. "In a
sense she was." Of course Jane was nobody's fictional character but a
living, breathing woman full of life and energy and purpose. Without
her, the Kurt Vonnegut we know would never have existed. To a great
extent, he was a character created by her. And yet what he said was
somehow true to the times in which they made their home and raised
their children. The men wrote the stories of their lives. The women
played their parts in them.

Kurt told Jane that a ten-year-old boy would be standing at the end of Scudder's Lane, the street where they had lived most of their years on Cape Cod. Standing on the boat ramp that reaches out into the pond, the boy would be sunburned and bored but happy. "I told Jane that this boy, with nothing better to do, would pick up a stone, as boys will. He would arc it over the harbor. When the stone hit the water, she would die."

•

Did Bernie really make rain? Scientists have been debating the efficacy of cloud seeding ever since Vincent dispensed dry ice over Mount Greylock in 1946, but the general consensus today is that in certain conditions it works in a limited way. The huge modifications Irving promised never came to pass. Immediately after GE shut down Project Cirrus, the military conducted six large-scale experiments. Five yielded inconclusive results, and one showed a positive result: the seeding of supercooled stratus clouds with dry ice and silver iodide. Officers from the Office of Naval Research consulted with Irving Langmuir on these experiments, though they would not reveal any specifics, and the results were classified until 1957. Irving had by then completed his magnum opus: his final report on Project Cirrus. But the nearly six-hundred-page treatise was classified as well. When it was finally published as volume 11 of his *Collected Works* in 1962, Irving was dead; he had died in 1957, with the work he considered his legacy to humanity unknown to science. Today, he is well-known among chemists, but his popular reputation died with his dream of widespread weather control.

Bernie's invention is the main legacy of Project Cirrus. Silver iodide remains the most widespread method of enhancing precipitation. Utilities in California have been using silver iodide to increase the winter snowpack in the Sierra Nevada since the early 1950s. The Desert Research Institute in Nevada has been using it to seed clouds since not long after that; currently, it has three operational programs in Nevada and California. In the 1960s, the Bureau of Reclamation conducted rainmaking experiments over reservoirs, with some apparent success, under the name Project Skywater. In the 1960s and 1970s, a joint U.S. Navy–Weather Bureau experiment called Project Stormfury attempted less successfully to modify hurricanes with seeding.

Research spending on weather modification dwindled after the 1970s. Factors blamed for the field's decline include early overpromising, the lack of rigorous research, environmentalist campaigns against altering nature, and Reagan-era reductions in government funding. Another key element: the early 1980s were an exceptionally wet period in the United States. The weather modifiers have a saying for this: "Interest in cloud seeding is soluble in rainwater."

Today's changing climate has renewed interest in weather modification. In the West and the Great Plains, severe drought and diminishing aquifers have led water utilities, hydropower producers, agriculture groups, and ski resorts to fund cloud-seeding programs. In Wyoming, Idaho, Colorado, California, Utah, and Nevada, rainmakers are hired to augment the snowpack. In Texas and Kansas, cloud seeders are at work to induce rain. In North Dakota, clouds are seeded to make them precipitate before they can produce crop-damaging hail. California, Nevada, and Arizona contribute funds to cloud-seeding projects over the Colorado River's upper basin, in hopes of increasing their water supply.

And yet many people today believe that weather modification is a hoax: the early overselling of rainmaking somehow caused it, down the line, to be grouped in the public mind with conspiracy theories about mind-altering "chemtrails," shock-jock speculation that the government manufactures tornadoes, and paranoid fantasies about "weather wars" involving earthquakes broadcast via the stratosphere. The reality is far less dramatic. A rigorous five-year randomized study sponsored by the Wyoming Water Development Commission and funded by the National Science Foundation is on track to yield results showing that seeding certain clouds can be expected to increase precipitation by about 10 to 15 percent.

As for Project Cirrus's widespread periodicities and whether they resulted from Bernie's little generator huffing away in New Mexico, the general consensus among those who've even heard of the experiment is that the periodicities were a freaky coincidence. The Weather Bureau meteorologist Roscoe Braham called Langmuir's experiment "one of those tantalizing things." The MIT meteorologist Henry Houghton called it "the most mysterious thing I have ever run up against . . . If it wasn't chance, it was a totally new effect." Another meteorologist in 1953 said the episode was "a great tragedy."

"If Langmuir actually influenced the weather," he said, "no one will believe him. If the periodicities were mere coincidence, nature played Langmuir a dirty trick."

Of course, nature plays dirty tricks on us all the time, if by that we mean that it shimmies out of grasp, foiling our urge to master and sometimes our desire to know.

"Beware of the man who works hard to learn something, learns it, and finds himself no wiser than before," writes Bokonon in *Cat's Cradle*. "He is full of murderous resentment of people who are ignorant without having come by their ignorance the hard way."

"Perhaps if he had comprehended fully the magnitude of atmospheric phenomena," the meteorologist Horace Byers wrote years later of Irving Langmuir, "he might have been discouraged from the start." But in one way Langmuir—and Bernie too—understood the magnitude of atmospheric phenomena better than almost anyone. They understood that the atmosphere was such a huge, complex, and dynamic system that we would never nail it down with numbers. The weather, Langmuir wrote in his great work, "is not definitely determinate. It depends in large part and essentially upon meteorological events that originate from small and unpredictable beginnings, such as the location and concentration of freezing nuclei that may set off chain reactions." Today we call this chaos.

Developed by the meteorologist Edward Lorenz beginning in 1960, chaos theory holds that in some huge systems—weather and other things like it—small contingencies cascade upward to produce large effects. Scientists named it "sensitive dependence on initial conditions." Norbert Wiener had already seen this in 1954, calling it "the self-amplification of small details in the weather map." Langmuir's theory of convergent and divergent phenomena was an early version of chaos theory, another startling intuitive achievement and one for which he has never been given credit. Langmuir and Wiener were right, and John von Neumann was wrong. The weather cannot be entirely solved by equation, because it is not deterministic. It's all flowing and blending; a touch in one place sets up movement at the other end of the earth.

The flutter of a butterfly's wing can touch off whirlwinds ten thousand miles away.

It's all an ocean, after all.

Weather prediction today combines von Neumann's mathematical approach with Wiener and Langmuir's probabilistic one. The weather can be predicted with a good degree of accuracy for about a week out. It can be predicted with somewhat less accuracy for up to two weeks. After that, it all falls apart, because the effects of very tiny disturbances multiply with great speed. Eventually, you get far enough out that statistics and probabilities smooth out the variations, and you can make largely accurate guesses about long-term climate, but in the zone between two weeks and two millennia it's still a mystery. The computer did not turn out to be Laplace's demon—the all-knowing consciousness of a clockwork universe—though hope that it might still morph into that being can sometimes be whiffed in the tech factories of Silicon Valley.

•

As for John von Neumann, in early 1955 he was appointed to the Atomic Energy Commission and moved to Washington. That June, he published an essay in *Fortune* called "Can We Survive Technology?" He outlined the sweeping technological advances about to transform the world: nearly free atomic energy, automation of everything, and global climate control. All of these advances, he acknowledged, had immense potential for harm as well as good. But that was the nature of science. To attempt to control or restrain it was impractical.

"For progress," he wrote, "there is no cure."

Kurt—and Bernie—would disagree. The cure for progress was simply remembering that we are human.

Not long after his essay appeared, von Neumann slipped and fell in a Washington hallway and was subsequently diagnosed with bone cancer, possibly due to his presence at so many early atomic tests. He died eighteen months later, under military guard with top clearance, for fear that in his agonized raving he should reveal military secrets. He was tormented beyond all reason by the fact that he, too, turned out to be frail, imperfect, inefficient, that for the progress of life there is no cure.

Before he died, the lifelong atheist requested the ministrations of a priest.

•

Harry Wexler eventually gave up his opposition to the idea of weather control. In 1959, he attended a meeting on weather modification chaired by Edward Teller, who had become a believer. Three years later, Harry gave a paper called "On the Possibilities of Climate Control" at the AMS meeting in Boston. The subject of weather control, he told the audience, was "now becoming respectable to talk about." Indeed, President Kennedy had called for international cooperation on climate control in his inauguration speech that year. The UN had also voiced hope that nations would cooperate on this front.

Wexler outlined some interventions in the climate that seemed to him feasible, given the greater climate understanding both satellites and computers were providing. But, he pointed out, "we are in weather control *now* whether we know it or not." Wexler talked about the dangers of inadvertent damage to the ozone layer via ozone-depleting chemical reactions. He noted the fact that "we are releasing huge quantities of carbon dioxide and other gases and particles to the lower atmosphere which may have serious effects on the radiation or heat balance which determine our present pattern of climate and weather." He was still investigating these phenomena just months later when he died, tragically, of a heart attack at age fifty-one. His research was largely forgotten until the 1970s. It would be interesting to know what might have happened had such a forceful character been around to advocate investigating the dangers of chlorofluorocarbons and greenhouse gases more than a decade before the majority of scientists thought to do so.

In fact, the most significant legacy of Project Cirrus might be that it laid the foundation for studying human impacts on the climate, a field previously considered the domain of science fiction. In 1978, Bernie explained,

Project Cirrus's investigations of ways that man can intentionally affect the weather cast a new light on how man's activities might unintentionally have a large influence on weather processes. Along with the scientific study of deliberate weather modification, a new vigorous research activity is developing to explore how man may be affecting his environment by the gases, aerosols and heat he emits into the atmosphere in the course of his many activities . . . In recent years several international workshops on inadvertent weather modification have been held. These are undoubtedly only the first of many similar ones that will be held in the future on this subject.

•

GE continued to move to the right throughout the 1950s, blacklisting employees who wouldn't cooperate fully with HUAC and gradually reining in its unions through tough negotiation tactics that came to be known as Boulwarism. Two years after Bernie left, GE hired an underemployed actor to serve as its public relations spokesman and to host the company television show *GE Theater*. Taken under the ideological wing of Lemuel Boulware, he was purged of his previous liberal convictions and indoctrinated in the virtues of unfettered markets. Ten years later, that actor, Ronald Reagan, would make a stunning speech in support of Barry Goldwater at the Republican National Convention, launching a conservative revolution and his own political career.

The nation by then had thrown itself so fully into the Cold War and the arms race that even the Republican president, Eisenhower, famously warned against letting the "military-industrial complex" have too much power. The hope shared by so many—including Kurt and Bernie—in the late 1940s, hope for peace through disarmament and world government, came to seem like a distant pipe dream. Kurt never stopped longing for America to be what he believed it could be—the progressive, freethinking nation that had given birth to the New Deal—and in his work he returned to the theme again and again. America, he wrote in novels and essays and newspaper columns, could live up to its promise if only people would embrace their better selves—the selves dedicated to equality and free speech and kindness and giving the downtrodden a hand. By the time Bernie gave him back the letter he had sent to Uncle Alex fifty years earlier, Kurt was growing disheartened. That old America, he told friends, was gone. In his novel *Galápagos*, in many ways a rewrite of *Player Piano*, he had proposed that humanity would only improve when humans evolved away from being big-brained tool users and into furry, fish-eating amphibians. As Bernie was dying, Kurt was working on *Timequake*, in which the entire planet is forced to repeat a whole decade, "betting on the wrong horse again, marrying the wrong person again, getting the clap again. You name it!" History is literally doomed to repeat itself, at least in a clockwork universe. The novel is a kind of thought experiment about what it might be like to inhabit a completely deterministic world. But, as if shaking off the ghost of John von Neumann, Kurt returned the world to its messy unpredictability in the end. There's even a glimmer of hope in the mantra Kilgore Trout and a crew of volunteers use to spur people back into action once the timequake has ended and free will has returned: "You were sick, but now you're well again, and there's work to do."

•

Bernard Vonnegut's last published work was about art. During his research at Arthur D. Little, he had been introduced to a technique for making dendritic electrical discharge patterns on blocks of transparent plastic—little lightning bolts preserved in plastic like fossils in amber. Contemplation of the branching images had changed his thinking about lightning. Later, he and a colleague made convective flow patterns between sheets of plastic using aluminum paint and kerosene. Eventually, just for the fun of it, he began making permanent patterns by squeezing paint between two smooth surfaces—ceramic tile or glass or plastic—then pulling the surfaces apart.

"Physicists may already know enough about the behavior of liquids to predict the patterns that form, based on such variables as the rate at which the surfaces are pulled apart, the thickness of the liquid film, the viscosity and surface tension of the liquid and the angle at which it wets the surfaces," he wrote in his piece. In other words, physicists would see this process as reducible to a series of equations, would understand the know-how. But what about the know-what? Would they note how it glowed?

Kurt would. Bernie sent some of his patterns to his brother and asked him, is this art? Kurt's letter back reads as if he still occasionally relished the chance to lecture Bernie. "This is almost like telling you about the birds and the bees," he began. Art, he told his brother, was in the eye of the beholder. Contemplating it was a social activity.

"You are a justly revered experimentalist," Kurt wrote. "If you really want to know whether your pictures are, as you say, 'art' or not, you must display them in a public place somewhere, and then try to judge whether or not strangers liked to look at them, were glad that you had made them. That is the way the game is played. Let me know what happens."

Bernie's dendritic prints might or might not have been art. But in calling his brother a "justly revered experimentalist," Kurt was admitting something he had probably known for a long time: his brother was an artist. Bernard's real art was in the pages of scientific journals. It was scrawled in his notebooks. It was in tubes and jars and Rube Goldberg contraptions cluttering his disaster of a desk. It was ice crystals glinting in the sunlight, gammas carved out of the clouds, a thunderstorm flipped on its back like a turtle. It was water summoned from a cloud-painted sky. There's more art to science than most of us believe.

According to Kurt, at the end of his life Bernie cherished a collection of favorite quotations by Albert Einstein. One of them was "Physical concepts are free creations of the human mind, and are not, however it may seem, uniquely determined by the external world."

Another was "The most beautiful thing we can experience is the mysterious. It is the source of all true art and science."

Bernie died not long after giving Kurt his old letter. Before dying, he told his brother, "If the superpowers decide to duke it out with silver iodide, I think I can live with that."

Four days after Bernie died, Kurt finished the highly personal *Timequake*, his fourteenth novel, and the last he would ever write.

"I was the baby of the family," he explained at the end. "Now I don't have anybody to show off for anymore."

Bernie's son Terry died not long after him, losing a long struggle with cancer. Family members took both their ashes up in a small plane. They flew to the vicinity of Mount Greylock, where it all began, and scattered father and son into the clouds.

Kurt published a tribute to Bernie in *The New York Times Magazine*.

Thinking back to those early days after Hiroshima, when the scientists first knew sin, Kurt declared that Bernard had "original virtue." And then he described New York City's rainmaking efforts of 1950, a story that somehow the city had forgotten. But Kurt had not. The deluge was beautiful. Sure, he allowed, it might have "washed away a lot of privies and gazebos or whatever. But it did fill the reservoirs to brimming.

"And what the heck," he concluded. "It was only water."

Notes

NCAR-PDT   Philip Duncan Thompson Papers, Archives, National Center for Atmospheric Research

NYPL-CC   Crowell-Collier Publishing Company records, Manuscripts and Archives Division, New York Public Library

NYPL-NY   *New Yorker* records, Manuscripts and Archives Division, New York Public Library

NYU-AS   National Council for American-Soviet Friendship Records, TAM 134, Tamiment Library/Robert F. Wagner Labor Archives, Elmer Holmes Bobst Library, New York University

PU-CS   Archives of Charles Scribner's Sons, Manuscripts Division, Department of Rare Books and Special Collections, Princeton University Library

RAC-DM   Papers of Duncan A. MacInnes, Rockefeller University Archives, RG 450, Rockefeller Archive Center

UP-LB   Lemuel R. Boulware Papers, Kislak Center for Special Collections, Rare Books, and Manuscripts, University of Pennsylvania

1. Autumn Fog

3   *At the bottom of a snowy hollow*: Much of my account of Vonnegut's personal war experience comes from his discussion in his interview for *The Paris Review* 69 (Spring 1977), reprinted in Allen, *Conversations with Kurt Vonnegut*. "It was nice there for a few minutes," he said. The porcupine image is his.

4   *He hadn't realized how much he needed that*: Kurt Vonnegut to Jane Cox, June 1944, Vonnegut family collection.

4   *Still, for the first time in his life*: Shields, *And So It Goes,* 56. Late in life, Kurt was asked to choose a single memory that he would want played endlessly in the afterlife: he chose the moment he rolled to the front, "where I was doing everything right, where I was beyond criticism . . . I was right where I belonged." J. Rentilly, "The Best Jokes Are Dangerous: An Interview with Kurt Vonnegut: Part II," McSweeneys.net, September 17, 2002, www.mcsweeneys.net/articles/the-best-jokes-are-dangerous-an-interview-with-kurt-vonnegut-part-two.

4   *"the incredible artificial weather"*: Vonnegut, *Slaughterhouse-Five*, 106.

4   *Come out, the Nazis ordered again*: Vonnegut, *Fates Worse Than Death*, 96.

4   *Then out of the predawn darkness*: "It was as if the sky fell in," recalled Sam Giles of the 423rd's Company K, in Szpek, Idzikowski, and Szpek, *Shadows of Slaughterhouse Five*.

5   *"A hurricane of iron and fire"*: Gunther Holz, quoted in Kershaw, *Longest Winter*, 79.

5   *General Eisenhower had a standing bet*: Dupuy, *Hitler's Last Gamble*, 5.

6   *During World War I*: Norway relied on its fishing fleet to keep its citizens fed. But when war broke out, the British—knowing the weather could provide a tactical advantage—classified their weather forecasts. The Norwegian fleet had always relied on the British forecasts; the new secrecy caused fishing hauls to plummet, and Norwegians began to starve. A group of scientists at the Geophysical Institute in Bergen offered to provide weather services to the government. These theoretical heavyweights brought a new rigor to the study of large weather patterns that came to be called air mass analysis. A thorough account of the rise of this school of meteorology is Harper, *Weather by the Numbers*.

6 *Petterssen told Eisenhower's team*: Petterssen's *Weathering the Storm* tells the story of this historic forecast in detail.

7 *The attack that would come to be called*: Dupuy, *Hitler's Last Gamble*, 18.

7 *Two-thirds of its troops*: Like many personal details from this period, Kurt's attempts to get transferred to public relations duty come from his unpublished letters to Jane Cox from the period; Vonnegut family collection. Idzikowski cites the low age of the 106th in his introduction to Szpek, Idzikowski, and Szpek, *Shadows of Slaughterhouse Five*, 22. Kurt would make note of this in the full title of his war book: *Slaughterhouse-Five; or, The Children's Crusade: A Duty-Dance with Death.*

8 *They wanted to go*: In *Slaughterhouse-Five*, Kurt has Edgar Derby, the high school teacher who is executed for stealing a teapot, recount a capture that is almost exactly his own story. In the end, "the Americans put their weapons down, and they came out of the woods with their hands on top of their heads, because they wanted to go on living, if they possibly could." Vonnegut, *Slaughterhouse-Five*, 107.

9 *"It's a nasty picture"*: A collection of the *Cornell Daily Sun* columns is in LL-KV; along with his letters to Jane from the same period, the columns give a lively picture of Kurt's undergraduate years.

9 *He'd been sixteen*: Kurt describes this 1939 trip in "The Rover Boys," an unpublished manuscript composed of his letters home. LL-KV.

10 *He bragged about that to Jane Cox*: Kurt Vonnegut to Jane Cox, multiple dates, Vonnegut family collection.

11 *In Ithaca*: "I was happiest here," he later told a Cornell audience, "when I was all alone—and it was very late at night, and I was walking up the hill after having helped to put the *Sun* to bed." Vonnegut, *Palm Sunday*, 60.

11 *Toward the end of high school*: Shields has Vonnegut landing a job offer from *The Indianapolis Star*. But the *Star* was the city's staunchly conservative paper; the Vonneguts were readers of *The Indianapolis Times*. In *Timequake*, Vonnegut declares that he was offered a position at the *Times* through the machinations of a lawyer friend of his father's. Vonnegut, *Timequake*, 154.

11 *Be anything, he said bitterly*: Shields, *And So It Goes*, 34.

12 *That, Kurt said later, "was his idea of me"*: Ibid., 35.

14 *even Kurt had to admit it*: Kurt met Bow while on leave from the Army and commented on her beauty in a letter to Jane, March 1944, Vonnegut family collection.

14 *"the Flying Icing Wind Tunnel"*: Ice Research Base report, May 7, 1945. MEG-VS. Another airplane was later given the same name.

14 *The sergeant would sit casually by the hole*: Robert Morton Cunningham, autobiography online, www.egoaltar.com/fogseeker/.

15 *"He attended Cornell University"*: *Indianapolis Times*, January 15, 1945, 3.

15 *"I am very favorably impressed"*: Bernard Vonnegut to C. G. Suits, February 15, 1945. MIS-GE. His correspondence with Langmuir and Schaefer is in MEG-VS.

16 *Sometimes they worked*: Icing would remain a problem for aviation. The 2009 crash of an Air France Airbus in the Atlantic was attributed to icing on the plane's pitot tube—a problem first diagnosed in the 1920s.

17 *He'd been playing around with aircraft deicing*: The friend was James V. Dotson. Jim Dotson was killed while conducting test experiment flights on a Lockheed Electra in 1943, and Bernie became deicing director. James V. Dotson obituary,

MIT Technology Review 46 (1944). Also Robert Morton Cunningham, autobiographical sketch dated August 7, 1997, MIT Museum.

17 *He sometimes joked*: Bernard Vonnegut, talk given at the Weather Modification Association meeting, Los Angeles, 1976. Copy in MEG-BV. He also discusses going to work with Jim Dotson and Henry Houghton at MIT.

18 *Once, when he was in his early teens*: Scott Vonnegut, interview with the author, July 2013.

18 *President Charlie Wilson*: There were two CEOs named Charlie Wilson at the time: Engine Charlie of General Motors and Electric Charlie of GE. Engine Charlie was later appointed secretary of defense by Eisenhower. The Texas politician Charlie Wilson, played by Tom Hanks in the film *Charlie Wilson's War*, is another Charlie altogether.

18 *He planned for GE*: Chauncey Guy Suits, oral history, IEEE Global History Network, www.ieeeghn.org/wiki/index.php/Oral-HistoryGuy_Suits.

18 *There he met some of GE's scientific luminaries*: The GE scientists' interview evaluations of Bernard are still in MIS-GE, as is his application form.

2. Precipitating Events

21 *Someone was knocking on the door*: The story of the run-up to the Russia trip was told in a letter from Dean Langmuir to Ruth Van de Water, June 18, 1945, and quoted at length in Rosenfeld, *Quintessence*, 282–92. The chemist Duncan MacInnes kept a very informative diary of the entire trip, RAC-DM.

25 *"Dear People," it began*: The letter was published posthumously. Vonnegut, *Armageddon in Retrospect*, 11–13.

26 *But Bernard didn't tell Kurt about it*: No one I talked to from Kurt's or Bernard's family was aware of the publication, and Kurt never mentioned it.

26 *Even before Kurt wrote to his family*: Vonnegut to Cox, May 25, 1945, Vonnegut family collection.

26 *She had graduated from Swarthmore*: Vonnegut, *Timequake*, 222.

27 *He insisted on taking the wheel*: The account of picking up Kurt and the car ride home was written by Alex Vonnegut to Ella Vonnegut Stewart, July 4, 1945. Wakefield, *Letters*, 9.

28 *It was hard to believe*: Vonnegut to Cox, August 2, 1945, Vonnegut family collection.

29 *He consoled himself*: Vonnegut to Cox, n.d., but from context late July 1945, Vonnegut family collection.

29 *While awaiting Bernie's arrival*: Indianapolis had three papers in the 1940s: the morning *Indianapolis Star*, the evening *Indianapolis News*, and the afternoon *Indianapolis Times*. The *Star* and *News* had conservative reputations, and elsewhere Kurt identified the progressive *Times* as his family paper. It printed a society page announcement of his wedding and was the only Indy paper to review *Player Piano*. But Kurt identified the *News* as the paper whose offices he visited in his *Paris Review* "Art of Fiction" interview, and it makes sense he would visit the city's largest paper, "the great Hoosier daily," to get a sense of what was printed. Allen, *Conversations with Kurt Vonnegut*, 175.

29 *Strategic bombing was the front-page story*: *Indianapolis News*, February 14, 1945.

30 *He called the family*: Vonnegut to Cox, August 7, 1945, Vonnegut family collection.

30 *The usually unflappable Bernie*: "My brother was utterly sickened," Kurt wrote many years later. "It hit him in the gut. I really had no idea how horrible the news was, except through his reaction." McCartan, *Kurt Vonnegut*, 148.

31 *"the battle of the laboratories"*: White House press release, August 6, 1945. Along with "the greatest achievement of organized science in history," this phrase from Truman's press release was widely quoted in newspapers across the nation, including Indianapolis's.

31 *"Scientists' Dream Comes True"*: *Indianapolis Star*, August 7, 1945.

31 *There was no keeping*: Kurt told Jane that there was no secret in an undated letter clearly written shortly after the bomb was dropped, Vonnegut family collection.

32 *Kurt and Jane took the small, leaky rowboat*: Kurt tells this story in *Fates Worse Than Death*, 51–52.

33 *The wedding had been moved*: Earlier newspaper announcements (as well as Shields) set the date on September 14. But *The Indianapolis Times*, *The Indianapolis News*, and *The Columbian* (the magazine of Indianapolis's posh Columbia Club) all reported on September 1 that the couple were marrying that day, and it was the date of their anniversary. Kurt wrote to Jane about the Miami orders in August, and Bernard wrote to Chauncey Guy Suits on August 28 from Cambridge, so it's a pretty safe assumption that the orders led to moving up the date. Ben Hitz reported that it seemed as if there were a dark cloud over Kurt on his wedding day, and he assumed it was the war. Shields, *And So It Goes*, 83.

33 *In the newspaper announcements*: *Indianapolis Times*, September 1, 1945, reported that Kurt "attended Cornell." The Filomena Gould write-up for *The Indianapolis Star*, September 1, 1945, is the one Kurt carefully saved. LL-KV.

33 *He'd get a good job*: Vonnegut to Cox, August 2 and 3, 1945, Vonnegut family collection.

34 *"It's all an ocean"*: Kurt told the scholar Donald Fiene that this was one of Jane's favorite quotations. Fiene, "Elements of Dostoevsky in the Novels of Kurt Vonnegut," *Dostoevsky Studies* 2 (1981): 135. I quote from the Constance Garnett translation, which would have been the one Kurt and Jane owned in the Modern Library edition.

34 *It made her happy to believe*: "Jane could believe with all her heart anything that made being alive seem full of white magic." Vonnegut, *Timequake*, 135.

34 *As a child, Kurt had drawn*: Allen, *Conversations with Kurt Vonnegut*, 232.

34 *This could only be the dream*: "A hammer is still my Jesus, and my Virgin Mary is still a crosscut saw," he wrote in a 1980 essay on how he lost his innocence concerning technology. It was a theme he returned to many times. "How sick was the soul revealed by the flash at Hiroshima? . . . It was so sick that it did not want to live anymore." Vonnegut, *Palm Sunday*, 62–63.

35 *"Some good sacred memory"*: Fiene, "Elements of Dostoevsky," 134.

35 *For his subject, he chose a chair*: Ibid., 131.

35 *Irving Langmuir took his seat*: David Lilienthal published his notes on this conference as appendix A in his journals. *Atomic Energy Years*, 639. My account of the conference also comes from Wittner, *The Struggle Against the Bomb*; Smith,

A Peril and a Hope; Ashmore, *Unseasonable Truths*; and Glenn T. Seaborg, "Premonitions After the Bombs," *Bulletin of the Atomic Scientists*, December 1985.

37 *Yet many of the Chicago scientists*: In June 1945, a group of the Chicago scientists led by Szilard, Eugene Rabinowitch, Arthur Compton, and James Franck had sent a document called the Franck Report to Secretary of War Henry Stimson. They had argued vigorously that the first atomic bomb should be dropped not on a Japanese city but on an uninhabited island or desert spot. Only if the Japanese still refused to surrender should it be dropped on an actual city. Truman and his advisers rejected the idea. After all, they only had two bombs.

37 *"The physicists have known sin"*: This widely quoted line seems to have first appeared in print in J. Robert Oppenheimer, *Physics in the Contemporary World* (Anthoensen Press, 1947), 11. *Life* magazine quoted it in 1949.

38 *He stuck to the script*: Langmuir's every pronouncement was widely reported in the media. "Langmuir Warns of Danger to U.S.," *New York Times*, October 9, 1945; "Langmuir Urges Atom Pact, Says War Might Strip Earth," *New York Times*, November 17, 1945; "Crisis by '55 Seen in Atom Disunity: Scientist Tells of Atomic Energy," *New York Times*, December 1, 1945.

39 *Kurt stood in the shower*: Kurt Vonnegut to Jane Vonnegut, October 6, 1945. Much of my understanding of this period in Kurt's life is based on his unpublished letters to Jane between 1941 and 1946, nearly daily during his time at Fort Riley, generously shared with me by the Vonnegut family. Sadly, Jane's letters were not preserved, so where I have described her response, it is because Kurt mentioned or described it in one of his letters.

40 *The day the acceptance letter arrived*: At least he remembered it as such later. Vonnegut, *Wampeters, Foma, and Granfalloons*, 177.

40 *He would study anthropology*: He planned to study anthropology before arriving at Chicago. Kurt Vonnegut to Jane Vonnegut, December 1, 1945, Vonnegut family collection.

40 *Kurt had thought about going to its law school*: He wrote this to Jane from the Army in 1944, Vonnegut family collection.

40 *One of the very first*: Kurt included "Palaia" in a list of stories he intended to write in a letter to Jane, October 9, 1945, Vonnegut family collection.

41 *Bernie was the great one*: Vonnegut to Cox, August 3, 1945, Vonnegut family collection. Protestations about his lack of genius were a regular theme in his letters to Jane from the Army.

3. Head in the Clouds

44 *One of the most famous stories told about Steinmetz*: This version is mostly cribbed from the MIT president Charles M. Vest's Charge to the Graduates, June 4, 1999, http://web.mit.edu/newsoffice/1999/vestspeech.html. The story is also frequently told in the self-help books for businessmen and Bible students commonly sold in airport bookstores.

45 *The rest of the time*: My information about Doc Whitney and the Research Lab comes largely from Wise, *Willis R. Whitney, General Electric, and the Origins of U.S. Industrial Research*, 77. It's interesting that tech companies have been given credit for inventing policies like Google's 80/20 rule—in which engineers spend

20 percent of their time working on things that interest them—when they are simply following the GE model.

46 *Albert Hull taught Greek*: Lee de Forest, quoted in Rosenfeld, *Quintessence*, 154.

47 *If he didn't find something quickly*: Bernard Vonnegut, typescript interview with Barrington Havens, February 12, 1952, MEG-BV.

48 *The horror of Hiroshima*: This brand of postwar optimism makes frequent appearances in Kurt's fiction and nonfiction. "Think of the new era that is being born," *Jailbird*'s narrator, Walter Starbuck, tells his wife, Ruth, right after the war. "The world has learned its lesson at last, at last. The closing chapter to ten thousand years of madness and greed is being written right here and now—in Nuremberg . . . It's the most important turning point in history." Vonnegut, *Jailbird*, 67–68. Kurt himself wrote to Marc Leeds in 1995, "Once the Great Depression and the Second World War were over, we planned to build a Garden of Eden here." Wakefield, *Letters*, 364.

48 *But there were also tedious scientific tasks*: "I was still cowed by the science thing," he later recalled. McCartan, *Kurt Vonnegut*, 134.

49 *The adviser had recommended cultural anthropology*: Vonnegut, *Wampeters, Foma, and Granfalloons*, 178.

49 *"Wailing Shall Be in All Streets"*: This essay would remain unpublished until 2008, after Kurt's death. Vonnegut, *Armageddon in Retrospect*, 33–34.

50 *Jane went through it*: A typed manuscript of this essay is in LL-KV; Edie Vonnegut identified the hand in which the edits were written as her mother's.

51 *Snow had brought Vincent*: Schaefer, "Twenty Years at Langmuir University."

52 *"Look, Vince," he said*: Vincent relates this conversation in a conversation with Bernie, Raymond Falconer, and Duncan Blanchard videotaped in 1989. "Conversations on the Early Days of Cloud Seeding and the Development of the Atmospheric Sciences Research Center," MEG-UA.

53 *Vince had an idea*: My account of the discovery of dry ice nucleation comes from Katharine Blodgett, "Vincent Schaefer and Snow Making," a paper read at a meeting of the Schenectady Fortnightly Club, February 2, 1948, MIS-GE; Schaefer, "Twenty Years at Langmuir University"; and Vincent Schaefer GE lab notebooks, MEG-VS.

55 *Together they went looking for her adviser*: Vonnegut, *Timequake*, 126.

55 *When he heard the whine of an airplane*: The early days of Project Cirrus have been reconstructed using Havens, Jiusto, and; Vonnegut, *Early History of Cloud Seeding*; Project Cirrus Occasional Reports; Project Cirrus Flight Data; and Vince and Bernie's lab notebooks, MEG-VS and MEG-BV. Also critical were Langmuir, *Cloud Nucleation*, and Langmuir's lab notebooks, LOC-IL. Bernie's lunchtime story is told in Steven Spencer, "The Man Who Can Make It Rain," *Saturday Evening Post*, October 25, 1947.

58 *"I could see it"*: Blodgett, "Vincent Schaefer and Snow Making."

58 *"Well, Schaefer made it snow"*: Havens, Jiusto, and Vonnegut, *Early History of Cloud Seeding*, 7.

58 *"Scientists of the General Electric Company"*: GE News Bureau press release, November 14, 1946.

59 *Letters and telegrams poured into the Research Lab*: Letters and clippings were collected by both Vincent and Bernie, MEG-VS and MEG-BV.

60 *"Time to go home, Barney"*: Blodgett, "Vincent Schaefer and Snow Making." My account of Bernie's discovery is also based on his papers and GE lab notebooks, MEG-BV.

62 *"Schaefer made some seeding runs"*: Langmuir to C. N. Touart, December 26, 1946, MEG-VS.

63 *Now Langmuir was talking in sweeping terms*: Horace Byers, "History of Weather Modification," in Hess, *Weather and Climate Modification*.

64 *"comprehend all the forces"*: Laplace, *Essai sur les probabilités*, 4. Quoted in Newton, *From Clockwork to Crapshoot*, 108.

64 *"He who would master nature"*: Cited in a memorial to Harry written by Francis Reichelderfer, *Monthly Weather Review*, October 1963.

64 *The GE scientists' revelations were the "outstanding contribution"*: Report to the Bureau Chief, LOC-HW. He would continue to denigrate their "naive" approach for years.

65 *"I promise to scrub the bathroom"*: Wakefield, *Letters*, 13–14.

66 *He wanted to be part of it*: "I looked on the University of Chicago community as a folk society—and I felt like an outsider in it . . . I wasn't treated badly, but they already had a family," Kurt wrote in "A Very Fringe Character," in McQuade, *Unsentimental Education*.

66 *he exhibited three paintings*: Kurt and Jane Vonnegut to Walt and Helen Vonnegut, September 1, 1947. Wakefield, *Letters*, 20.

4. Bolt of Lightning

68 *He was thinking about computers*: Cited by George Dyson, son of Freeman Dyson, in *Turing's Cathedral*, ix. My background data on von Neumann come from Macrae, *John von Neumann*; and Heims, *John von Neumann and Norbert Wiener*.

68 *Now he was refining the architecture*: There is some confusion about the name of the institute computer. Early on, some people would refer to it as "Johnniac," then later "MANIAC." Ultimately, it was simply known as the IAS machine. The name "Johnniac" was later used officially for a Rand computer, and "MANIAC" was used for one built at Los Alamos, both using the institute machine's design, which came to be known as the von Neumann architecture.

68 *And that's where Harry Wexler came in*: My account of the institute's Meteorology Project is based on Harper, *Weather by the Numbers*; Nebeker, *Calculating the Weather*; George Dyson, *Turing's Cathedral*; oral histories at NCAR-AMS; papers at NCAR-PDT, LOC-FR, and LOC-HW; and 2014 interviews at the Institute for Advanced Study with Freeman Dyson, who came there as a young scholar during the Meteorology Project.

69 *In October 1945, Zworykin issued*: Vladimir Zworykin, "Outline of Weather Proposal" (white paper, October 1945), reprinted in *History of Meteorology* 4 (2008).

70 *"first steps towards influencing"*: Harper, *Weather by the Numbers*, 102–103.

70 *It was just the kind of experiment he liked*: Kurt calls Bernie's approach to science "a form of practical joking" in a 1987 interview with Hank Nuwer. Allen, *Conversations with Kurt Vonnegut*, 246. Bernie's son Scott recounted his father's earthy sense of humor, interview with the author, July 2013.

71 *He did it over and over*: Blodgett, "Vincent Schaefer and Snow Making."

71 *Instead, flight experiments would be "conducted by the government"*: Quoted in Havens, Jiusto, and Vonnegut, *Early History of Cloud Seeding*, 8–9.

72 *Just to be safe, Irving resigned his sponsorship*: Irving Langmuir to William Howard Melish, March 31, 1947, NYU-AS. Irving was one of the earliest to resign; later, its long list of scientific and artistic members would dwindle to nearly none as people scrambled to avoid persecution in the McCarthy era.

72 *In keeping with their new publicity aims*: "Army and GE Join to 'Make Weather,'" *New York Times*, March 14, 1947.

73 *He'd applied for a job*: Kurt recounts this in a letter to Knox Burger, July 2, 1949, NYPL-CC.

73 *In the solicitation letter*: Wakefield, *Letters*, 16. The letter to General Motors that Wakefield prints is an exact duplicate, but for the name, of the one Kurt sent to GE, which was generously shared with me by Mark Vonnegut.

74 *As Rear Admiral Luis de Florez had written*: "Weather—the New Super Weapon," *American Magazine*, September 1946.

74 *That's what he'd tried to do earlier that month*: "GE Rainmakers' Aid Sought to Quell California Fire," *Schenectady Gazette*, August 8, 1947.

75 *General George Kenney, of the Strategic Air Command*: "28,000,000 Urged to Support MIT," *New York Times*, June 15, 1947.

76 *It was an overpriced French joint*: Kurt calls it a "clip joint" in his letter to Walt and Helen. Wakefield, *Letters*, 19.

77 *But the couple would have to face*: Dan Wakefield writes, "Kurt's classmate Victor Jose told me that 'if they stayed in Indianapolis, they feared that Jane would be expected by her family to join the Junior League, and she and Kurt didn't like that "socialite" kind of life. They both were rebels even then.'" Ibid., 5. They were, but Jane still joined the Junior League in Schenectady, where they worked hard to fit in.

77 *Bernie had already told George*: Kurt mentioned Bernie's recommendation in his letter to General Electric. Also, Shields, *And So It Goes*, 94; and Wakefield, *Letters*, 19.

5. Eye of the Storm

79 *"I own a home now"*: Wakefield, *Letters*, 23.

79 *He felt manly enough*: Shields, *And So It Goes*, 96.

81 *There, it became part*: Nye, *Image Worlds*, 60.

81 *His new bosses gave him a physical*: Kurt Vonnegut to Jane Vonnegut, dated only Friday, Vonnegut family collection. Writers on Vonnegut almost inevitably fail to be clear about the distinction between GE (whose motto was "Progress is our most important product"), the GE Research Lab (called the House of Magic), the Schenectady Works (the plant itself), and the Schenectady Works Lab (like the many GE plants, the Schenectady Works had its own separate research lab). Many critics and biographers repeat not only the incorrect statement that Kurt worked for the GE Research Lab but also the erroneous claim that he wrote publicity for Project Cirrus.

82 *Stories about things*: The GE sales force refrigerator that walked and talked was featured in an unsigned story in *The GE Monogram* in January/February 1949 that was likely written by Kurt. It eventually morphed into female form and became the subject of Kurt's short story "Jenny," unpublished until the posthumous *While Mortals Sleep*.

82 *"A hurricane is a complicated thing"*: My account of the hurricane seeding comes from Havens, Jiusto, and Vonnegut, *Early History of Cloud Seeding*; Schaefer, *Final Report Project Cirrus*, Part 1; and Schaefer, "Twenty Years at Langmuir University."

84 *The steering committee drew up an official plan*: Irving Langmuir, "The Control of Hurricanes" (white paper, December 15, 1955), MEG-BV.

84 *"We accomplished our purpose"*: The press conference was reported in many newspapers, but the most complete account was the front-page story in GE's hometown paper. "Hurricane Study Only Begun, Says Schaefer," *Schenectady Gazette*, October 17, 1947.

84 *That's not what* The New York Times *had reported*: "Hurricane Sweeps into Atlantic Leaving Florida Widely Flooded," *New York Times*, October 13, 1947.

84 *"The next great tropical storm"*: "Hurricane Busters Ready to Test Chemical Seeding," *Rome Sentinel*, September 8, 1947.

84–85 *The steering committee composed a press release*: It's unclear if this press release was ever issued. Undated draft of Project Cirrus press release, MEG-BV.

85 *Nevertheless, when the Project Cirrus team*: Mobile *Press-Register*, October 12, 1947.

86 *"pretty sore at the army and navy"*: Quoted in Fleming, *Fixing the Sky*, 152.

86 *"low Yankee trick"*: "Science: Yankee Meddling?," *Time*, November 10, 1947.

86 *The sheriff of Savannah*: Schaefer, "Twenty Years at Langmuir University."

87 *"Did science, for the first time"*: *Schenectady Gazette*, October 31, 1947.

87 *"Perhaps you saw the news reports"*: Wakefield, *Letters*, 23. In this letter, Kurt also discusses his plans to take his master's exams and work on finishing his thesis at Columbia.

89 *He submitted them all*: A rejection letter for "Basic Training" from *Redbook* dated August 4, 1949, is in the rejection letters file, LL-KV. Based on the juvenile style and comments in letters to Jane, I believe Kurt actually started the novella in Indiana, before going to Chicago, but could not confirm it definitively.

89 *They put candles*: Yarmolinsky, *Angels Without Wings*, 7.

89 *He was looking forward*: Bernard Vonnegut, interview with Havens, February 12, 1952. This account was also put together using Bernard's paper "Experiments with Silver Iodide Smokes in the Natural Atmosphere," *Bulletin of the American Meteorological Society* 31, no. 5 (May 1950): 151–57; Schaefer, *Final Report Project Cirrus*, Part 1; and flight data from "Data, Catalogue of Data for PC 1950" folder, MEG-BV.

90 *"The photograph of General Electric's Dr. Bernard Vonnegut"*: Wakefield, *Letters*, 25.

91 *And at some point, he gave it to Bernie*: Kurt included the letter with a typed explanation in his papers, LL-KV. He also recounted the letter's journey from Alex to Bernie to him in the epilogue to *Timequake*.

91 *Langmuir was giving the keynote address*: "A hectic day," Irving wrote in his diary after his day with the GE legal team, LOC-IL. Also, Rosenfeld, *Quintessence*,

300. Irving's paper was published as "The Growth of Particles in Smokes and Clouds and the Production of Snow from Super-cooled Clouds," *Proceedings of the American Philosophical Society* 92:3 (July 1948).

92 *Project Cirrus was wading*: Byers gives an account of meteorologists' response to Langmuir's talk in "History of Weather Modification," 14.

93 *Chief Reichelderfer convened an advisory committee*: He sent Langmuir an invitation to join but then never invited Langmuir to attend a single meeting. Irving Langmuir lab notebook, LOC-IL. Other facts about the Weather Bureau's anti-Cirrus campaign have been collected from LOC-HW and LOC-FR.

94 *"Some 15 different types of finely divided soil"*: GE News Bureau press release, April 22, 1948, initialed KV, MIS-GE.

94 *He didn't love playing in the snow*: Local newspapers reported on the snowmaking scientist's broken ankle with great glee.

94 *GE cultivated this obsessiveness*: Kurt described the Research Lab as a playground in the essay "Think Bank." *Forbes ASAP*, May 31, 1999.

94 *They were in the business of seeking truth*: "Buggering truth for money" is Kurt's phrase, from the introduction to his second short story collection, where he attributes it to a college professor talking about public relations men and writers of slick fiction. Vonnegut, *Welcome to the Monkey House*, xiv.

95 *He stayed lost in thought*: Rosenfeld, *Quintessence*, 304.

95 *Kurt could get annoyed*: Scott Vonnegut tells a funny story about how even when they were old, Kurt sometimes had to work to get a word in edgewise, once even interrupting Bernie by jumping up and down and yelling, like a small child, "You never let me speak!" in a half-serious parody of his own younger-brother frustration. Interview with the author, July 2013.

95 *If subjected to enough pressure*: Ice-2 crystals are now recognized to have the shape of a rhombohedron—a prism with six rhomboid faces.

96 *And who knew*: Today, scientists have identified more variant forms of ice than of any other known material. Normal ice is known to science as ice-1h. After that, it has variants from ice-1 all the way through ice-15.

98 *The songbook also had the words*: Vince's songbook and commemorative booklet are in MEG-VS. The script of the 1948 pageant is in UP-LB.

99 *Mr. Bullshit was more like it*: In a 1983 letter to *The Washington Spectator*, the former GE employee David Anderton wrote, "Boulware's first name was, I am certain, Lemuel. He was known to the union then as 'Mr. Bullwhip' and to some of us in a GE Management course as 'Mr. Bull——t.' Ask Vonnegut." Kurt cut this letter out and saved it in his files.

99 *GE wouldn't be caught dead*: Vonnegut, *Bagombo Snuff Box*, 8.

99 *In Monday morning staff sessions*: Reminiscences of Ollie Lyon and Bob Pace from *Happy Birthday, Kurt Vonnegut*, a birthday festschrift put together by his second wife, Jill Krementz, for his sixtieth.

100 *Frequently, they didn't even know the cause*: A new young physicist at GE named Robert Vought was denied security clearance for mysterious reasons and had been struggling unsuccessfully for more than a year to clear his name. Guy Suits eventually suggested he look for another job. See Wang, *American Science in an Age of Anxiety*, 102–17.

100 *They didn't know that the FBI was compiling dossiers*: I received the FBI dossier on Irving Langmuir through the National Archives after filing a Freedom of Information Act request with the FBI. The FBI would neither confirm nor deny that it had a file on Bernard Vonnegut: its letter said that potentially relevant records were destroyed in 1987.

100 *"GE Disease"*: Krementz, *Happy Birthday, Kurt Vonnegut.*

101–102 *Acting president of the tiny New Mexico School of Mines*: Jack Workman ended up at the New Mexico School of Mines after launching a research and development division at the University of New Mexico physics department, where he originally taught. During the war, Workman and his team developed the proximity fuse, bringing in a huge influx of government money, and in 1946 the University of New Mexico tried to force them to share it with the rest of the school. Jack and most of his division resigned and moved to the School of Mines. Chew, *Storms Above the Desert,* chapter 2.

102 *Everyone was terrified except Irving*: Schaefer, "Twenty Years at Langmuir University."

103 *"The odds in favor of this conclusion"*: Langmuir, "Results of the Seeding of Cumulus Clouds in New Mexico," Research Laboratory Report No. RL: 364, June 1950.

6. Watersheds

104 *"If you think that's bad"*: This comment captured something about Bernie for Kurt, who repeated the story in a number of interviews and essays, as he often did his best material. "Address to the American Physical Society" (1969), in Vonnegut, *Wampeters, Foma, and Granfalloons,* 93. Duncan Blanchard, Bernard's young colleague at GE, also described for me the chaotic danger zone of Bernie's work space.

105 *You turned on the tap*: The remark about "nothing" coming out of the taps sounds like Bernie's sense of humor, and the reporter clearly spent much of his time with the Project Cirrus team. The quip is in the same section as a description of the team's new quarters. "300 Tour Main Wing of GE Research Lab," *Schenectady Gazette,* December 3, 1948.

105 *"You'll know when I'm retired"*: Havens, Jiusto, and Vonnegut, *Early History of Cloud Seeding,* 11.

107 *As Kurt and Jane prepared to go out*: Ollie Lyon recalls this incident in John Dinsmore, "Kurt and Ollie," *Firsts,* October 1992. The *Schenectady Gazette* always printed guest lists for Junior League dances; the list of November 26, 1948, includes Mr. and Mrs. Kurt Vonnegut but not Mr. and Mrs. Ollie Lyon. Majie Failey describes Alice Vonnegut wearing sneakers with an evening gown in *We Never Danced Cheek to Cheek,* 58.

108 *On weekdays in Building 6*: My account of Kurt's early work is based largely on his short story drafts, LL-KV. Some of the PR work he did at GE can be found in MIS-GE.

108 *So in the evenings and on weekends*: Shields, *And So It Goes,* 101.

108 *A smooth, steady clacking*: Jane describes listening for the rhythm of his typing in Yarmolinsky, *Angels Without Wings,* 5.

108 *They knew they'd find Kurt*: John Dinsmore, "Kurt and Ollie," *Firsts*, October 1992. This interview with Ollie Lyon, a colleague of Kurt's at the GE News Bureau, is a rare account of the work environment there. It is also probably the source of a frequently repeated mistake: the claim that Kurt wrote most of the publicity for Project Cirrus. Initialed GE press releases prove that in fact the company seems to have deliberately avoided having one brother write about the other.

109 *When Jane gave him a grocery list*: Rejection letters folder, LL-KV.

109 *He had a sneaking suspicion*: "We are what we pretend to be, so we must be careful what we pretend to be." Epigraph to Vonnegut, *Mother Night*.

110 *And so, right there in Building 6*: Some short paragraphs from early drafts of "Mnemonics" are written on a Building 6 notepad.

112 *"There is no use worrying"*: Langmuir, "Large-Scale Seeding of Stratus and Cumulus Clouds with Dry Ice." Stenographic record of paper given at the January 1949 AMS meeting, LOC-IL.

112 *And it was simply outrageous*: Langmuir, *Cloud Nucleation*, 556.

112 *"The experiments showed"*: Richard Coons, R. G. Gentry, and Ross Gunn, *Second Partial Report on the Artificial Production of Precipitation: Cumuliform Clouds, Ohio* (U.S. Weather Bureau, 1949).

113 *After the talk, Irving took Reichelderfer aside*: An account of this conversation is in Langmuir, *Cloud Nucleation*, 213.

113 *"Rain-Making Held of No Importance"*: *New York Times*, January 26, 1949.

114 *The Navy and the Signal Corps liked his silver iodide generator*: R. W. Larson to Ruth Dwyer, GE memo, February 1, 1949, MEG-BV.

114 *They simply assumed*: Project officer (Naval Science Division, Office of Naval Research), to Bernard Vonnegut, January 21, 1949, MEG-BV.

114 *"The policy of the government itself"*: "A Scientist Rebels," *The Atlantic*, January 1947.

115 *Wiener's letter had made*: It also had a big effect on Harry Wexler, who found it infuriating. He and one of the researchers at the Institute for Advanced Study began calling it "the affair of Wiener," NCAR-PDT. In essays and interviews, Kurt frequently discussed the GE scientists' interest in ethical questions.

115 *Two years of debate*: Kurt mentions the Wiener essay in several interviews, including one with *Playboy*. Vonnegut, *Wampeters, Foma, and Granfalloons*, 269. The *Bulletin of the Atomic Scientists* would have been widely read in Schenectady; it's reasonable to think that Kurt would have seen the follow-up essay or heard about it. He discussed Wiener's refusal directly in a 1980 interview with Robert Musil, published in *The Nation* and later collected in McCartan, *Kurt Vonnegut*, 73.

115 *"The degradation of the position"*: Norbert Wiener, "A Rebellious Scientist After Two Years," *Bulletin of the Atomic Scientists* 4, no. 11 (1948).

116 *Kurt's new story*: In interviews later in life, Kurt would refer to "Report on the Barnhouse Effect" as his first story. It would be his first published story, but the manuscripts prove it was far from the first he wrote. Still, a surprising number of literary critics have taken him at his word, failing to perceive the long, grueling apprenticeship that led to it. The drafts at LL-KV show the story's painstaking evolution. The only lines I quote are those that are consistent in early drafts and in the final published version in Vonnegut, *Welcome to the Monkey House*.

118 *"It is not possible"*: William Lewis to Irving Langmuir, memo, June 23, 1949, LOC-IL.

119 *It had proved*: "Trial by Newspaper," *Scientific American*, February 16, 1949.

120 *The stories were brisk*: Russell to Vonnegut, February 18, 1949, rejection letters folder, LL-KV.

120 *That month, three thousand delegates*: Robbie Lieberman, "Does That Make Peace a Bad Word? American Responses to the Communist Peace Offensive, 1949–1950," *Peace & Change* 17, no. 2 (April 1992).

120 *"This is a little sententious for us"*: This undated letter from Knox Burger is in the general rejection letters file at the Lilly and is quoted by Shields, *And So It Goes*, 101. However, by cross-referencing the note with Kurt's own scrupulous records of his early stories and their submissions, one can see that the story he sent to *Collier's* in April was "Report on the Barnhouse Effect," not "Mnemonics," as Shields has it. Burger's letters in NYPL-CC show that Vonnegut sent him "Mnemonics" after they met for lunch in July.

121 *Clams, cigars, cocktails*: Kurt literalized the idea of the corporate clambake as a kind of funeral in the famous clambake celebrating Kilgore Trout and memorializing American eloquence threaded throughout his valedictory last novel, *Timequake*.

121 *George Burns was a photographer*: Kurt's first letter to Knox Burger begins, "George Burns, who, never having read anything of mine, takes a casual interest in my writing career, allowed as to how he had a friend on *Collier's* fiction staff who might be able to give me some help. The friend turned out to be you." NYPL-CC, and Wakefield, *Letters*, 26. Wakefield, like Shields, seems to have taken the name George Burns to refer to the popular comedian—an understandable mistake, because Vonnegut sometimes referred to the famous George Burns as well. However, the letter only makes sense if referring to his acquaintance George Burns.

121 *After flying over Nagasaki*: "G-E Photographer Takes Pictures of Atomic-Bombed City," *Schenectady Works News*, September 21, 1945.

122 *Once, Knox had even taken Kurt's suggestion*: Shields, *And So It Goes*, 40.

122 *"Sorry you didn't care"*: Wakefield, *Letters*, 26. Kurt's underlining of "typewritten" is not reproduced in Wakefield, though it would seem to be essential to understanding his tone. The original letter is in NYPL-CC.

122 *He would see if he could do anything*: Account taken from Bernard Vonnegut interview, 1952, and Data: GE Research Notepad, July 19, 20, and 21, 1949, both MEG-BV. Also Schaefer, *Final Report Project Cirrus*.

122 *If the bureau scientists were using other compounds*: Bernard Vonnegut, "Note on Nuclei for Ice Crystal Formation," *BAMS* 30, no. 5 (May 1949).

123 *That meant the winds were carrying*: "Whooping it up" is Bernie's phrasing from his lab notebook, MEG-BV.

124 *"You were running the generator today?"*: Bernie recounted these conversations with Langmuir in his February 12, 1952, interview with Havens.

125 *"Taking all in all"*: Quoted in Langmuir, *Cloud Nucleation*, 208.

125 *The FAA had ruined flying for him*: Vincent recounts this fact in "Twenty Years at Langmuir University."

125 *"What river is that?"*: Langmuir, *Cloud Nucleation*, 110.

126 *As Langmuir enthused*: Teller, *Memoirs*, 253. Teller places this meeting in 1947; however, it seems clear from context that he must be misremembering the date.

126 *"In phase," he would chant*: Rosenfeld, *Quintessence*, 183. Vonnegut relates the charlatan comment in *Palm Sunday*, 145.

128 *The next day, Knox returned "Mnemonics"*: Vonnegut to Burger, July 1, 2, 6, 17, and 20, 1949; Burger to Vonnegut, July 8, 1949; Gertrude Buckman to Vonnegut, July 14, 1949, all NYPL-CC.

129 *Unless he wrote in a secretary*: Burger to Vonnegut, July 13, 1949, LL-KV.

129 *"I told him"*: Burger to Vonnegut, July 19, 1949, NYPL-CC, and quoted in Shields, *And So It Goes*, 108. Kurt's much-edited draft of his response is in LL-KV.

130 *"the net result lacks conviction"*: Burger to Vonnegut, August 1, 1949, NYPL-CC.

130 *Knox returned it almost immediately*: Vonnegut to Burger, July 20, 1949; Burger to Vonnegut, July 26, 1949, NYPL-CC.

130 *He figured it had the best chance*: Vonnegut to Littauer, August 18, 1949, LL-KV.

130 *Collier's itself had recently run*: "UN Is Doing a Job," *Collier's*, July 9, 1949.

131 *No editor would stand for*: Littauer to Vonnegut, LL-KV.

132 *"Only the descendants"*: Albany *Times-Union*, August 28, 1949.

7. Rainmakers

133 *Ever since the Project Cirrus team had returned*: Bernie's activities were recorded in his lab notebook, MEG-BV. Irving wrote up his Crown Island experiment and his conclusions in his own lab notebook, LOC-IL. Guy Suits described his meeting with all three scientists in a letter to Irving cc'd to Vince and Bernie. Suits to Langmuir, August 26, 1949, MEG-BV.

135 *"in which the behavior"*: These definitions are quotations from his paper "Science, Common Sense, and Decency," first given in 1942 and published as chapter 1 of his book *Phenomena, Atoms, and Molecules* (1950), but he had been developing the idea much earlier, including in his 1934 paper "Science as a Guide in Life."

136 *It was simply a matter of knowing*: Freeman Dyson, who heard von Neumann speak on the topic around 1950, summarizes Johnnie's attitude as "All processes that are stable we shall predict. All processes that are unstable we shall control," in *Infinite in All Directions*, 182. Dyson's paraphrase of Johnnie's attitude has often been incorrectly attributed to von Neumann as a quotation.

136–137 *There would never be*: Wiener had begun insisting in *Cybernetics* that weather prediction should be undertaken not in a deterministic way but in a probabilistic one. Von Neumann and his chief meteorologist, Jule Charney, disagreed. The argument flared up periodically at conferences and meetings. Charney even heard that Wiener considered Johnnie and him to be *gonifs*—Yiddish for "scoundrels"—in their attempt to hoodwink the world into believing that they could turn the weather into an equation. Jule Charney, "Conversation with George Platzman," in Lindzen, Lorenz, and Platzman, *Atmosphere*, 57.

137 *The idea he came up with*: I discussed Langmuir's experiment with Freeman Dyson. "It was the right approach," he said, "to produce a signal." Interview, February 2014.

137 *"should be carried out"*: Suits to Langmuir, cc'ed to Vonnegut and Schaefer, August 26, 1949, MEG-BV.

138 *"Why doesn't he use his real name on the story?"*: Burger to Littauer, October 13, 1949, NYPL-CC, and quoted in Shields, *And So It Goes*, 109.

139 *Kurt knew in his heart*: Letters between Vonnegut and Littauer are in the short story files, LL-KV.

139 *But as Jane giddily told a neighbor*: Shields, *And So It Goes*, 110.

139 *"I think I'm on my way"*: Wakefield, *Letters*, 27.

139 *"An oath, an oath"*: Vonnegut, *Fates Worse Than Death*, 26.

140–141 *His paper came*: Harry Wexler, trip report, March 10, 1949, LOC-HW.

141 *Had Project Cirrus been around in World War II*: C. Lester Walker, "The Man Who Makes Weather," *Harper's*, January 1950.

141 *It was Kenneth collecting*: Kurt's earlier rejections are in a separate file in LL-KV. The rejections sent to Littauer are in NYPL-CC and NYPL-NY.

142 *There was even a hilarious playlet*: "Das Ganz Arm Dolmetscher" was ultimately published as "Der Arme Dolmetscher" in *The Atlantic* in July 1955 and in Vonnegut, *Bagombo Snuff Box*, in 1999, 228.

142 *In fact he'd spent*: Vonnegut to Miller Harris, May 19, 1950, LL-MH.

143 *And now, at the annual AMS meeting*: Irving noted that it was the most important paper of his career in his lab notebook. The paper, "Control of Precipitation from Cumulus Clouds by Various Seeding Techniques," was published in *Science*, July 14, 1950.

146 *Langmuir triumphantly took William Lewis out to lunch*: Langmuir recounts this conversation in his lab notebook.

147 *"a graduate of the University of Chicago"*: *Schenectady Gazette*, February 3, 1950.

148 *He was, Kurt grumbled, turning to Yaddo again*: Vonnegut to Miller Harris, February 16, 1950, in Wakefield, *Letters*, 32.

149 *First noticed by a scientist at Bell Labs*: Harry Wexler wrote to the Bell Labs scientist M. W. Baldwin Jr. in November 1948 asking him for a copy of his original paper about the "ghosts." LOC-HW.

149 *Kurt made his main character*: Vonnegut, "Thanasphere," in *Bagombo Snuff Box*.

151 *"a competent meterologist"*: *The New York Times*, February 16, 1950.

152 *But after the war*: Eventually, Sverre Petterssen would write a corrective memoir that historians of meteorology consider authoritative: *Weathering the Storm*. James Rodger Fleming has written a succinct summary of the debate: "Sverre Petterssen, the Bergen School, and the Forecasts for D-Day," *Proceedings of the International Commission on the History of Meteorology* 1, no. 1 (2004).

152 *"using GE and the names Langmuir, Schaefer and Vonnegut"*: Hammond to Langmuir, cc'ed to Bernard Vonnegut, February 3, 1950, MEG-BV.

152 *a "new way" to make rain*: "New Way Is Found of Producing Rain," *New York Times*, December 24, 1949.

152 *Then Langmuir took him aside*: Langmuir lab notebook.

153 *Dr. John Herbert Hollomon invited Kurt*: "Dr. Hollomon at Home," a press release signed by Vonnegut with photos signed by Burns, March 1950, MIS-GE.

154 *"A one-armed robot on wheels"*: GE News Bureau press release initialed "KV," March 14, 1950.

155 *Kurt couldn't blame the inventors*: "To have a little clicking box make all the decisions wasn't a vicious thing to do. But it was too bad for the human beings who got their dignity from their jobs." Kurt Vonnegut, interviewed by David Standish, 1973, in Allen, *Conversations*, 93.

155 *Langmuir and Katharine Blodgett*: "Conversations on the Early Days of Cloud Seeding and the Development of the Atmospheric Sciences Research Center."

155 *"Are machines smarter than ME?"*: "Mechanized Math Shark: The Computer," *GE Monogram*, March–April 1950.

155 *Wiener defined cybernetics*: The definition was the subtitle of *Cybernetics*.

156 *Kurt named his story*: "EPICAC" was collected in Vonnegut, *Welcome to the Monkey House*.

157 *Knox returned it with notes*: Burger to Vonnegut, undated letter filed with "EPICAC" drafts, LL-KV.

157 *The first flight of New York's rainmakers*: My account of New York City's rainmaking is compiled from the near-daily newspaper stories on it at the time, mostly in *The New York Times*, but also the New York *Daily News*, the *Schenectady Gazette*, *The Kingston Daily Freeman*, and the *Catskill Mountain News*. The story is also recounted briefly in Galusha, *Liquid Assets*.

159 *"no vested property rights"*: *Slutsky v. City of New York*, 97 N.Y.S.2d 238 (Sup. Ct. 1950).

160 *"No," he had said*: Kurt told this story, and the story of Langmuir's idea, repeatedly throughout his life, including in a 1974 interview with Joe David Bellamy and John Casey reprinted in Allen, *Conversations*, 161.

161 *At the stroke of twelve*: The image is reminiscent of the famous "Doomsday Clock," visualizing how close the world is to precipitating Armageddon, printed on every issue of the *Bulletin of the Atomic Scientists*.

161 *Still, he thought it was the best thing*: He says so in a May 19, 1950, letter to his Cornell friend Miller Harris, LL-MH.

162 *"There is nothing moral"*: *General Office News*, May 19, 1950.

162 *He would write a novel*: Vonnegut to Miller Harris, May 19, 1950, LL-MH.

163 *"I have made rain"*: "Dr. Howell Yields: Yes, He Made Rain," *The New York Times*, August 8, 1950.

163 *When Irving found out, he was furious*: Langmuir lab notebook.

8. Out of the Blue

164 *Then he was taken*: GE News Bureau press release, May 24, 1950. The prime minister's visit was also covered extensively by newspapers.

165 *He figured that's what he'd been writing*: "I hope to build a reputation as a science-fiction writer. That's the pitch," he wrote to Miller Harris on February 28, 1950. Wakefield, *Letters*, 32.

166 *"I haven't given it a thought"*: Kurt described this talk many years later in an address to the American Physical Society in 1969. Vonnegut, *Wampeters, Foma, and Granfalloons*, 100. A detailed account of the talk ran in the *Schenectady Gazette*, March 8, 1950.

166 *He wanted to write*: "I cheerfully ripped off the plot of *Brave New World*," Kurt declared in the *Playboy* interview. Vonnegut, *Wampeters, Foma, and Granfalloons*, 263.

166 *He was going to bite the hand that fed him*: "I bit the hand that used to feed me," Kurt wrote in the introduction to *Bagombo Snuff Box*, 8.

167 *"The first industrial revolution"*: Wiener, *Cybernetics*, 37. I cite the 1948 edition that it is likely Kurt read.

167 *The job was making him crazy*: "K. has got to quit before any such gigantic length of time," Jane wrote to Fred Rosenau around this time, after he suggested that Kurt's success might take years, "because this idiotic job of his is such a drag on his spirit. It's making us both psychotic." Shields, *And So It Goes*, 112.

170 *"the property of the client"*: "Weather Control and Augmented Potable Weather Supply," joint hearings on S. 5, S. 222, and S. 798 before subcommittees of the Committees on Interior and Insular Affairs, Interstate and Foreign Commerce, and Agriculture and Forestry, 82nd Congress (March 14, 15, 16, and 19, and April 5, 1951).

170 *A high school senior headed for Caltech*: Langmuir lab notebook.

171 *He had chosen to sleep in*: Schaefer, "Twenty Years at Langmuir University."

173 *"The cold resolve deserted Kelly"*: "White King" was eventually published as "All the King's Horses." Vonnegut, *Welcome to the Monkey House*, 102.

173 *While they were in Gloucester*: Mark Vonnegut identified this painting as having been done in Gloucester, and Edie Vonnegut generously let me see it. Kurt always liked clowns. Humor was one of the few things in the world in which he never lost faith. "Historians of the future, in my opinion," he would write when old, "will congratulate us on very little other than our clowning and our jazz." Vonnegut, *Palm Sunday*, 127.

174 *"Many farmers, ranchers and civic-minded people"*: Quotations from Bernie's speech appeared in "Rainmaker Licenses Seen by GE Weather Scientist," *Schenectady Gazette*, August 26, 1950.

174 *"He has been known to sit for half an hour"*: *Time*, August 28, 1950.

175 *"Ice-9," Kurt's story about a scientist*: Kurt Vonnegut to Ben (Hitz?). The letter is an undated draft but mentions that it is written on the evening of Kurt and Jane's fifth wedding anniversary, hence August 31, 1950. LL-KV.

176 *That was highway robbery*: Vonnegut to Littauer and Max Wilkinson, draft letter, n.d., LL-KV. It's fortunate "Ice-9" was not sold to *Astounding Science Fiction* (as it was retitled in 1938); if it had been, *Cat's Cradle* would never have been written.

176 *"I am a registered Democrat"*: Vonnegut to Burger, October 31, 1950, in Wakefield, *Letters*, 37.

176 *Kurt had been looking*: An article in *Scientific American* two years earlier, "The Army Ant," June 16, 1948, might have suggested the topic. It made an interesting connection between some of the more irrational behaviors of ants and of men. Kurt almost surely saw this piece: he read *Scientific American* regularly at GE as part of his job (Vonnegut, *Wampeters, Foma, and Granfalloons*, 84), and the echoes of this feature in his story are many. Kurt took notes on Wheeler, which are preserved in "The Ants of Erz Gebirg" file in LL-KV. It's notable that Wiener used ants as frequent examples in *Cybernetics* as well.

176 *Like "Ice-9," the new story*: All quotations are from "The Petrified Ants," published posthumously in Vonnegut, *Look at the Birdie*. The published story is one of the many story drafts in LL-KV. It's impossible to tell if it is the last one.

177 *The story is set in the Erzgebirge*: As usual, the location has personal significance for Kurt: he had been marched into the Erzgebirge, half-starved, as the Red Army approached Dresden. It also demonstrates how attuned he was to political events: the Russians really did search for uranium in the region.

177 *Josef tells Peter that he mustn't speak*: Josef's explicit instructions and Peter's seeing him as "frail" and compromised are in early manuscripts, then excised, then put back in. They are in the version of the story that was ultimately published in Vonnegut's posthumous collection of short fiction, *Look at the Birdie*.

178 *He saw it as a chance*: Byers, "History of Weather Modification."

179 *"It seems to me"*: Reichelderfer to Charles Brooks, September 27, 1950, LOC-HW.

179 *He had Weather Bureau charts*: Vince Schaefer describes the presentation, calling it a "spectacular demonstration," in "Twenty Years at Langmuir University."

179 *Bernie was back at work by then*: "Seven Day Periodicity in Weather in 1950," *BAMS*, March 1951. Letters between Reichelderfer and Langmuir and Robert G. Stone and Langmuir are in MEG-VS.

179 *"It is hoped"*: Copies of Bernie's letters and some of the replies are in MEG-BV.

180 *The storm intensified that night*: My information about the floods comes from the U.S. Geological Survey water-supply paper "Floods of 1950–51 in the Catskill Mountain Region, New York" (U.S. Government Printing Office, 1957), as well as local newspapers, *The New York Times*, and Galusha, *Liquid Assets*.

181 *They disagreed on whether cloud seeding was sufficiently proved*: Harry Wexler, trip report, December 8, 1950, LOC-HW.

181 *He also suggested Kurt try*: Burger to Vonnegut, September 13, 1950, LL-KV.

9. Cold Fronts

184 *Eventually, he would give up on it*: Kurt never saw "From Timid to Timbuktu" in print; it was published only posthumously. Given that he doesn't seem to have shopped it around, it's reasonable to think he probably wouldn't have liked it being published.

186 *Eventually, more than 130 upstate clients*: *Catskill Mountain News*, March 23, 1951.

187 *He was even asserting*: Langmuir wrote a paper about Hurricane King that remains unpublished to this day. A typescript of the first part was preserved by Bernie; MEG-BV. A typescript of the second part is in MIS-GE. Irving continued to try to get people to take his conclusions about the hurricane seeding seriously up to his death, even mentioning it again when appearing on the *Today* show following a vicious hurricane in 1956.

188 *When a young meteorologist at an MIT symposium*: The insulted party, Charles Hosler, was taken aside afterward by Henry Houghton, chair of the MIT meteorology department, who explained that Langmuir was so abrupt because he felt his whole career was defined by his cloud-seeding work. Hosler recounted the event for James Fleming, who repeats it in "The Pathological History of Weather and Climate Modification," *Historical Studies in the Physical and Biological Sciences* 37, no. 1 (2006): 12.

188 *Harry Wexler spent Valentine's Day in Princeton*: Harry Wexler, trip report, February 21, 1951, LOC-HW. The ENIAC logbook is in MIT-JC. Harper writes about this visit as well, though she never mentions the discussion of the periodicities, or any of the Project Cirrus work, in *Weather by the Numbers*.

190 *It was spring*: Kurt wrote a letter to Miller Harris on the back of a *New Yorker* rejection slip, saying that they would be in New York staying at the Algonquin on March 29–31. Vonnegut to Harris, February 26, 1951, LL-MH. Kurt and Knox exchanged letters about having had drinks with Jane afterward, NYPL-CC.

191 *But what the hell?*: In later years, Kurt himself had a slightly dismissive attitude toward much of his early magazine work. He included neither "Mnemonics" nor "Little Drops of Water" in the only collection of short fiction he ever put together

himself, *Welcome to the Monkey House.* In 1999 he declared that "no matter how clumsily I wrote when I was starting out, there were magazines that would publish such orangutans." "Coda to My Career as a Writer for Periodicals," *Bagombo Snuff Box*, 349. He dedicated this collection to the memories of Littauer and Wilkinson, "who taught me how to write."

193 *Just focus on the carpenter story*: Knox called the Dresden story "risky" in a letter (jokingly) dated April 5, 1961, NYPL-CC.

193 *Kurt invited Knox to come visit*: Kurt told Knox he was selling his house in a letter on April 14, 1951; LL-KV. Knox congratulated Kurt on selling it at a profit in a letter in which he also commented on "More Stately Mansions," May 22, 1951, LL-KV. Jane wrote to her mother that they moved to Provincetown expecting to roam the East Coast looking for a house that fall (September 15, 1951, Vonnegut family collection). So it's clear that Kurt and Jane decided to leave Alplaus and sold their house that spring, not in the fall, as Shields has it.

193 *Collier's intended to convey*: Notes from the editorial meetings for Operation Eggnog, including many statements of intent and correspondence with a host of potential writers, are all in NYPL-CC.

193 *The Atomic Energy Commission was ramping up*: The Enewetak (then spelled Eniwetok) tests in April and May were known as Operation Greenhouse, and they were not secret. Details were released by the government in June. As was common, many newspapers ran a front-page story and photograph of the mushroom cloud. "Tests Prove Gains in Hydrogen Bomb," *New York Times*, June 14, 1951.

194 *"You say here"*: "Weather Control and Augmented Potable Weather Supply," joint hearings on S. 5, S. 222, and S. 798 before subcommittees of the Committees on Interior and Insular Affairs, Interstate and Foreign Commerce, and Agriculture and Forestry, 82nd Congress (March 14, 15, 16, and 19, and April 5, 1951).

195 *In November, he had visited Schenectady*: Langmuir lab notebook.

197 *It was a PR disaster*: Reichelderfer was still stewing about the fist pounding nearly a year later, noting in an internal memo on February 20, 1952, that the Weather Bureau had lost funding after the hearings and that it had been scrambling to improve its reputation ever since. LOC-HW.

200 *Condon had won the battle with HUAC*: Even Irving knew to keep a low profile as far as HUAC was concerned. He had recently been asked by a lawyer to provide a character reference for another scientist who was being investigated, and he had insisted that his name be kept out of it. He would rather avoid publicity, he said. He didn't want to end up like Edward Condon. Langmuir to General Edward Greenbaum, February 2, 1951, LOC-IL.

202 *But after the hearings ended*: The Department of the Army's letter on behalf of the Department of Defense was added to "Weather Control and Augmented Potable Water Supply," 34.

202 *He was writing about what might be*: The foreword to *Player Piano* declares, "This is not a book about what is, but a book about what could be." All quotes are from Vonnegut, *Player Piano*.

202 *He saw it as an American version*: Kurt made this connection in an unfinished early description of the book. LL-KV.

203 *His desire for the cat*: The moment is eerily redolent of the many deaths on the electric fences of German death camps, a parallel Vonnegut does not push too

hard. But it does hint, as do the early drafts of "Mnemonics," at the deeper meaning of his mistrust of the Works and its world.

206 *"Any labor that accepts the conditions"*: Wiener, *Cybernetics*, 37.

207 *Ten thousand farms*: NOAA report, www.crh.noaa.gov/mbrfc/flood51.pdf.

207 *Senator Kem asked them to draft a statement*: Langmuir lab notebook.

207 *Meanwhile, the governor of New Mexico*: Roscoe Braham, interview, June 19–21, 2002, NCAR-AMS.

208 *Irving thought this was an excellent idea*: Langmuir lab notebook.

208 *Vincent went to the meeting instead*: Langmuir lab notebook.

208 *Now the undersea warfare*: R. W. Larson to Captain C. L. Murphy (head, Undersea Warfare Research, Office of Naval Research), June 25, 1951, MIS-GE.

209 *Besides, getting involved*: Suits to Vonnegut, July 16, 1951, MIS-GE.

209 *Don't come to Provincetown*: Jane Vonnegut to Mariah Cox, September 15, 1951, Vonnegut family collection.

210 *Kurt would probably need to fly to New York*: Edie Vonnegut, interview with the author, October 2013.

10. Shifting Winds

214 *Bernard entered the East Ballroom*: The meeting was written up, with a photograph of all attendees, in *Weatherwise* 4, no. 6 (December 1951).

214 *The only other serious researcher*: Appalled that the panel was all "rainmakers," Chief Reichelderfer pulled strings with the AMS president to get Thom added to the roster. Memo to Harry Wexler, September 20, 1951, LOC-HW.

214 *Bernie was going to outline the construction*: Program and abstracts ran in *Bulletin of the AMS* 32, no. 7 (September 1951).

215 *But if Bernie wasn't*: Lab notebook entries throughout July and August 1951 document Langmuir's frustration and his conversations with Bernard.

215 *"Project Cirrus is supported by the public"*: Bernard Vonnegut to Michael J. Ference Jr., October 3, 1951, MEG-BV.

217 *That, Kurt knew, was why*: Kurt wrote a sullen letter to Knox Burger about the whole affair the following April, declaring, "Wild as my stories may be, I would never make World War III seem little more hazardous than and as interesting as an automobile trip from New York to Los Angeles in a Stutz Bearcat." As if that weren't enough, a sarcastic parody of the story's dialogue followed. Wakefield, *Letters*, 42. In a letter the same month to Harry Brague, Kurt complained that *Collier's* was growing so conservative his stories were no longer welcome there. Vonnegut to Brague, April 16, 1952, PU-CS.

218 *When he started the novel*: Kurt's early outlines, notes, and drafts are in LL-KV.

218 *Dr. Paul Proteus having quit*: Vonnegut to Brague, October 18, 1951, PU-CS.

218 *The loudspeaker at the Meadows*: In one of the last pre-galley typescripts of *Player Piano*, Kurt cut out the team songs and replaced them with new ones that are even more similar to the actual fight songs from Camp GE in 1948. Because Vincent, Herb Hollomon, and Roger Hammond of the News Bureau all attended that summer, it seems clear that at some point during the revising of the manuscript, Kurt got his hands on one of their songbooks, but I could not confirm this. Photographs of the skit from that session also show a godlike figure attaching tinsel

stars to the set sky and what appears to be a trial. This sounds exactly like the skit depicted at length in the novel. Photographs of Camp GE are in UP-LB. Vince's Camp GE songbook is in MEG-VS.

220 *Ludwig von Neumann is so unlike John von Neumann*: Kurt was very likely familiar with John von Neumann and his work. Von Neumann gave frequent talks at the same conferences as Bernie, and Project Cirrus received regular reports from the Institute for Advanced Study's Meteorology Project. Distribution list, IAS.

222 *Weather Bureau analysts were double-checking*: According to his own handwritten notes, when he got wind of a meeting Langmuir scheduled with Henry Houghton of MIT to discuss the report he was writing, Harry called Hurd Willett, his mentor at MIT, and suggested that Willett attend the meeting and propose an alternative explanation for the periodicities. He then called Henry Houghton and arranged for him to see the Weather Bureau statistical data on the periodicities. LOC-HW. By the time Langmuir sat down with Houghton and Willett, they had been converted to the Weather Bureau's position. A baffled Irving called the meeting "very unsatisfactory" in his lab notebook entry of June 30, 1951.

223 *Doc Whitney's question, "Are you having fun today?"*: Vincent Schaefer writes about the changing feel of the lab in "Twenty Years at Langmuir University."

223 *Visitors and colleagues*: Many of the arrangements are reported in Irving's notebooks. Also Anthony Hall, "A Laureate's Lake," *Lake George Mirror*, July 10, 2011.

225 *"Our papers have been making"*: Wiener, *Human Use of Human Beings*, 210.

226 *On perhaps the last innocently joyous night*: Vonnegut, "Rover Boys," LL-KV.

227 *But even now, before that triumph*: Harry Wexler, trip report, May 7–10, 1952, LOC-HW.

228 *"A tidal wave of computational power"*: Julian Bigelow, the chief designer for von Neumann's computer, quoted in George Dyson, *Turing's Cathedral*, 153.

228 *Guy Suits had asked Bernie*: Bernie recounted this conversation, and his feelings about GE then, in an interview with Earl Droessler, May 9, 1993, NCAR-AMS.

229 *He was corresponding with Bill Hubert*: Hubert to Vonnegut, June 13, 1952, MEG-BV.

231 *It's unclear what set Wiener off*: Conway and Siegelman, *Dark Hero of the Information Age*, 287.

231 *"he cannot with impunity"*: Wiener to Hope English, July 17, 1952, MIT-NW. Quoted in Conway and Siegelman, *Dark Hero of the Information Age*, 288.

231 *He apologized for having innocently given offense*: Vonnegut to Wiener, July 26, 1952, MIT-NW.

232 *He pulled them from his personal store*: Once, over lunch in Tulsa, a magazine editor told me he had always been baffled by Vonnegut's location of the demonology institute in Verdigris, Oklahoma, in "Armageddon in Retrospect." Instinctively, I responded that the place must mean something to him. More than a year later, when I first read the manuscript "The Rover Boys," it became clear what that was: on his road trip in 1939, he and his two friends stayed not far from Verdigris on the Woolaroc Ranch. While enjoying that paradise for sixteen-year-old boys, they heard on the radio that Hitler had invaded Poland. His own personal demonology began there.

232 *George M. Helmholtz*: Helmholtz Watson is also the frustrated writer character

in *Brave New World*; all citizens in Huxley's imagined world have names taken from historical figures because real families no longer exist.

232 *Not one bookstore in GE's company town*: Norman Snow to Henry Hohns, memo, September 3, 1952, PU-CS.

233 *Bernie went down to the beach*: Bernard Vonnegut, abstract of "A Possible Mechanism for the Formation of Thunderstorm Electricity," *BAMS* 34 (1953), and "Giant Electrical Storms," in *Recent Advances in Atmospheric Electricity*, ed. L. G. Smith (Pergamon, 1955). Meteorologists were at first skeptical of Bernie's estimate, but later improvements in wind-speed detection established that his estimates were close to correct. I am grateful to Scott Vonnegut for drawing my attention to the Worcester Twister as a formative event for his father.

234 *"I believe the best way"*: Bernie wrote to W. E. Williamson, clerk of the Committee on Interstate and Foreign Commerce, on March 12, 1958, asking to testify; his statement is also in his files, MEG-BV.

234 *That same year, Commander William Kotsch*: Kotsch to Vonnegut, September 8, 1958, MEG-BV.

235 *"I'm [just] trying to find out"*: Quoted in Michael Lopez, "Talk Soup," *Albany Times Union*, April 13, 1997.

236 *He had even purchased a television*: Kurt's teleplays are in the unprocessed files, LL-KV. They include an adaptation of *Player Piano* and a teleplay called "Slaughterhouse 5" that is nothing like the novel. In a letter to Harry Brague, February 7, 1954, Kurt complains of having "squandered all my time on short stories and scripts that haven't sold." Wakefield, *Letters*, 52. He writes to Knox Burger about having bought a television on May 11, 1954. Wakefield, *Letters*, 57.

237 *"What is God? What is love?"*: Vonnegut, *Cat's Cradle*, 55. The Clare Boothe Luce story is told in Rosenfeld, *Quintessence*, 321.

239 *"Let us remember how good it was once here"*: Dostoevsky, *The Brothers Karamazov*, 895. This is the Constance Garnett translation that Kurt would have read. Later in the same speech Alyosha says, in another passage demonstrating the book's lifelong impression on Kurt, "Let us be, first and above all, kind."

240 *Thanks to the way the human mind lets us*: "Everything about that lake was imprinted on my mind when it held so little and was so eager for information, it will be my lake as long as I live," he wrote in *Architectural Digest*. "I have no wish to visit it, for I have it all right here." Reprinted in Vonnegut, *Fates Worse Than Death*, 50.

Epilogue: Rainbow's End

241 *He had handed the letter to Kurt*: Kurt set this scene in a typed explanation dated April 13, 1997, included with Uncle Alex's letter in his files, LL-KV.

242 *Cape Cod wasn't quite ready*: Shields, *And So It Goes*, 142–44. Kurt later speculated in jest that the dealership failure had cost him the Nobel Prize. "Have I Got a Car for You!," *In These Times*, November 24, 2004.

242 *He even designed and tried to market*: Notes and samples of the game are in LL-KV.

242 *He was working on it when he and Jane*: The smallest child was subsequently adopted by another relative in a traumatic family event.

243 *They were too focused on the fasinating things*: McCartan, *Kurt Vonnegut*, 148.

243 *Bernard was horrified*: Kurt discusses Bernie's reaction to the news in ibid.

Bernard's sons have confirmed this. "He was very much against it," Scott Vonnegut said. "He was very, very much against the war . . . He wanted it used for agriculture, or for snowpack, for water." Interview with the author, July 2013.

244 *"My brother knew early on"*: He gets the location wrong, but a colleague Bernie worked with while at Hartford-Empire in Connecticut was based in Butler, Pennsylvania. The address was reprinted in Vonnegut, *Fates Worse Than Death*, 117.

245 *"one who declines to work on weapons"*: Walter Sullivan, "Strike to Protest 'Misuse' of Science," *New York Times*, February 6, 1969.

246 *"I told Jane that this boy"*: Vonnegut, *Timequake*, 135.

246 *Five yielded inconclusive results*: The Weather Bureau seeded clouds in Oregon and Washington with dry ice on a randomized basis with inconclusive results. Scientists at the University of Chicago, funded by the Department of Defense, seeded warm clouds in the Midwest and the Caribbean with water and dry ice, getting a positive result too small to be statistically significant. The Navy collaborated with NYU on Project Scud, an attempt to modify the development of nineteen large-scale extratropical cyclonic systems utilizing dry ice from airplanes and seventeen silver iodide generators scattered from Florida to New York. The Air Force collaborated with the Stanford Research Institute to study the physics of ice fogs. The Army, with Arthur D. Little, studied methods of dispelling warm fogs and stratus. And the Army Signal Corps conducted an extensive flight program to study seeding of supercooled stratus clouds with both dry ice and silver iodide, the one of these projects to get a positive result. The results were ultimately declassified and published as *Cloud and Weather Modification: A Group of Field Experiments*. Meteorological Monographs. Vol. 2, no. 11 (AMS, 1957). See also Byers, "History of Weather Modification."

246 *Officers from the Office of Naval Research*: Irving guessed, correctly, what each of these projects was. Langmuir lab notebook, September 14, 1953.

247 *A rigorous five-year randomized study*: Daniel Breed, "Design and Preliminary Results of the Wyoming Weather Modification Pilot Program Randomized Seeding Experiment," Research Applications Laboratory, National Center for Atmospheric Research. For an overview of the program, see http://ral.ucar.edu/projects/wyoming/.

247 *"one of those tantalizing things"*: Oral history with Roscoe Braham, 2002, NCAR-AMS.

248 *"If Langmuir actually influenced the weather"*: This meteorologist remained anonymous in the article, but his generosity toward Langmuir rules out anyone at the Weather Bureau. It could have been Wallace Howell, or even Vince or Bernie. "Tomorrow's Weather," *Fortune*, May 1953.

248 *"Perhaps if he had comprehended fully"*: "History of Weather Modification," in Hess, *Weather and Climate Modification*.

248 *"is not definitely determinate"*: Langmuir, *Cloud Nucleation*, 456–57. Von Neumann's key meteorologist, Jule Charney, later acknowledged that "in some fundamental way Wiener was probably right . . . Wiener I think anticipated the unpredictability of the atmosphere that Lorenz later formulated rigorously." George Platzman, Conversations with Jule Charney (NCAR Technical Notes, 1987).

249 *The computer did not turn out to be Laplace's demon*: See, for instance, theories

about the "singularity" by the techno-utopian and Google director of engineering Raymond Kurzweil. Kurzweil credits John von Neumann with the original idea in his foreword to von Neumann's unfinished lecture series, published as *The Computer and the Brain* (Yale University Press, 2012).

250 *"we are releasing huge quantities of carbon dioxide"*: Typed and handwritten lecture notes, LOC-HW.

250 *"Project Cirrus's investigations of ways"*: Epilogue written by Bernard in Havens, Jiusto, and Vonnegut, *Early History of Cloud Seeding*.

251 *That old America*: Loree Rackstraw recounts a letter in which Kurt says *Timequake* "has to do with the disappearance of the America I tried to write for." *Love as Always, Kurt* (Da Capo, 2009), 182. Kurt writes something similar to Marc Leeds in 1995, describing the mood of his generation as "wry disappointment with what the world has actually become, so inhospitable and snide. Once the Great Depression and the Second World War were over, we planned to build a Garden of Eden here." Wakefield, *Letters*, 364.

251 *In his novel* Galápagos: Interestingly, this idea too was proposed in *Cybernetics*. Wiener spends part of a late chapter considering the possibility that the human brain had grown too large to be efficient anymore and that humans might "be facing one of those limitations of nature in which highly specialized organs reach a level of declining efficiency and ultimately lead to the extinction of the species." Wiener, *Cybernetics*, 180. This is, in a nutshell, the premise of *Galápagos*.

252 *"Physicists may already know enough"*: Bernard Vonnegut, "Adventures in Fluid Flow: Generating Interesting Dendritic Patterns," *Leonardo* 31, no. 3 (1998): 207.

252 *Kurt's letter back*: Describing Bernie's question and quoting from his own reply in *Timequake*, Kurt says, "I was pleased to reply with an epistle which was frankly vengeful, since he and Father had screwed me out of a liberal arts college education." Vonnegut, *Timequake*, 167. But of course the Kurt Vonnegut in Vonnegut's fiction was a satirical version. The tone of the real Kurt Vonnegut's letter is ultimately not vengeful at all: it is unmistakably loving.

253 *"If the superpowers decide to duke it out"*: Kurt told this story a number of times, including in an interview published in *Stop Smiling Magazine*, August 2006.

254 *"washed away a lot of privies"*: Kurt Vonnegut, "Bernard Vonnegut: The Rainmaker," *New York Times Magazine*, January 4, 1998.

Bibliography

Allen, William Rodney, ed. *Conversations with Kurt Vonnegut*. University Press of Mississippi, 1988.

Ashmore, Harry. *Unseasonable Truths: The Life of Robert Maynard Hutchins*. Little, Brown, 1989.

Bates, Charles, and John F. Fuller. *America's Weather Warriors, 1914–1985*. Texas A&M University Press, 1986.

Birr, Kendall. *Pioneering in Industrial Research: The Story of the General Electric Research Laboratory*. Public Affairs, 1957.

Boyer, Paul. *By the Bomb's Early Light: American Thought and Culture at the Dawn of the Atomic Age*. University of North Carolina Press, 1984.

Brands, H. W. *American Dreams: The United States Since 1945*. Penguin, 2010.

Chew, Joe. *Storms Above the Desert: Atmospheric Research in New Mexico, 1935–1985*. University of New Mexico Press, 1987.

Coe, Jerome. *Unlikely Victory: How G.E. Succeeded in the Chemical Industry*. Wiley, 2000.

Conway, Flo, and Jim Siegelman. *Dark Hero of the Information Age: In Search of Norbert Wiener, the Father of Cybernetics*. Basic Books, 2006.

Cotton, William R., and Roger A. Pielke Sr. *Human Impacts on Weather and Climate*. Cambridge University Press, 2007.

Cox, John D. *Storm Watchers: The Turbulent History of Weather Prediction from Franklin's Kite to El Niño*. John Wiley & Sons, 2002.

Dickstein, Morris. *Leopards in the Temple: The Transformation of American Fiction, 1945–1970*. Harvard University Press, 2002.

Donner, Leo, Wayne Schubert, and Richard Somerville. *The Development of Atmospheric General Circulation Models*. Cambridge University Press, 2011.

Dostoevsky, Fyodor. *The Brothers Karamazov*. Translated by Constance Garnett. Signet Classics, 2007.

Dupuy, Trevor. *Hitler's Last Gamble: The Battle of the Bulge, December 1944–January 1945*. HarperCollins, 1995.

Dyson, Freeman. *Disturbing the Universe.* Harper & Row, 1979.

———. *Infinite in All Directions.* Harper & Row, 1988.

Dyson, George. *Turing's Cathedral: The Origins of the Digital Universe.* Vintage Books, 2012.

Evans, Thomas. *The Education of Ronald Reagan: The General Electric Years.* Columbia University Press, 2008.

Failey, Majie Alford. *We Never Danced Cheek to Cheek: The Young Kurt Vonnegut in Indianapolis and Beyond.* Hawthorne, 2010.

Fleming, James Rodger. *Fixing the Sky: The Checkered History of Weather and Climate Control.* Columbia University Press, 2010.

Fussell, Paul. *The Boys' Crusade: The American Infantry in Northwestern Europe, 1944–1945.* Modern Library, 2003.

Galusha, Diane. *Liquid Assets: A History of the New York City Water Supply.* Harbor Hill Books, 2002.

Gleick, James. *Chaos: Making a New Science.* Penguin, 1987.

Hammond, John Winthrop. *Men and Volts: The Story of General Electric.* J. B. Lippincott, 1941.

Harper, Kristin. *Weather by the Numbers: The Genesis of Modern Meteorology.* MIT Press, 2012.

Havens, Barrington, James E. Jiusto, and Bernard Vonnegut. *Early History of Cloud Seeding.* Langmuir Laboratory, Atmospheric Sciences Research Center, and GE, 1978.

Hawkins, Lawrence. "The Story of G.E. Research." Pamphlet published by GE. MIS-GE.

Heims, Steve J. *John von Neumann and Norbert Wiener: From Mathematics to the Technologies of Life and Death.* MIT Press, 1980.

Hess, Wilmot, ed. *Weather and Climate Modification.* John Wiley & Sons, 1974.

Kershaw, Alex. *The Longest Winter: The Battle of the Bulge and the Epic Story of World War II's Most Decorated Platoon.* Da Capo Press, 2005.

Klinkowitz, Jerome. *Kurt Vonnegut's America.* University of South Carolina Press, 2009.

Klinkowitz, Jerome, and John Somer, eds. *The Vonnegut Statement: Original Essays on the Life and Work of Kurt Vonnegut Jr.* Dell, 1973.

Krementz, Jill, ed. *Happy Birthday, Kurt Vonnegut.* Delacorte Press, 1982.

Langmuir, Irving. *Atmospheric Phenomena.* Vol. 10 of *Collected Works.* Pergamon Press, 1962.

———. *Cloud Nucleation.* Vol. 11 of *Collected Works.* Pergamon Press, 1962.

Laskin, David. *Braving the Elements: The Stormy History of American Weather.* Doubleday, 1995.

Lilienthal, David. *The Atomic Energy Years.* Vol. 2 of *The Journals of David Lilienthal.* Harper & Row, 1964.

Lindzen, Richard S., Edward N. Lorenz, and George W. Platzman, eds. *The Atmosphere, a Challenge: The Science of Jule Gregory Charney.* American Meteorological Society, 1990.

Lingeman, Richard. *The Noir Forties: The American People from Victory to Cold War.* Nation Books, 2012.

Lynch, Peter. "The ENIAC Forecasts: A Re-creation." *Bulletin of the American Meteorological Society,* January 2008.

Macrae, Norman. *John von Neumann: The Scientific Genius Who Pioneered the Modern Computer, Game Theory, Nuclear Deterrence, and Much More.* American Mathematical Society, 2000.

Mariner, Rosemary, and G. Kurt Piehler, eds. *The Atomic Bomb and American Society: New Perspectives.* University of Tennessee Press, 2009.

McCartan, Tom, ed. *Kurt Vonnegut: The Last Interview and Other Conversations.* Melville House, 2011.

McQuade, Molly, ed. *An Unsentimental Education: Writers and Chicago.* University of Chicago Press, 1995.

Meisler, Stanley. *United Nations: The First Fifty Years.* Atlantic Monthly Press, 1995.

Mergen, Bernard. *Weather Matters: An American Cultural History Since 1900.* University Press of Kansas, 2008.

Miller, John A. *Men and Volts at War: The Story of General Electric in World War II.* Bantam, 1948.

Monmonier, Mark. *Air Apparent: How Meteorologists Learned to Map, Predict, and Dramatize the Weather.* University of Chicago Press, 1999.

Nebeker, Frederik. *Calculating the Weather: Meteorology in the Twentieth Century.* Academic Press, 1995.

Newton, Roger G. *From Clockwork to Crapshoot: A History of Physics.* Belknap Press, 2007.

Nye, David. *Image Worlds: Corporate Identities at General Electric, 1890–1930.* MIT Press, 1985.

Petterssen, Sverre. *Weathering the Storm: Sverre Petterssen, the D-Day Forecast, and the Rise of Modern Meteorology.* Edited by James Rodger Fleming. AMS Historical Monographs, 2001.

Phillips-Fein, Kimberly. "American Counterrevolutionary: Lemuel Ricketts Boulware and General Electric, 1950–1960." In *American Capitalism: Social Thought and Political Economy in the Twentieth Century*, edited by Nelson Lichtenstein. University of Pennsylvania Press, 2006.

Rhodes, Richard. *The Making of the Atomic Bomb.* Simon & Schuster, 1986.

Rosenfeld, Albert. *The Quintessence of Irving Langmuir.* Pergamon Press, 1966.

Schaefer, Vincent. *A Field Guide to the Atmosphere.* Peterson Field Guides. Houghton Mifflin, 1981.

———. *Final Report Project Cirrus Part 1: Laboratory, Field, and Flight Experiments.* GE Research Laboratory Report No. RL-785, 1953.

———. "Twenty Years at Langmuir University." Unpublished autobiographical manuscript. MEG-VS.

Schatz, Ronald W. *The Electrical Workers: A History of Labor at General Electric and Westinghouse.* University of Illinois Press, 1983.

Sheets, Bob, and Jack Williams. *Hurricane Watch: Forecasting the Deadliest Storms on Earth.* Vintage Books, 2001.

Shields, Charles. *And So It Goes: Kurt Vonnegut, a Life.* Henry Holt, 2011.

Smith, Alice Kimball. *A Peril and a Hope: The Scientists' Movement in America, 1945–47.* University of Chicago Press, 1965.

Sumner, Gregory D. *Unstuck in Time: A Journey Through Kurt Vonnegut's Life and Novels.* Seven Stories, 2011.

Szpek, Ervin, Jr., Frank Idzikowski, and Heidi Szpek. *Shadows of Slaughterhouse Five: Recollections and Reflections of the Ex-POWs of Schlachthof Fünf, Dresden, Germany*. Self-published, 2008.

Teller, Edward. *Memoirs*. With Judith Shoolery. Perseus, 2001.

Vonnegut, Kurt. *Armageddon in Retrospect*. Berkley Books, 2008.

———. *Bagombo Snuff Box*. 1999; Berkley Books, 2000.

———. *Breakfast of Champions*. 1973; Dial Press, 2011.

———. *Cat's Cradle*. 1963; Dial Press, 2006.

———. *Fates Worse Than Death*. Berkley Books, 1991.

———. *Galápagos*. 1985; Dial Press, 1999.

———. *Jailbird*. 1979; Dial Press, 2011.

———. *Look at the Birdie*. 2009; Dial Press, 2010.

———. *A Man Without a Country*. Seven Stories, 2005.

———. *Mother Night*. 1961; Dial Press, 2009.

———. *Palm Sunday*. 1981; Dial Press, 2011.

———. *Player Piano*. 1952; Dial Press, 2006.

———. *The Sirens of Titan*. 1959; Dial Press, 2009.

———. *Slapstick*. 1976; Dial Press, 2010.

———. *Slaughterhouse-Five*. Dell, 1969.

———. *Timequake*. Berkley Books, 1997.

———. *Wampeters, Foma, and Granfalloons*. 1974; Dial Press, 1999.

———. *We Are What We Pretend to Be: First and Last Works*. Vanguard, 2012.

———. *Welcome to the Monkey House*. 1968; Dial Press, 2006.

———. *While Mortals Sleep: Unpublished Short Fiction*. 2011; Dial Press, 2012.

Vonnegut, Mark. *The Eden Express*. Dell, 1975.

Wakefield, Dan. *New York in the Fifties*. Houghton Mifflin, 1992.

———, ed. *Kurt Vonnegut: Letters*. Delacorte, 2012.

Wang, Jessica. *American Science in an Age of Anxiety: Scientists, Anticommunism, and the Cold War*. University of North Carolina Press, 1999.

Wiener, Norbert. *Cybernetics; or, Control and Communication in the Animal and the Machine*. John Wiley & Sons, 1948.

———. *The Human Use of Human Beings*. Houghton Mifflin, 1950.

Wise, George. *The G.E. Story*. Unpublished manuscript history of GE. MEG-GW.

———. *Willis R. Whitney, General Electric, and the Origins of U.S. Industrial Research*. Columbia University Press, 1985.

Wittner, Lawrence. *One World or None*. Vol. 1 of *The Struggle Against the Bomb*. Stanford University Press, 1993.

Yarmolinsky, Jane Vonnegut. *Angels Without Wings: A Courageous Family's Triumph over Tragedy*. Houghton Mifflin, 1987.

Acknowledgments

This book is a history. I have stuck to documented and verifiable fact, reconstructing the day-to-day activities of historical figures through published works, interviews, and archival sources. Where there is dialogue in quotation marks, it is because someone, somewhere, transcribed it. Some of my sources are Kurt Vonnegut's stories and novels. His entire oeuvre—short stories, novels, essays, lectures—can be read on one level as an autobiographical collage, a memoir unstuck in time. However, I have only attributed to him feelings he claims for himself, the author, not feelings or thoughts he ascribes to his characters.

As for the scientists in this book, I have found their published papers surprisingly helpful in developing an understanding of who they were. Their lab notebooks provided data about their activities but also conveyed—through handwriting, underlining, and asides—when they felt excited or rushed or cautious. I was also fortunate to find many oral histories, interview transcripts, and videos to help me get to know the people behind this story. All of these are listed in my sources.

Perhaps most essential in developing a feeling for these wonderfully complex characters was the generous and heartfelt assistance of the Vonnegut-Adams family, as nice a tribe as one could imagine. In particular, Scott Vonnegut, Edie Vonnegut, Kurt Vonnegut III, and Mark Vonnegut corresponded with me, met with me, shared family photographs and documents, and exchanged ongoing e-mails to help me understand the facts and the people behind them. It is not easy to share one's family with the public, and they have done so with kindness and grace. I also owe a huge debt to Bernard Vonnegut's esteemed colleagues Sally Marsh and Duncan Blanchard for spending lavish amounts of time with me to help me understand a man they both knew so well. Bernard's student Tony Grainger not only talked to me about his mentor but did his best to explain cloud physics to me. I am indebted to the meteorologists Arlen Huggins, Jeff Tilley, and Don Griffin for helping me get a grip on weather modification and what it can do. I am grateful to the Weather Modification Association for allowing me to attend its annual meeting and plague the weather modifiers with endless questions. Dan Wakefield, a friend of Kurt Vonnegut's, was an especially delightful and informative correspondent. And I was thrilled when Freeman Dyson turned up at an early talk on this project. He gave me an inside look at the Institute for Advanced Study's Meteorology Project and the people he knew there as a young upstart.

This book would not have been possible without archives and the dedicated professionals who make them accessible. Perhaps most central were the papers of Bernard Vonnegut and Vincent Schaefer at the M. E. Grenander Special Collections at the SUNY Albany Science Library. Jodi Boyle and Geoffrey Williams were invaluable guides there. Equally critical were the manuscripts and papers of Kurt Vonnegut at the Lilly Library, Indiana University, Bloomington. Special thanks to the Lilly Library for a Helm Fellowship to help me spend sufficient time with its amazing collection, and to Cherry Williams, Joel Silver, Craig Simpson, and the staff of its beautiful reading room.

Another invaluable resource was the General Electric Archives at the Museum of Innovation and Science (formerly the Schenectady Museum) in Schenectady. I am grateful to the curator Chris Hunter for helping me find things in his treasure trove of GE materials. Visiting the manuscripts room at the Library of Congress, as I did to access the papers of Irving Langmuir, Vannevar Bush, Francis Reichelderfer, and Harry Wexler, makes one proud to be a taxpayer. Jennifer Brathovde, in particular, went above and beyond in an effort to help me make the most of my time there.

The Manuscripts and Archives Division of the Stephen A. Schwarzman Building of the New York Public Library provided access to the Crowell-Collier files, including the separate Operation Eggnog files, and the *New Yorker* files. Princeton University's Rare Books and Special Collections Department allowed me to use the Scribner files. Special thanks to Nora Murphy at the MIT Institute Archives and Special Collections, home to the papers of Jule Charney and Norbert Wiener, for helping me on-site and for continuing to help me remotely. The Grems-Doolittle Library of the Schenectady County Historical Society was helpful in understanding the history of the Electric City, and the Indiana Historical Society was essential in finding newspaper resources. I must also thank Kate Legg at the National Center for Atmospheric Research Archives at the University Corporation for Atmospheric Research, Julia Whitehead at the Kurt Vonnegut Memorial Library in Indianapolis, Christine Di Bella and Erica Mosner at the Shelby White and Leon Levy Archives Center at the Institute for Advanced Study, Michael Miller at the American Philosophical Society, Nancy Shawcross at University of Pennsylvania Special Collections, Chela Scott Weber at NYU's Tamiment Library, Deborah Douglas at the MIT Museum, and Lee Hiltzik, who directed me to many things I might not otherwise have found at the Rockefeller Archive Center.

Writing this book required access to local newspaper archives in a variety of cities. In many cases, this involved using microform archives held by public libraries or universities and retrieved via interlibrary loan at the New York Public Library. This is one of the many special features of a strictly research library that makes maintaining the integrity of the Stephen A. Schwarzman Building as a research library absolutely essential to people like me.

I completed the first draft of this book while living in Portland, Oregon, as Tin House/Portland State University writer in residence. My thanks to the PSU faculty and the editorial staff of *Tin House* for a perfect place to work and for listening to endless Vonnegutian ramblings and to my MFA students there for making me think hard about what nonfiction is. This book has also benefited from the unstinting intelligence of my editor at FSG, Ileene Smith, and the wisdom and enthusiasm of my agent, Jin Auh. And as always, I could not have done it without the support, love, and understanding of Robert Brown, who always comes along for the ride, no matter how bumpy. God bless him.

Index